Why Beauty Matters

Why Beauty Matters

KAREN LEE-THORP &

CYNTHIA HICKS

NAVPRESS
BRINGING TRUTH TO LIFE
NavPress Publishing Group
P.O. Box 35001, Colorado Springs, Colorado 80935

The Navigators is an international Christian organization. Our mission is to reach, disciple, and equip people to know Christ and to make Him known through successive generations. We envision multitudes of diverse people in the United States and every other nation who have a passionate love for Christ, live a lifestyle of sharing Christ's love, and multiply spiritual laborers among those without Christ.

NavPress is the publishing ministry of The Navigators. NavPress publications help believers learn biblical truth and apply what they learn to their lives and ministries. Our mission is to stimulate spiritual formation among our readers.

© 1997 by Karen C. Lee-Thorp and Cynthia B. Hicks
All rights reserved. No part of this publication may be reproduced in any form without written permission from NavPress, P.O. Box 35001, Colorado Springs, CO 80935.
Library of Congress Catalog Card Number: 96-36906
ISBN 08910-99794

Cover design: David Carlson
Cover photo: David Hanover/Tony Stone

Some of the anecdotal illustrations in this book are true to life and are included with the permission of the persons involved. All other illustrations are composites of real situations, and any resemblance to people living or dead is coincidental.

Unless otherwise identified, all Scripture quotations in this publication are taken from the *HOLY BIBLE: NEW INTERNATIONAL VERSION* ® (NIV®). Copyright © 1973, 1978, 1984 by International Bible Society. Used by permission of Zondervan Publishing House. All rights reserved. Other versions used include: the *New American Standard Bible* (NASB), © The Lockman Foundation 1960, 1962, 1963, 1968, 1971, 1972, 1973, 1975, 1977; the *New Revised Standard Version* (NRSV), copyright 1989, by the Division of Christian Education of the National Council of the Churches of Christ in the USA, used by permission, all rights reserved; and *The New English Bible* (NEB), © 1961, 1970, The Delegates of the Oxford University Press and The Syndics of the Cambridge University Press.

Library of Congress Cataloging-in-Publication Data
    Why beauty matters / Karen Lee-Thorp and Cynthia Hicks.
      p.   cm.
    ISBN 0-89109-979-4
    1. Women—Religious life.   2. Beauty, Personal.   3. Christian life.   I. Hicks, Cynthia. II. Title.
BV4527.L468   1997
248.8'43—DC21   96-36906
                                                    CIP

Printed in the United States of America

1 2 3 4 5 6 7 8 9 10 11 12 13 14 15 / 99 98 97

FOR A FREE CATALOG OF
NAVPRESS BOOKS & BIBLE STUDIES,
CALL 1-800-366-7788 (USA)
or 1-416-499-4615 (CANADA)

CONTENTS

ACKNOWLEDGMENTS

Body image is a hard subject to discuss openly in our culture. Few of us want others to know about our pride, shame, fear, or envy; nor do we want to advertise in print the ways we have been hurt by other people's attitudes. Consequently, we have changed the names in most of the stories in this book. Although we cannot name them here, we want to express our gratitude to the many beautiful women who allowed us to tell their stories.

We also want to thank the men who helped us make sense of men's response to women's appearance, especially Chris Knippers, Stan Thornburg, Tom Whiteman, and Cinny's husband, Bob.

Cinny is especially grateful for her daughters, Charis and Ashley, for their courage to expose her hypocrisy around beauty, for their forgiving love, and for their encouragement to change. She applauds their confidence to be and look like themselves.

Karen wishes to thank those who helped her believe in her beauty, particularly the three Susans, Roxanne, Laura, Joanne, Cindy, Maryln, Don, Jim, and Paul. And to the women who discussed body issues with her week in and week out for eighteen months—Arlene, Pat, Kim, Heidi, Kitty, and Carmen—a special hug of thanks.

We are grateful for the editorial skill of Roy Carlisle, who helped us get this book off the ground, and we offer three loud cheers to Liz Heaney, without whose editorial wisdom and encouragement it would never have landed safely. Betsy Sellick and Soozi Bolte were generous enough to critique a draft of the manuscript, and the final version gained a great deal from the revisions they suggested.

PART ONE

WHY WE WANT TO LOOK GOOD

CHAPTER ONE

DOES ANYONE ELSE FEEL THIS WAY?

KAREN'S STORY

At the age of thirty, I (Karen) began to be beautiful. Don't laugh. I'm not speaking simply of "the unfading beauty of a gentle and quiet spirit,"[1] although inner beauty is certainly part of it. I'm talking about the kind of physical transformation that made a man I'd worked with for years whisper to a coworker, "What's happened to Karen? She looks great!"

It wasn't just an external change, a "makeover," as the beauty industry likes to call the wizardry of cosmetologists and fashion consultants. It was an inner revolution that manifested itself in the way I dressed and moved, the shape of my body, the quality of my smile, the light in my eyes. At the age when some women begin to fear their youthful glow is slipping away, I saw myself glow for the first time. Our culture deems it vain to say so, but today I feel beautiful.

While for some women that statement might reflect arrogance, I think for me it represents resurrection. As a child I felt invisible to my busy family, noticed only by the person who incested me. I made the queer, contradictory judgments many molested children make: that I was fundamentally invisible and ugly, but also that my feminine attractiveness had invited the abuse.

11

Attractiveness, then, seemed both dangerous and out of my reach.

As a teenager I shunned makeup. I wore limp clothes in drab colors that accentuated the pale complexion I cultivated through compulsive undereating. In college I abandoned my contact lenses in favor of glasses. By graduation I weighed ninety-seven pounds at five-foot-five, and for several years in my twenties I shrank even more. Chronic soul ache registered on my face as a cerebral, detached expression. If asked, I would have said that my indifference to appearance came from my decision to pursue God rather than worldly approval. Doesn't that sound spiritual? But there was nothing godly about my hatred of my body, nothing Christlike about a look that held people at bay.

But love changed me—inwardly and outwardly—over the span of a few years. Some of God's people loved me to life, and the effects are visible. In part, this book is about the power of love to make a woman beautiful even when she feels beyond hope of ever believing in her beauty. It's also about how a woman like me can learn to handle her beauty once she has it. Beauty matters because how we view and treat it is a barometer of our spirits.

Some readers may recoil from that word *beauty*. Our cultural and religious traditions send women confusing messages about beauty: that how we look determines what we're worth or, at the other extreme, that if we want to be seen as beautiful, then we're vain and unspiritual. In fact, even the word *beauty* has been so trivialized that it embarrasses us; we might acknowledge the importance of "positive body image," but what Christian woman would admit to wanting to be beautiful?

Let's talk, then, about body image. A 1995 study found that 48 percent of American women felt "wholesale displeasure" about their bodies. That is, about half of us utterly detest our appearance, while many more merely dislike our weight or breasts or thighs. This self-hatred has spiraled up from 23 percent in 1972 and 38 percent in 1985.[2] In 1985 I would never have acknowledged feeling wholesale displeasure about my body (that would have meant admitting to a vain preoccupation with looks), so I wonder if even these shocking figures understate the truth.

Something is broken in the spirits of women if in 1995 at least one out of every two of us hates the body God gave her. Every one of us knows someone who feels this way, openly or secretly. Where does that hatred come from, and what can we do about it?

CINNY'S STORY

My (Cinny's) experience of body image is about as different from Karen's as it could be. Raised in the Deep South by a mother who always looked first-class, I knew what was expected of me. And growing up with a fraternal twin sister who was always the cute little thing while I shopped in the chubbette department and had glasses and braces by the first grade, I struggled to measure up. The number 103 remains burned into my brain: I will never forget being the only fifth-grade girl in my class to weigh over 100 pounds. From that day on, I thought of myself as a fat person, with all the shame that carries in our culture.

As a teenager I loved water sports and prided myself more on my athletic prowess than on my appearance. When I was fourteen I was brushing my hair one day when my sister commented, "You look like an Amazon with those arms!"—arms toned from swimming, diving, and water skiing. Humiliated again, I committed myself to slimming down and giving up sleeveless blouses. When I look at my old pictures now, I realize I had the toned, muscular body that is so in vogue today. I guess I was ahead of my time!

Because I thought of myself more as a jock than a beauty queen, I was surprised when my sorority sisters chose me to enter the Miss University of Florida contest—and more startled when I finished as fourth runner-up. But my mother had taught me how to look beautiful, and I could do it when I tried.

During my first twenty years of marriage, I felt caught between the image of the well-groomed southern woman I was raised to be and the realities of living with small children, a husband in ministry, church activities, and part-time jobs. My weight crept up and frustrated my attempts to control it. For a while I could barely afford creme rinse, let alone compete in the Dallas beauty race. Later, I sensed that as a minister's wife I might appear vain and materialistic if I dressed with too much flair. When I entered the business world in my early forties, however, my ability to look great suddenly became one of my best assets.

While I was feeling more confident about my appearance, my daughters began to labor under pressure from both the media and me to be thin. I started to see that by watching me diet and talk about weight for years, they had picked up my distorted thinking. They struggled with feelings of inadequacy and mild eating disorders. If I was going to be of any help to my daughters, I had to admit I'd been trying to impose upon them my unconscious obsession with appearance. I had to face my fears that society would reject them if they didn't meet its beauty standards, and that their failure would reflect badly on me as their mother. I had to acknowledge that while my desires to be proud of them and to protect them from pain were normal, I had let those desires blind me to my girls' real needs. When I realized I was measuring my own appearance, my daughters', and that of every other woman by an exacting and impossible standard, I felt stunned. I was never satisfied, and my daughters knew it.

> "Is shapeliness now next to godliness?"[3]

Now that I'm almost fifty, I've begun to make peace with my body. I'll never again have the body I had as a college student, but I can choose either to deal with the feelings that fact churns up in me or to pretend those feelings don't exist. This book is about becoming conscious—conscious of how big an issue appearance is for me and the women around me, and of how profoundly I can affect what my daughters, friends, and even total strangers believe about themselves, just by how I respond to how they look. Beauty matters because it's intertwined with fear and love.

OTHER WOMEN'S STORIES

As we have talked with women, we've heard them echo our feelings of shame, anxiety, loss, confusion, and even body-hatred. For example, Alison wants to get married. At the age of thirty-five, she looks longingly at other people's kids. Yet she is invisible to the men in the singles group at her church. These guys walk right by her to pursue the outer beauty of the women with perky features and appealing figures. By contrast, the woman she sees in the mirror has a prominent nose, sparse hair, and a lumpy body.

A couple of years ago, Alison went on a singles' retreat sponsored by a Christian conference center. Although the activities were fun, the retreat as a whole painfully reinforced her sense of being unwanted as a woman. "The guys all went for the Southern Belles—the girls who talked sweetly and looked pretty. It was partly personality, of course; they knew how to flirt. Even at dinner the men showed no interest in getting to know me. My roommate was a college-age cutie; the guys just hovered around her. She already had a boyfriend, but the guys never stopped yakking with her."

For Alison, the hardest part of a situation like this is wondering whether men ignore her because she's doing or being something "wrong." "You don't know if it's you," she says. "You wonder what signals you're sending, what kind of walls you're putting up. Do I keep guys away because I want to protect myself?" Second-guessing herself can be agonizing. Alison works hard to be likable, and she's a good friend, but the "men game," as she calls it, eludes her. Part of her lack of confidence in the game stems from her belief that she's simply not pretty enough to compete. For a woman who wants to marry, looks matter.

In another arena, the job market, consider Tomika. She has won her colleagues' respect for her polished professionalism that gets results. Everyone on the sales staff in her company invests heavily in grooming, but as an African American, Tomika knows that clients may be especially inclined to evaluate her based on how she looks. Tomika estimates that she spends one out of every four dollars she earns on clothes, jewelry, hair straightening, makeup, and other grooming needs. Is she doing this because of vanity and pride, or because these efforts are necessary to make an impression on clients who, right or wrong, judge a salesperson on her physical appearance? Tomika wants to live by biblical values, but she also wants to keep her job.

Tomika's concerns are realistic. In her 1990 bestseller, *The Beauty Myth*, journalist Naomi Wolf documented that "urban professional women are devoting up to a third of their income to 'beauty maintenance', and considering it a necessary investment."[4] Why? Evidence of the rewards of attractiveness abound.

In one study, viewers were asked to rate the physical attractiveness of women in photographs. The ratings were then compared with those women's participation in the labor force, with their incidence of being hired for jobs they applied for, and with the incomes of their husbands. The study found that women perceived as being less attractive had a lower incidence of participation in the labor force and married men whose earning ability was less than that of other men.[5] Another study found that attractive people were considered sexually warm, responsive, sensitive, kind, interesting, strong, poised, modest, social, outgoing, and smart.[6] Several studies show that people are more likely to buy products advertised by salespersons whom they perceive as physically attractive. Finally, a study of people making hiring decisions found they were likely to perceive attractive applicants as more qualified than their less attractive competition.[7] "Studies show that you are less likely to be considered a job candidate if you are overweight, and if you do get the job, instead of focusing on being successful in your career, you have to work hard to get within 'normal' weight standards."[8] American Airlines flight attendants had to wage a seventeen-year legal battle to strike down company weight standards.

How should all this evidence affect Tomika's buying decisions and what mothers tell their daughters about weight?

A DIRTY SECRET?

When women are anxious and confused about matters of appearance, it doesn't help to tell them, "Inner beauty is all that matters; how you look doesn't count." Looks obviously do count, both at work and in relationships, yet people often pretend they're "above all that." We've heard women deny that body image is an issue for them, yet fork out the money to have their hair colored, pay someone else to do their nails and use expensive creams to moisturize the wrinkles on their face and around their eyes. We've sent women transcripts of our interviews with them and received requests that we delete certain quotations that make them sound, well, a little too vain. It seems that appearance is such a shameful issue in our culture that many women are chagrined to admit they have ever been ashamed of their looks. Vanity is as embarrassing a "sin" as adultery.

Why are women so ashamed to admit they care deeply about how they look? Sometimes Christians think shame is the appropriate antidote to pride. One woman told us that when she was a child, she sat at the dinner table across from a large framed picture that mirrored her image back to her. When her mother noticed her admiring her face in the glass and playing with her hair, she moved the girl to a different seat at the table, permanently. "You're so vain!" her mother scolded. This woman recalls hearing that rebuke repeatedly during her teen years, and while it hurt and angered her, being labeled "vain" did nothing to dampen her enthusiasm for clothes and makeup.

The Bible offers rich insights into the complex interplay of pride, shame, and humility around physical appearance, insights that can guide mothers who worry that their daughters are "vain." Sadly, most of us have distorted notions of what the Bible says about beauty, so we're at a loss when a daughter goes on a crash diet, a friend confides that she hates her body, or we find ourselves nervous when another birthday rolls around.

MIXED MESSAGES

It's not surprising that women are confused. The Christian community sends at least three conflicting messages about appearance.

Silence

The first is silence. Neither of us has ever heard a sermon about body image in a Sunday morning service, even though we're willing to bet that nearly every man in the congregation has evaluated some woman's attractiveness (or lack thereof) sometime during the service, and nearly every woman has evaluated her own looks — and possibly those of the women around her — during the same time period. The pulpit may be silent, but homes reverberate with cries of "I have nothing to wear to church!" The top five cosmetics companies racked up $30 billion in 1996 in the USA alone,[9] but the implications of this mega-business rarely register concern in the church. Half the women in America hate their bodies, but few people consider that this could be relevant to their spiritual health.

The Traditional View

Christian women have an especially hard time seeing the connection. After all, no self-respecting Christian would admit to being among the half with the "problem." That's because the second, strong message we often get is that physical appearance is unimportant; mature followers of Christ don't care about how they look. According to this line of reasoning, the only people concerned about their looks are the hypocrites and those who find their identity in other people's approval rather than in Christ. If you hate your body, you're just not right with God.

One of the passages that springs to many people's minds when you ask them what the Bible says about physical appearance is 1 Peter 3:3-5—

> Your beauty should not come from outward adornment, such as braided hair and the wearing of gold jewelry and fine clothes. Instead, it should be that of your inner self, the unfading beauty of a gentle and quiet spirit, which is of great worth in God's sight. For this is the way the holy women of the past who put their hope in God used to make themselves beautiful.

Another is Proverbs 31:30:

> Charm is deceptive, and beauty is fleeting;
>   but a woman who fears the LORD is to be praised.

These passages seem to say that inner beauty is what counts. How you look doesn't matter. Don't pander to men's lust or your own vanity by primping in front of some mirror. But is that what the apostle Peter and the writer of Proverbs are really saying? How do other biblical texts address the beauty question: the account of Eve created in the image of God; Sarah's and Esther's experiences in oriental harems; the rape of Tamar; and the Song of Songs's wild celebration of a woman's beauty, to name just a few. And what exactly is "the unfading beauty of a gentle and quiet spirit" anyway?

The Contrary View

Just when we think we've gotten a clear message from the church that we should give away our curling irons, we get a different message entirely. We pick up a Christian women's magazine and observe a lovely woman on the cover whose hair and makeup are perfect and whose head and body are tilted to flatter her elegant bone structure. We scan a row of CD covers promoting Christian recording artists, and we see more beautiful people attractively presented.

Is it sinful to use an artist's physical attractiveness to sell Christian music? Is it wrong for a photographer to use all her skill to make a magazine cover beautiful to the eye?

Then there's the new twist on the old fundraiser. For a mere thirty-five dollars, a church in Colorado Springs offered photo sessions like those advertised by Glamour Shots, promising the prints would be ready in time for Valentine's Day. Curious, I (Karen) signed up. When I arrived on the appointed Saturday morning, hair and face clean and unadorned as instructed, a Mary Kay consultant guided me and the other assembled women in choosing and applying makeup. "You need twice as much for the camera as you would wear on the street," she said. (Make that several times as much as I would be caught dead in.) A hairstylist rolled, teased, fluffed, and sprayed my hair into rock-star proportions, then sent me toward a pile of jewelry and an assortment of shimmering or feathery wraps I could use to present the illusion that I was wearing an elegant gown.

The photographer (a church member) took eight different poses, and the results were impressive. The frosted camera filter had faded the garish makeup into subtle highlights and had left my skin with an even, milky glow. Gone were blemishes and even an inch-long scar on my throat.

The traditional Christian view of beauty would call this fundraiser a sellout to worldly values. Is it that? Or is it a bunch of women having some harmless fun? Perhaps the matter is more complex.

A NEW RELIGION

Beauty has become a religion in our culture. Consider the 1989 ad that labels a photo of a chocolate sundae TEMPTATION and a photo of 70-calorie Alba® Fit'n Frosty™ Shake SALVATION. Or observe the rise of evangelically inspired weight-loss books and groups that claim to offer Jesus' system of weight loss, including such titles as: *God's Answer to Fat—Lose It*; *Pray Your Weight Away*; *More of Jesus and Less of Me*; *Free to Be Thin*; and *Help, Lord, the Devil Wants Me Fat*. These books imply that obesity is a sin, or evidence of the Devil's attack, but isn't it something far more complicated?

> "40% SIN. 60% FORGIVENESS. Yes, we freely confess that a full 40% of Country Morning® Blend is real butter. . . . Rich, creamy, wickedly delicious Land O Lakes butter. But the other 60% is pure, saintly corn oil margarine that means a comforting 60% less cholesterol. Enjoy buttery bliss with Country Morning Blend. Live it up and all will be forgiven. Well, mostly."[10]

Maribel Morgan's *The Total Woman* riveted the attention of conservative Christian women when it was released by an evangelical publisher in 1973. As a young wife, I (Cinny) saw *The Total Woman* as the model of what I should be. Morgan warned women that outer beauty was critical to their marital security:

> One of your husband's most basic needs is for you to be physically attractive to him. He loves your body; in fact, he literally craves it. The outer shell of yours is what the real estate people call "curb appeal"—how the house looks from the outside. Is your curb appeal this week what it was five years ago?[11]

Beware, Morgan said, of letting your husband spend all day among "dazzling secretaries who emit clouds of perfume," only to come home to a grubby you.[12] The implication was clear: If you're "dumpy, stringy, or exhausted" when he comes home, you may be setting him up for an affair or even a divorce.

Morgan even portrayed primping as Christlike other-centeredness: "When you look smashing, you can forget yourself and concentrate on the other person. In marriage, that's the name of the game—to concentrate on the other person!"[13] She claimed that even with two small children, she still took a bubble bath every evening before her husband came home. She once greeted him at the door in pink baby-doll pajamas and white boots. "Your husband needs you to fulfill his daydreams,"[14] she said, urging women to dress up in various costumes in order to appear to be a different woman every night.

We may dismiss Morgan's ideas, but at the time they were hugely influential. Witness the 1990s film *Fried Green Tomatoes*, in which Kathy Bates's character, a Southern woman in the 1970s, fantasizes about greeting her husband at the door wrapped in cellophane. According to Morgan, a woman who had taken her course at a Southern Baptist church "welcomed her husband home in black mesh stockings, high heels, and an apron. That's all. He took one look and shouted, 'Praise the Lord!'"[15]

In another Christian bestseller thirteen years later, *His Needs, Her Needs: Building an Affair-Proof Marriage*, Willard F. Harley, Jr., repeated Morgan's doctrine. Harley said that a good-looking wife is one of a husband's top five needs. "This isn't some quirk or whim. It's something he needs *very* badly. . . . By taking care of your body you take care of your husband."[16] Harley continued,

> I'm often challenged when I list an attractive mate as one of a man's five most basic marital needs. Surely, I'm told, men must have more important needs than fulfilling some kind of fantasy or sense of vanity. Besides, doesn't this just play into the hands of the beauty/youth movement across America and put tremendous pressure on every wife to try to look like a beauty queen? What if she simply doesn't have the equipment?
>
> By calling for a wife to be attractive I mean she should take pains to look something like the woman her husband

married. After all, that was the woman he fell in love with, not a movie star or some other fantasy.

Does this mean a woman must stay eternally young? Of course not, but getting old provides no excuse for letting weight creep up and up, not fixing your hair, and dressing like a bag lady.[17]

Harley stated two reasons why a man needs an attractive wife. First, men are stimulated visually, so if a man's wife looked bad, he had reason to be turned off and prefer to look elsewhere. A wife should stay attractive in order to guard her husband from being vulnerable to an affair. Second, "A man also wants an attractive wife as a pure and simple matter of pride. . . . Juvenile as it may sound, people often *do* judge the ability and success of a man in terms of his wife's appearance."[18]

Harley said that any woman can enhance her attractiveness to her husband, and he recommended books, videos, and other products designed to help his readers "shape up, dress with style, color their hair properly, and so forth." He insisted that weight control was simply a matter of discipline: "thirty minutes of aerobics four to five times a week" to lose weight. Further, "with our modern multi-billion-dollar cosmetics industry no woman has the excuse that help is not available." Harley also urged women to choose their hairstyles and color according to their husband's preference. "If he doesn't like a certain hairstyle and color, abandon it." Likewise, "Dress to be attractive to your man. . . . A woman should pay as much, if not more, attention to her choice of nightgown or pajamas as she does to what she wears in public. When she dresses for bed, she dresses strictly for her husband." While Harley preferred diet and exercise to cosmetic surgery, he did recommend surgery for "prematurely wrinkled women. While this procedure must be repeated every few years, it is relatively safe and effective. I also recommend nose surgery if a client has an abnormally shaped nose."[19]

> "There are no ugly women, only lazy ones."

He concluded with Harley's Sixth Law: "An attractive woman is made, not born."[20] This law reminds us of cosmetic magnate

Helena Rubinstein's famous statement: "There are no ugly women, only lazy ones."[21]

We have quoted Morgan and Harley not to deride them but to illustrate that the Christian community does not speak with one voice on the subject of beauty. Harley's book, of which more than 500,000 copies are in print, still sells in Christian bookstores alongside such books as *Beauty and the Best*, in which Debra Evans details the dangers of plastic surgery, the deceptions of the cosmetics industry, and the delusions of pursuing physical beauty. A Christian college bookstore displays *Beauty from the Inside Out: A Guide for Black Women*, which explains that care of one's appearance is necessary for self-esteem. Christian romance novels, with their pretty-but-virtuous heroines on the cover, sell like ice cream in August. And most speakers at Christian women's conferences put as much effort into their appearance as any secular speaker would.

One conference organizer, whom we'll call Sharon, was thrilled that one of her spiritual heroines was speaking at her conference. Sharon confided to this famous woman that she, too, was about to begin a speaking career. Sharon's heroine replied, "You know, of course, that the audience isn' going to respect what you have to say."

"What do you mean?" asked Sharon.

"They'll take one look at you and realize you lack self-discipline. Why should they listen to what you have to say?"

Sharon cringed. She was at least seventy-five pounds overweight, and to this woman with a reputation for spiritual maturity, Sharon's appearance was clear evidence of something lacking within.

Perhaps neither the traditional nor the contrary view of beauty is sufficient, and it's time to break the silence and talk honestly about what's going on. Beauty matters for spiritual people in relationships, at work, at church, and alone with themselves. Until we put this issue on the table, hypocrisy will flourish.

CULTURAL CONFUSION

To some degree, the Christian woman's confusion about beauty simply reflects the ambivalence of our culture. The world sends double messages that are hauntingly like those we hear from Christians. For instance, Ann Hopkins used to be a consultant for

Price Waterhouse, a large accounting firm. However, Hopkins was denied a partnership because "she needed to learn to dress more femininely." Teresa Fischette was a Continental Airlines ticket agent at Boston's Logan Airport but was fired when she refused to obey the company's new rules "requiring female employees who deal with the public to wear foundation makeup and lipstick." On the other hand, the Oakland, California Police Department fired Nancy Fadhl because her hair and makeup made her look "too much like a lady."[22] Just as Christians have varying views on how a wife should look, so people in the world have differing pictures in their minds of how an accountant, airline representative, or police officer should look.

Remember Marcia Clark, the prosecutor in the O. J. Simpson trial? While any male prosecutor would have had to endure public scrutiny of his professional performance, Clark also had to undergo scrutiny of her hairstyle.

> The verdict is in: Marcia Clark's new hairdo is a winner. After very public trial and error since the O. J. Simpson case began last June, Clark swapped her curly perm a week ago for a softer style and a deep auburn color. "She looks much more pulled together," says tress expert Kenneth Battell, of Kenneth's in Manhattan. "I hated that frizzy mall hair." Clark's mane man . . . has fielded more than 30 interview requests since the makeover. "This is just huge," he says. Spectators applauded when Clark walked into court, prompting her smiling response, "Get a life."[23]

In our culture women are expected to make themselves attractive in order to catch a man or keep a job. But when they do this, it becomes their fault if they're judged as vain or harassed sexually. Beautiful women report having their competence questioned when they're successful; people suspect them of using their looks to get ahead. Author Naomi Wolf decided to research and write *The Beauty Myth* after a clash with a male fellow student. She challenged something he said in class, and in response he taunted that she'd won her Rhodes Scholarship because she was gorgeous.

CLOUDED MIRRORS

It's no wonder women are uncertain about whether they're too ugly to get a man, anxious about how to raise their daughters, and ashamed to admit they care a lot about looking good. How can we not be confused in a world in which people may shame us for being too pretty, too heavy, too careful with our appearance, or not careful enough?

The apostle Paul compared our current understanding of reality to what one saw in a first-century mirror. "For now we see in a mirror dimly," he said, and his term *dimly* in Greek was literally, "in a riddle."[25] The glass mirror had not been invented yet (flat, clear glass was nearly impossible to make), so mirrors of Paul's day were simply polished metal. Try looking at yourself reflected in the bottom of a scoured pan. Can you tell if the face looking back at you is beautiful or not? Can you discern the image of God, or is the image clouded, like a riddle?

Much of the time, when we look at our friends and ourselves, our view is clouded by shame, anxiety, envy, and hurt.

> http://hillaryshair.com —Web site where viewers could vote on the best and worst of Hillary Clinton's hairstyles, and even create their own look on a bald Hillary head.[24]

The tension between inner and outer beauty seems like a riddle. Paul said we would never fully solve such riddles in this life, but we can learn to see ourselves and each other more clearly the more we understand the nature of the clouds that obscure our sight.

One might define the biblical notion of *the world* as those traits in a given culture that bend and distort the mirrors, that make sin look normal and wisdom look crazy. In this book, we hope to equip women to sort out the wise from the crazy in magazines, television ads, men's remarks, their mother's comments, and their daughter's habits. In the next five chapters we'll examine four reasons why physical appearance matters so much to women:

- Our longing for love
- Our yearning for respect
- Our response to the instincts wired into men
- The spiritual yearnings built into every human

Once it's clear where beauty gets its power, we'll explore how this force easily becomes an object of idolatry for both women and men, with disastrous consequences. Finally, we'll examine two alternate responses to the danger beauty poses. One is to reject and veil it, as I (Karen) did for many years. The other is to become aware of our emotions and temptations regarding appearance, to grieve over the ways we've sinned and been sinned against, and to let ourselves be loved until we glow with the beauty of love.

Love, then, will be both the goal of our journey and its beginning. Love is a woman's strongest yearning, so we will look first at the link between beauty and love.

A CLOSER LOOK

Throughout this book you'll find quotations set off in boxes to spark your thinking. Many of them will be advertisements we found in women's magazines. Our goal is to help you notice, laugh over, and get mad at the hype that bombards you.

If you haven't done so already, start paying close attention to what television and magazines are telling you about beauty. What beliefs about female appearance are advertisers and producers trying to sell you? How do you feel about yourself after being immersed in this stuff? You may feel fabulously feminine, ashamed of your failure to measure up, or something else entirely. If you keep a journal, jot some notes, or tell a friend what you've observed.

CHAPTER TWO

THE FACE OF LOVE

Once there was a young girl whose mother died, leaving her to a stepfamily who treated her cruelly. But she was good and prayed three times every day at her mother's grave. When she grew to be a young woman, she wanted to go to a party the king was giving so his son could meet "all the beautiful maidens in the country" and choose one of them for his bride. (Beauty was the only criterion for admittance.)

The good girl's family tried to keep her from going to the party, saying she didn't have the right clothes or shoes and would embarrass them, but divine intervention provided her with the most fabulous designer outfits anyone had ever seen, and the girl sneaked into the ball. The prince was smitten by her beauty, danced with her for three nights in a row, and by then was determined to marry her. He had to work a bit to distinguish her from some impostors (her stepsisters), but eventually he identified her by her teeny, tiny feet. For their wickedness, the stepsisters were punished with bodily mutilation, and the good girl lived happily ever after.

Those are the highlights of the Grimm's version of "Cinderella," a tale that parents have read to little girls for generations.

It consistently resonates with girls, who go wide-eyed at the terror of losing Mom and having no one to love them, and who hope beyond hope that someday they will have the beautiful clothes and the tiny feet, and a prince will choose them over all the other girls. If they're very, very good, then maybe magic will strike and make them beautiful enough to win the prince's love. For beauty, of course, is the key.

THE LINK BETWEEN BEAUTY AND LOVE

Women hunger for love. From babyhood we experiment with strategies to win the love we crave: smiling at Mom, batting our lashes at Dad, performing at school and church, being good at home. Countless books have described how women become "performance oriented" in order to earn love. The same voracious need for love drives many girls to become what we might call "appearance oriented."

Do attractive people get more love than less attractive ones? Studies confirm what most of us intuitively sensed as children: Mothers and day-care workers smile, coo, kiss, and hold pretty babies more than plain ones. Fathers are more involved with attractive babies. Smiling and holding are the ways a baby learns to feel loved, so these early responses have enormous consequences for the child's sense of security as he or she grows up.[1]

> "A girl learns that stories happen to 'beautiful' women whether they are interesting or not. And, interesting or not, stories do not happen to women who are not 'beautiful.'"[2]

Many children's stories reinforce this impression that attractiveness is the secret to love. The prince wasn't enraptured with Cinderella's intelligent, sensitive conversation. Snow White and Sleeping Beauty netted their men while comatose. Rapunzel had great hair. What child wouldn't conclude that beauty is the key to people's hearts?

The Bible affirms that, sadly, the beauty-love connection is a fact of human nature. When the writer of Genesis introduces the sisters Leah and Rachel, he says nothing about their character. He simply notes that Leah, the older sister, "had weak eyes, but

Rachel was lovely in form, and beautiful. Jacob was in love with Rachel" and wanted to marry her.[3] By declaring Jacob's love right after commenting on the two sisters' looks, the author strongly implies that Rachel's beauty was at least a partial cause of Jacob's love. Since the rest of the story highlights Rachel's petulant, conniving character, it's hard to conclude that Jacob preferred her because she was the more godly of the two. Beauty often wins love. It just does.

Imagine Leah's sorrow. God did. In compassion, "When the LORD saw that Leah was not loved, he opened her womb, but Rachel was barren."[4] When her son was born, Leah acknowledged God's intervention even as she showed that her heart's deepest longing was for her husband's love: "It is because the LORD has seen my misery. Surely my husband will love me now," she said.[5] Evidently he didn't, for when her next child was born she said, "Because the LORD heard that I am not loved, he gave me this one too."[6] She expressed the same yearning for Jacob's heart at the birth of her third child. Leah represents all women who have been unloved and undervalued among humans because God did not make them beautiful.

THE EYE OF THE BEHOLDER

Although beauty often wins love, that's not the end of the story. It's said that "beauty is in the eye of the beholder." That is, when a person looks at another, his perceptions are strongly influenced by the emotions he feels for the one he sees. To love someone is to see her as beautiful. Moreover, studies suggest that *being* objectively attractive is less important to a child's well-being than *feeling* attractive and *being treated as* attractive by some loving beholders. "More than intelligence, athletic competence, and other areas of self-content, how people think they look is highly related to their self-esteem," says psychologist Susan Harter. "It is true for groups as varied as the male and the female, the handicapped and the gifted." Susan wonders "whether self-esteem is only skin deep. Why should one's *outer* physical self be so tied to one's *inner* psychological self?"[7]

Dr. Nancy Poland works with expectant parents at the Brazelton

Institute, preparing them to understand that the baby they actually bear may not look exactly like the baby of their imaginations. She says that if parents don't adjust their dreams of how their baby should look to the appearance of the actual child, "then the baby feels unimportant, unnoticed, invisible, and grows into a child who doesn't feel accepted for who he or she is. . . . Even children with defects, who are deformed, can turn out okay. . . . It's the love and the nurturing that they get from parents. They've been made to feel beautiful."[8]

IN PURSUIT OF THE LOVING GAZE

In short, children don't need to be beautiful, but they do need to be loved in ways that make them feel beautiful. The same is true of grown women. Hear the stories of four women who have struggled with the longing to be loved in this way.

Nancy: Filling a Hole in the Heart

What happens to a woman who grows up lacking the precious sense that she is beautiful in the eyes of at least one loving beholder? Nancy Friday, bestselling author of *My Mother/My Self*, is one such woman. She wrote her 589-page tome, *The Power of Beauty*, to explain what she freely admits has been a lifelong addiction to being found beautiful. She begins, "I am a woman who needs to be seen. I need it in a basic way, as in to breathe, to eat."[9] Her explanation? Her father abandoned her family shortly after her birth. "There is nothing like the mystery of an absent father to addict you to the loving gaze of men."[10] Nancy grew up knowing her mother considered her older daughter pretty, but Nancy was unattractive until she blossomed in her late teens. By then she was a confirmed exhibitionist, devoted to drawing the loving gaze of anyone from her nurse to her grandfather, and eventually a dizzying string of lovers.

Before puberty, Nancy found what she calls a "father substitute" in "the loving eye of God."[11] But when she discovered boys at the age of twelve, she felt forced to choose between pursuing the magic of their adoration and sticking with God. Boys won. Only in her forties, she says, did she mature enough to find the loving gaze from inside herself, to be her own loving beholder.

Vive narcissism. Much of Nancy's book flaunts her sexual exploits and the charge she has gotten out of alluring one man after the next to adore her body, so although she did spend ten years and a lot of money gathering research on beauty, we can't recommend her book.

Ellen: On Becoming Ugly

On the other hand, Ellen Lambert's story moves us with its keen insight into Cinderella's sorrows. As a professor of English and long-time feminist, Ellen believed "that women's traditional concern for their appearances was a part, and perhaps the most pernicious part, of the patriarchal legacy that demanded a woman's subordination of her own self to masculine imperatives."[12] However, when she lost a breast to cancer, she realized that these high-sounding abstractions—"patriarchal legacy" and "masculine imperatives"—had nothing to do with the terror she felt about facing her desecration in the mirror. Rereading the novels of nineteenth-century women like Jane Austen with new eyes, Ellen finally admitted to herself that she and most of the women she knew longed to be loved as whole persons, body and soul, inside and out. As much as she trusted her mate, a primal fear rose up in her that her mutilation might have made her too ugly to love. Ellen had the courage to face down feminist dogma and ask why this fear was so potent.

She begins her book *The Face of Love* by describing photographs of herself as a child. Until the age of eight, little Ellen appears with "grave tenderness" looking outward upon the world, or with "a dazzling smile." She is often reaching toward or entwined with another family member: her mother or her sister. She is a beautiful, lively child. But at eight years old, Ellen's beauty vanishes. Photographs portray a withdrawn, awkward body and a guarded, neutral face. In one picture she scowls at the camera, her hair disheveled. Her arms are "stiffly braced by [her] sides," her foot thrust out "as though I were about to kick something."[13]

As an adolescent, Ellen says, "My face was too thin, my eyes too close together, my nose too long, my breasts (when they came) too small, my hips too large. . . . It all added up to my sense of myself as graceless, undesirable, ugly."[14]

What accounts for this transformation? When Ellen was eight, her beloved mother died:

> I understand now that the transformation of myself from a beautiful child to an ugly one is so distressing to me because deep down I have known all along what it was: neither an accident nor the fulfillment of an inevitable destiny but a response to an overwhelming loss. When I look at those early photos of myself I realize that what I am seeing and responding to so positively is the way delight and security inform a child's whole physical aspect. Looking at the photographs closely, I realize how many of the details I read as "beauty" can be referred back to the love at the center of that charmed circle . . . all those outward-reaching, confident gestures, of a body at peace with itself in the world. And so it comes to me now, with the same rush of understanding, that what I am responding to, when I look at the images of myself sitting awkwardly on someone else's porch, with the wrong dress and the wrong hairstyle, and features which seem to have lost their right relation to one another, is the enormity of the loss that wrought such a change. . . . I didn't just *become* ugly; my ugliness in those later childhood years was a response—in a sense *the most powerful response* I could make—to the turning upside down of my whole life.[15]

From the changes she observed in her own appearance, Ellen theorized that beauty was the outward expression of an inward harmony—in her case, the security of knowing she was loved. Young Ellen was beautiful because she was looked upon and made beautiful by "the face of love"—her mother's loving face that saw Ellen as beautiful because she loved her.

If beauty is in the eye of the beholder, then a loving beholder somehow has the power to bring out the beauty in the beloved. The loved girl or woman radiates the beauty of security, and so her beautiful face can also be called "the face of love." More than that, the loved woman also acquires the face that is itself "animated by love. Thus as a small child I gave back to the world the reflection of the love I had received, and in so doing I was beautiful."[16] The face of love, then, is the face of one who loves because she is loved.

God gives every parent a godlike task: to love a tiny immortal in an intensely physical way, and thereby to make that little one believe in her beauty. What true mother would say she loves her daughter's soul but finds her body distasteful? She loves that little body that wets, messes, bleeds, and nurses. She counts her toes, smiles into her eyes, and watches for her ever-shifting expressions. To her, that face is the beautiful face of love.

> YOU'RE NEVER TOO OLD FOR BARBIE™
> "She's back—but not for long. In her satin gown and furry stole, Enchanted Evening® Barbie® doll is the epitome of elegance. As a girl, you couldn't resist that intoxicating glamour. Now, with this Collector Edition reproduction of the 1960 beauty, you can preserve her pristine perfection, shoes and all."[17]

Mary Anne: The Face of Unlove

But some of us, for whatever reason, do not receive the face of love from our parents, or having had it, like Ellen, we lose it tragically. Ugliness is in the eye of the beholder who does not love. Mary Anne Tabor recalls:

> There was never a day in my childhood years when I thought that I was attractive, let alone beautiful. . . .
> I accepted the words I heard from the grownups in my world that I was an unattractive child. I was told I was too dark, my nose too flat, my eyes too small, my ears too cupped, my feet too long and narrow, and that I walked "pigeon-toed."
> I believed all of this, to my own inner agony.[18]

Unlike Ellen, Mary Anne had not lost the loving mother who made her believe in her beauty. Rather, Mary Anne never had such a mother: her mother taught her to believe in her ugliness. Was Mary Anne really "too dark" to be beautiful, or did her mother simply believe that fair European skin was better than dark Filipino skin? Mary Anne's ugliness was in the eye of a beholder who could not love her daughter well because she could not love herself.

Consequently, Mary Anne learned to see ugliness in her own face, which she could not love:

> I remember when I would go to the bathroom and look long and hard at myself in the mirror, staring into my own eyes to determine if I had any beauty. No, I did not see the same sight. The beauty I was seeking was not there. It did not dawn on me, for many years, that what I was seeking was an inner beauty which was connected to kindness and love. Those feelings were missing in my life, and when those feelings came my way via another person, well, to me that person was beautiful. In my own eyes I saw only ugliness, because I believed I was ugly, and hidden beneath that belief were feelings of sadness and anger. My eyes looking back at myself were filled with doubt. I could not love that face which brought no feelings of happiness or joy, and I could understand why my mother thought me to be ugly too.[19]

In part, Mary Anne saw herself as ugly because she felt no joy at the sight of herself and because she saw what her elders had taught her to see. She saw the ugly little girl anyone would have seen: a child whose face was marred by sadness, anger, and doubt. No inner beauty of a kind, loved-and-loving girl warmed those eyes or smiled out from that mirror. She saw only the face of unlove.

> "Plain women know more about men than beautiful women do."
> —Katherine Hepburn

Pat: Beauty as Manipulation

I (Cinny) remember the first time I met Pat. I was in a dressing room shopping for college clothes when Pat entered the opposite dressing room. My mother said, "There goes one of the best-dressed and most beautiful women in town." Pat was wearing an animal-print dress, had beautiful dark brunette hair, and exuded confidence and presence. She was one of the most glamorous women I had ever seen.

Pat, now sixty-four, told me, "The more attractive a woman is when younger, the more difficult it is to get older. My appearance is not the focus of my life, but as I get older, it certainly is important. I don't like the lines on my face and the roll around my middle.

"Before I became a Christian, my appearance *was* the focus of my life. I always dressed with a great deal of flair, too much flair. When a child is pretty and grows up with too much praise, she always works hard at being pretty.

"Dad talked about how I looked more than my mother did. I was very close to him. I felt being pretty was how I got accepted by him. He told me that when one was pretty she had a lot more responsibility to look pretty. As a result, I felt other areas of my life didn't get developed. Dad called me 'Princess.' I grew up thinking that when you're pretty, you get treated like a princess.

"I was an only child. Mom would shop for weeks for my party dresses. That seemed to be her hobby. I had to have the perfect dress, the perfect shoes, the perfect earrings, the perfect everything. The funny thing was that as hard as my mother worked to get me dressed, she never complimented me on how I looked. She used to say that 'pretty is as pretty does.'"

Young Pat suffered from double messages about her beauty. She didn't bask in the security of her parents' love but rather learned that beauty was a responsibility she had to work hard at in order to earn the right to be treated like a princess. Her father's approval never made her feel secure because she was always aware it might be withdrawn as quickly as it came; her mother's approval was even more elusive. "I felt hurt," said Pat. "I could never understand why she worked so hard on my appearance when she never said anything about it. She talked a lot about inner beauty and kindness, but she sent me a double message between her words and her actions that confused me.

"As I got older and learned to use attractiveness as a tool, I was able to get lots of pats on the back. Beauty can become very manipulative. That's what Dad meant when he said that beauty was a responsibility. I had to choose how to use it.

"When I had my thirtieth birthday, I stayed in with the covers over my head all day. A few days before, a boy in the grocery

store had called me, 'Ma'am' instead of 'Miss.' Then for my birthday, my sister-in-law gave me some beauty cream for around my
eyes. This panicked me, and I felt old for the first time in my life."

When beauty is the chief tool in a woman's strategy to earn
love, aging is a crisis. With all her money, Nancy Friday happily
claims that she can fend off that crisis indefinitely through plastic
surgery and hard work with a personal trainer, but Pat has chosen
instead to face her hunger for love and ask whether there is a better way to deal with it than through obsession with her appearance.
It's not easy to tell the truth as Pat did about her childhood hurts,
her fear of aging, and her habit of manipulation. Not easy, but
essential to real growth.

SHOULD GOD BE ENOUGH?

Some would say that what women like Nancy, Ellen, Mary Anne,
and Pat need to do is spend an hour each day alone with God and
a Bible, and tape a note to their mirrors that reads, "God loves me.
It doesn't matter what people think." That method works for some
people: the annals of the saints record the stories of countless
women who have become recluses to meditate on the love of God
until divine love alone sustains them. However, all the women who
told us that appearance isn't an issue for them have at least one
flesh-and-blood human being in their lives who loves them well,
who treats them as beautiful.

Not long ago, Barbara celebrated her sixtieth birthday. Three
generations of her family were gathered as her husband raised a
toast: "To Barbara, the most beautiful woman in the world." This
mature Christian woman, a role model for both her daughters
and the many other young women she mentors, felt her face flush.
After all these years, words like that still matter to her. Barbara is
not vain; she simply retains the human longing to be seen as beautiful in the eyes of a loving beholder.

A little girl parades her new dress in front of her daddy, hoping to bask in his delight. A woman beautifies herself before a
date, hoping he will see her with the eyes of a loving beholder.
These people may or may not understand the difference between
the life-giving truth that "I am beautiful to the one who loves me"

and the often sad fact that "I will be loved if I am beautiful." Yet in the gap between these two statements, thousands of women live in fear and sorrow.

The more confident we are in God's loving gaze, the less driven we will be to win the loving gaze of others, yet until resurrection we will probably always flourish best when we are experiencing God's love not just by faith but also through the eyes of human beholders. Even Adam was not complete until he had a fellow human whose beauty he could enjoy and who could enjoy his beauty. And even Adam had another deep longing, the longing for respect. That's the subject we'll explore in the next chapter.

A CLOSER LOOK

What messages did you receive about your beauty or lack of it from your mother when you were a child? What about from your father? (If one of them was not around, how did that affect your sense of security about being loved and/or being beautiful?) What messages did you receive from any other significant adults in your life?

Look at yourself in a mirror, preferably one that shows your entire body. How easy is it for you to look at yourself and say, "Behold, a loved woman"? Are you aware of being seen as beautiful by God? What about by other people in your life? How does that awareness or lack of it affect the way you live and the way you look? When you see your face in a mirror, do you see the face of love, or the face of unlove?

CHAPTER THREE

RESPECT

MAKING AN IMPRESSION

I (Cinny) have worked for years in sales and marketing, and as a public speaker. My most ambitious opportunity came when I auditioned to be a spokesperson for the QVC shopping network. Knowing how important appearance is in television work, I had my hair and makeup professionally done for the "head shot" (photograph) I sent to QVC with my resume.

The photo and resume won me an invitation to the second step of the audition: two five-minute taped presentations of products. Needless to say, I was extremely nervous and needed all the help I could get to sustain my confidence. I was up against professional actors who had done national television commercials or even hosted their own shows. To get the job, I had to walk into that studio and command respect just by the way I looked. I not only had to earn the respect of the producers but also had to look like someone who could win the respect of the QVC audience. Nobody buys from a salesperson they don't respect.

I turned to my red "power suit." Image consultants know that colors affect both wearer and viewer psychologically, and red expresses confidence and power. I always feel strong and assured when I wear it. I spent an inordinate amount of time on my makeup, had a great hair day, and when I arrived at that audition, I felt like a million bucks; I looked like a woman who knew what she was doing, even though she didn't.

I guess that red suit did the trick because I got a call back for the third step in the audition process. In the end I didn't make the final cut, but I had a great time and despite my lack of television experience, I felt I held my own.

Were the extra efforts on my hair, makeup, and choice of clothing just expressions of vanity or a sellout to a worldly industry like television? Or were they realistic efforts to win respect from a potential employer? As we've talked with women, respect seems to be as strong a motive as love in the drive to look good.

RESPECT GOES TO WORK

Humans need respect as we need air. Ask a girl why she joins a gang; it's partly because she needs somebody to watch her backside when everybody else belongs to a gang, but it's mostly because she's dying for respect. Her gang sisters respect and value her as one of them, and outsiders know they'd better treat her with respect.

In a world where nearly everybody judges books by covers, appearance heavily affects respect. One study found that "the classroom teachers of the early adolescents rated physically attractive students as more scholastically, socially, and athletically competent . . . than physically unattractive students."[1]

Consequently, when a woman is trying to make a living, respect feels more important even than love. A survey of 8,000 female executives found seventeen percent had wardrobe consultants.[2] Image consultants unanimously urge "investing" in professional clothing. Emily Cho of New Images/Emily Cho of New York thinks ten percent of one's salary is a reasonable amount to spend on clothing and image: "Whether you are vying for a promotion, competing for a new account, or moving from a corporate job into a business of your own, how effectively you attain your goals can depend quite significantly on how well your image is projected."[3] Susan Holland, president of a Chicago executive recruiting firm, concurs: "There is much more competition out there now. Companies want a lot of reasons to hire you—and keep you—and how you look is one of them."[4]

The respect game is even more complicated because, as Naomi Wolf discovered, a woman who is "too" attractive may lose respect if she is judged vain or less intelligent than more ordinary-looking women. For example, Elaine is a television newscaster in a major market. At forty-two she remains an attractive blonde, tall, slim, and happily married to her high school sweetheart. Many women with fewer advantages might envy her, but to Elaine, beauty has been a mixed blessing where respect is concerned: "In our business, the better you look, the more intimidating you are to co-workers. If one is particularly attractive and stylish, people tend to discount her credibility. Many people have a hard time believing you can be beautiful *and* smart. People tend to try to tear down people who seem to have everything."

If people believe a woman got her job through beauty rather than brains, she's lost. So women pick their way through a minefield, trying to look good enough but not too good, and the standard is constantly shifting. An Air Force major told us what a relief it is to wear a uniform: she always knows what's appropriate, and respect comes because of the symbols on her shoulders, not from her skill in shopping.

But in business, subtle variations in clothing and hairstyles can make all the difference in whether a woman is judged appropriately feminine or merely frivolous. Business attorney Nancy Cahill tells us that in her industry, attorneys wear long jackets; only support personnel would be seen in a cropped jacket. A tailored look is essential. Attorneys wear "serious" colors like navy, black, and more recently, red. An attorney in a cream-colored or apricot suit would find it very hard to cut a business deal. No one would be interested in her protests: "But I'm a Spring! Those are my colors!" Light colors simply do not command respect in the business world.

Business gurus pound women with the message that dressing for success is a life-or-death matter. Joely Beatty, senior partner in a California management consulting firm, says, "Updating your image, especially in light of a promotion, will not only give you

new self-confidence but will signal subordinates to take you seriously. . . . They might have difficulty accepting you in your new
role if you don't change."[5] That's quite a threat to an aspiring
worker: upgrade your image or forfeit the respect of your subordinates. We are reminded of Melanie Griffith's character in the
film *Working Girl*, who had to cut her hair and totally change her
look in order to be taken seriously as a mergers-and-acquisitions
negotiator rather than dismissed as a secretary.

Respect equals dollars. Studies in 1986 and 1989 found that
with each additional attractiveness point on the researcher's scale,
a woman gained $2,000 in ongoing yearly salary. "By 1993, people
perceived as good-looking — men and women — were earning at
least 5 percent more than those labeled average-looking."[6]

Respect can exist among equals and partners, but in a business
environment it often involves competition and hierarchical status.
Only one person gets the job or the promotion. Bosses have higher
status than subordinates. In such an environment, appearing to
have higher status counts. And dressing for status isn't cheap. Part
of the message that dressing well gives is: "I have the money to
afford these clothes because I am a high-status person." Carrying
this message off can be especially burdensome for young women
in entry-level positions, who are expected to project just as polished an appearance as someone earning twice their salary. A
manicure or a Liz Claiborne suit costs the same whether one is a
secretary or a manager.

Further, women who have appearance-status liabilities may
have to work extra hard and spend extra money to earn respect.
Large women, for example, have to overcome our society's tendency to disrespect women of their size. Sharon, the aspiring
speaker in Chapter 1, slammed hard into this fact. Minority women
have to counter the suspicion that they're less qualified than a Caucasian might be. Disfigured or physically impaired women must
deal with people's tendency to dismiss or even avoid them.

Talk about pressure! If you don't spend thousands of dollars
a year on your clothes, accessories, makeup, and hair, then your
coworkers will ignore you, your clients will leave you, and your
boss will pass you over for a promotion. If you're large, black, or

handicapped, you'll have to work twice as hard for half the respect. But don't worry; God loves you.

THE MALL AND THE CHURCH

I (Karen) have an automatic habit of adjusting my appearance when running errands, depending on the response I want. If I want to roam a mall without being bothered by salespeople, a T-shirt and unpainted face usually guarantee I'll be ignored. I look low-status, so salespeople don't respect me enough to assail me. On the other hand, if I want service, and especially if I want to have a store error redressed or to request something out of the ordinary, I put on my makeup, do something with my hair, and wear office clothes. Retailers tend to respect my professional look.

Recently I was out and about and needed to find a public restroom. My options were few, so I decided to march into a five-star hotel and find the meeting floor, where there would definitely be public restrooms. I knew I could carry this off partly because I looked like I belonged. An African-American male wearing anything but an immaculate suit would have been noticed and watched.

Appearance has always been a crucial signal of status. Medieval noblemen passed "sumptuary laws" that regulated the amount of silk, gold and silver thread, velvet, and fur each rank of person might wear.[7] However, appearance is even more essential in a culture of strangers such as ours. In earlier times, most people married people they had grown up with and known their whole lives. Most people did business with people they had known for years. People moved much less than they do now, so when people looked at a woman, they knew not just her exterior, but a great deal about her character as well.

In a stable culture it is much easier for a plain woman to win love and respect for her good nature, relational skills, and strength of character. But in a mobile urban culture, people know the woman who walks into their classroom or office only by her appearance. A saleswoman has to look trustworthy to clients who haven't known her long enough to have other evidence that she is trustworthy. A job applicant has to look like a desirable employee. A speaker has to look like someone worth listening to when her audience has never met her before. And men looking for mates are encouraged to judge by appearance when they have no other information about women they meet at social gatherings.

It's no wonder that women's desire to earn respect by their looks spills over into church. In many congregations it's normal for women to arrive in their Sunday best, carefully painted, coiffed, and accessorized. While some of this may be intended to express respect for God, most of us know we're at least as eager for the other worshipers to respect us. The pastor's wife and elders' wives often have to look like they deserve our respect. As in business, these women walk a tightrope that no one discusses openly. I (Cinny) sweated to choose clothes that would look neither too dowdy nor too flashy: respectable, whatever that meant in this particular church in this particular part of the country.

If church members don't know each other well, they can't possibly earn each other's respect by a lifetime of open-hearted acts done in humility. But even when we do know each other and have seen one another's character in action, it's easy for our human need for respect and our tendency to judge by appearance to drive us into a competition for the best hair—or at least into a valiant attempt to hold our own. We'd sound vain if we talked about it, so we go right on struggling to keep up, wondering if we're the only one who feels weighed down by relentless, silent expectations.

Ultimately, of course, we want to mature to a point where we are secure in God's respect of us. God views each one of us as highly valuable creatures. God takes us seriously. Nevertheless, most of us still need to see God's respect reflected to us through the eyes of His people. Paul instructed believers to "Honor one another,"[8] to show each other respect. He didn't tell them, "Treat others like dirt; it will make them more spiritual." Paul understood that his readers weren't spiritual giants. They yearned to be taken seriously by their brothers and sisters. If people don't automatically treat us with respect just because we're fellow humans, then we'll feel tempted to earn their respect by any available means, including appearance.

In our efforts to win respect in the arenas of work, church, and romance, we put on what we might call a public face or mask.

Because of Jesus' harsh words against the Pharisees, who put on false public images in order to hide their cold hearts and exalt themselves above others, Christians tend to be suspicious of public faces, even while we've raised masking to an art. We have a love-hate relationship with hypocrisy. We are wise to be cautious, but let's consider the value a mask can have when used appropriately.

> "When you were growing up, did you know what you wanted to be? A mother? A dancer? A glittering success? And did you know that whatever your path, something inside you would always shine through? **ghost myst**. . . . The first fragrance to celebrate your inner beauty."[9]

THE MASK

Psychologists use the term *persona* to name the outer self of a person, often a false self that hides the true, inner self from view. However, the original term described an outer face that revealed a person's true character. *Persona* is Latin for "mask," the mask that an ancient actor wore in sacred theater. The Greeks and Romans believed that when an actor put on the mask of the king Agamemnon, he became Agamemnon. They did not think of the mask as hiding the actor's true self but as revealing the character of the king. The mask was created to be a perfect outer representation of the character's inner self.

Because we are so aware that a mask or outer appearance can hide and lie about a person's inner beauty or ugliness, we often underestimate how important a public face is, how much it can reveal about the inner person, and how much it affects the way people think about others and about themselves. Mask-making is a sacred act, the creation of a public face that offers some parts of one's soul to the world while protecting other parts that should be kept private.

My (Cinny's) makeup and red suit used color to convey the confident, energetic side of my inner self. This mask effectively revealed a part of me I chose to make public, while hiding my nervous self. I knew I was playing a role on a stage and never lost sight of the total me behind the mask.

On the other hand, I (Karen) believed for years that my plain look was more honest than a professional mask, when in fact I was hiding behind the appearance of "unworldliness." Curiously, my natural look was more hypocritical than Cinny's carefully chosen professional costume. I believed my mask was me; Cinny knew hers was only a piece of her. Cinny was honest with herself about wanting respect, while I imagined I was above all that.

In a way, the mask is like skin. People say, "Beauty is only skin deep." While this may be true, it actually underscores beauty's importance. Our skin is the largest organ of our bodies. It shields us from outside harm and reveals a lot about our internal health. For example, stress depletes both minerals and water from our bodies; our skin is quick to reflect that depletion. A person can live relatively well with significant loss of kidney or liver function, but an equal loss of skin plunges her into agony and probable death. We should never underestimate the significance of anything that is skin deep. God created us to wear our public masks not as deceptive shells but as living skin, an essential organ of our personhood.

Mary Anne Tabor tells a potent story about using makeup, clothing, and jewelry to speak silently both to others and herself about who she was:

> The mirror reflected a woman intense and confident. Her skin appeared flawless and the contrast of her red lipstick and her black eyeliner was dramatic. She decided to use no blushing powder, so as to achieve a look of contrast and drama. She applied her mascara carefully to separate each lash, both upper and bottom lashes, and smudged just a little green eyeshadow at the outer corner of her eyelids to emphasize the apple green Ching dynasty earrings she wore that day. She studied herself. Her eyes looked angry. Good, she thought, for she was after all quite angry. She looked cold, aloof, unreachable. Then she bent forward and brushed her thick, black, permed hair from underneath. She brushed more than a hundred times, very deliberately, to achieve a hairdo akin to a lion's mane.

She stood very straight, checked herself in the mirror again and knew what she must wear that day. She chose a black knit fitted dress, very expensive, which was mid-calf in length with three-quarter length sleeves. She did not want too much flesh to show anywhere, yet she wanted the effect of showing off her small waist while mildly emphasizing her bust line and hips.[10]

Here Mary Anne portrays herself like a warrior arraying herself for battle against the internationally known attorney for whom she was press secretary. She was about to confront the wrongdoing of a powerful, controlling man, so she used a beauty mask to declare to both herself and her adversary that her true self at this moment was intense, confident, angry, aloof from manipulation, and completely feminine in her strength. The mask hid parts of her—the nervous, intimidated, self-doubting parts—but the aspects it revealed were just as true. In both hiding and revealing, protecting and offering different parts of a woman's self, the beauty mask serves as essential a function as skin.

> "New Ultress® lets you express your inner self. Or perhaps we should say selves."[11]

EXPRESSING OURSELVES

The mask's purpose is to express the aspect of our identity that is appropriate to the occasion (work, sports, church) and to win us respect in that identity. Our culture has raised self-expression to heights of absurdity, but at core, the desire to express ourselves flows from the desire to be known and embraced for who we are, to be noticed and respected. A mass, anonymous culture makes it hard for us to feel that people see, know, and acknowledge us, so people depend greatly upon expressing themselves visually. While the desire to express oneself, visually or otherwise, can become an unhealthy obsession, it is basically a normal human impulse. In fact, it is essential to humanness, for in it we reflect God's desire to express Himself through creating and loving us.

Makeup parties and shopping expeditions are standard forms

of female recreation. One woman bubbled to us about the fun she has trying on new cosmetics; she feels a childlike joy in playing dress-up, in trying on new identities and saying in effect to friends and strangers, "Look at me!" This woman is young and pretty, with a husband, family, and friends who love her. Nonetheless, she pursues self-expression passionately. Listening to her, we could imagine God smiling with amusement at her streak of youthful exhibitionism. It doesn't appear to control her. On the other hand, women who have received little attention and respect in their lives may feel far more driven to be seen at any cost. We can imagine God grieved by their drivenness, and even more grieved by the world that has starved them of what God knows they need.

We can see the potent ways in which self-expression and respect interweave in a single aspect of the mask: face paint. Face painting is common in many societies, and paint or its absence sends a variety of messages. In many cultures, men, women, or both paint their faces to say something about their prowess as warriors, their sexual availability, their status in society, and so on. In eighteenth-century Europe, for instance, both men and women wore powder and rouge, or even painted their faces with "enamels made from egg whites or a combination of lead and vinegar"[12] to signal that they belonged to the aristocracy or the rising business class as well as to hide the effects of smallpox. A century later, such painting represented the kind of aristocratic pretense scorned especially in North America but also in Europe. A woman who wore rouge or lipstick sent the message, "I am a prostitute," while a man who did so declared himself far outside the mainstream of society. While in 1750 men rouged themselves in order to win respect for their identities as aristocrats, in 1850 they avoided rouge in order to win respect for their identities as serious and masculine.

Today, powder, rouge (demurely renamed "blush"), and lipstick all signify mainstream femininity. A woman who wears no makeup may be perceived as unprofessional, masculine, or purely intellectual, unless she's a natural beauty. A man who wears makeup outside a theater or film studio is seen as effeminate. (However, both men and women are now permitted to color their hair.) Each industry and region has a slightly different standard for appropriate women's makeup: more makeup in Dallas than in Vermont; more in computer sales than in chemical engineering. In short, while the fundamental reason for wearing cosmetics is to attract love, a second but strong reason is simply to fit in, to be respected in one's chosen identity.

Cosmetic companies work hard to convince women that we must wear makeup to fit in and to express our true selves. Both pieces of this message are crucial: Women want to believe that their public faces express who they really are; they also want to be respected for being that person. If a woman feels that her made-up mask is a false front, hiding the real her, then any respect she receives feels empty. She wants to be seen and acknowledged for herself, and makeup helps her attain those goals.

An article in the *Journal of Psychology and Marketing* highlights the way modern women use makeup both to find out who they are and to seek respect for that person. As they interviewed women on their makeup histories, Drs. Stacey Fabricant and Stephen Gould identified four basic styles of makeup use.

Devotees used a lot of makeup (more than four products at once) nearly all the time. The thought of going out in public without makeup made them as nervous as the suggestion that they run through the streets naked. Their painted face felt like part of who they were, and they doubted people would respect them without it.

Habituals wore a little makeup nearly all the time; they wanted to look "natural" (as though they were wearing no makeup), but were as uncomfortable as Devotees at the thought of actually wearing no makeup in public. Again, they believed respect depended upon presenting their slightly painted face.

Creatives often wore no makeup, but when they did paint themselves for special occasions, they wore a lot "as a form of creative and social expressiveness."[13] They might feel a little anxious if they showed up for certain occasions, such as work or class, without makeup, but they would quickly forget about it. They were somewhat concerned about losing respect in those situations but not as concerned as Devotees or Habituals. Creatives put the most thought into how much was right for what occasion, varying their mask according to the situation.

Finally, *Avoiders* "felt awkward with makeup on, were conscious of it being on their faces, and sought a natural look by refraining from using it as much as possible."[14] For Avoiders, camouflaging facial flaws was at least as important a reason for painting as was expressing themselves. As a former Avoider, I (Karen) can say that I craved respect as much as any Devotee, but I was nervous about drawing attention to my femininity. Other Avoiders with a more secure sense of themselves might genuinely not care what other people think, but I was not one of those.

Whatever look each woman in this study chose, she did so because she believed it brought out the real her. For all but the Avoiders, the women believed wearing no makeup actually hid the real them by making them look less alive and attractive than they really felt inside. They believed the mask revealed their true identity, the one the world would welcome and respect.

Fabricant and Gould traced how each woman in their study learned her makeup style. Role models like mothers and sisters set examples of how one should use makeup to send the message, "I am the kind of woman our family approves of." The media and children's toys also told the women that being a grown-up-but-not-over-the-hill woman required wearing makeup.

> If the barn
> needs painting,
> paint it?

I (Cinny) recall learning painfully in the summer before ninth grade that makeup was essential for respect. I lived in Florida but was visiting old friends in Tulsa, Oklahoma. At the time I was interested in sports, especially swimming and diving, and I was rapidly growing interested in boys. My girlfriends and I went to a country club for a day, and I noticed the gap between how I spent the day and how my friends did. They passed the time in the clubhouse flirting with boys, their faces heavily made up and every frosted blond hair in place. When I joined them at the end of the day, my face bare and my wet brown hair combed behind my ears, I felt unsophisticated, unfeminine, and insecure—the country mouse compared to my city friends with their cosmopolitan style. I tried to blend into the background. I returned to Florida committed to never feeling so completely out of it again.

To this day I am a Devotee and feel insecure in public without my face on. As I've become aware of this insecurity, I've chosen regularly to run errands without wearing makeup, and I'm becoming more comfortable letting people see me like this. For a Southern woman, this is a big step of faith!

The Fabricant and Gould study also revealed that makeup signified rites of passage from one identity to another, such as the transition from girlhood to womanhood or from single to married. Unmarried Marie Bloom was an Avoider, but when she became Marie Bloom-Hansen, she became a Creative, experimenting with how the new Marie should look.

Alternatively, makeup signified a woman's varied selves: different looks for "the day versus night self, the work versus fun self, the feminist versus nonfeminist self."[15] Adorning herself for a date might put a woman in a romantic mood, while grooming for work helped adjust her feelings and thought patterns for the business ahead. A woman might use her beauty mask as a shield to hide behind, or as a way to play with different identities and change character.

With some frustration, the women in the study talked about the minefield that the quest for respect through beauty could be. They generally agreed that they needed to play down their attractiveness in order to get ahead at work and play up their attractiveness in order to get ahead in social relationships with men. However, Marie Bloom-Hansen's boss actually asked her to wear makeup and skirts in order to be attractive enough for a sales position. She attributed her power, self-confidence, and success in sales to her beauty mask. At the age of nineteen or twenty, she says, she reduced several men to "babbling, bumbling idiots" because of her beautiful suit and perfect makeup. Bursting with pride, she crowed: "The colors, the lips were really there, the whole thing made a great sale!"[16]

For women who feel chronically undervalued, such potent attention feels intoxicating. Like the biblical Queen Esther, who put on her best face and clothes before she approached her husband with a dangerous request, Marie used beauty as a mask of power when seeking the favor of men. In future chapters, we will explore the ethical dilemma Marie's story illustrates: is it appropriate to try to look our best in order to influence clients and others? At what point do we cross the line into manipulation or pandering to a person's weaknesses?

For good or ill, wearing cosmetics is about putting on a culturally appropriate face in order to be respected. Challenge a woman's makeup routine, and be prepared for a fight.

SCANDAL IN CORINTH

Interestingly, alongside the well-known New Testament warnings against conforming to the ways of the world, in one case the apostle Paul actually urged women to conform to cultural customs of appearance. In the Roman Empire women normally grew their hair long and, when in public, bound it on top of their heads and covered it with a veil. Prostitutes set themselves apart by going out in public unveiled.

Certain women in Corinth decided that freedom in Christ liberated them from all constraints of culture. They expressed their freedom by shedding their veils when praying to God in church meetings. We can imagine how shocked both outsiders and fellow worshipers were. An equivalent display might be a modern woman's decision that freedom in Christ authorized her to come to church bare-chested.

Paul was horrified. In his response he wrote of short hair or a bare head on a woman as a disgrace, as improper (*improper* means contrary to custom), and as against nature. His final ruling on the subject was, "We have no other practice"—that is, veiling is standard practice or custom.[17]

This ruling remained the custom in churches around the world until the 1920s. In that decade North American and European women began to express their liberation from social constraint by removing their hats and cutting their hair. Many people were scandalized, and the custom in churches remained that women should wear hats while men should remove them. Hats in public became customary again from the 1930s through the 1960s, at which time hats fell victim to a general social upheaval.

Today most churches accept the culture's customs and see

nothing wrong with women wearing their hair short and coming hatless to church. In fact, women who refrain from cutting their hair and continue to veil themselves are in the minority. Most churches teach that Paul was urging women to conform to their culture's standard of propriety in order to win respect for the gospel. If short hair or a bare head signifies prostitution or wanton defiance in a given society, then women should avoid those styles of appearance. The important thing is not the style itself, but rather the message it sends to onlookers.

A person's public face or appearance sends strong nonverbal messages to anyone who sees her, so it makes sense that she thinks carefully about what message she wants to send and how best to send it to the society in which she lives. She may wear short sleeves in Southern California but not in Saudi Arabia in order to send the same message about her moral character, because in California bare arms are appropriate, while in Saudi Arabia they are not.

> Women working outside the home spend an average of almost $2,000 per year on career clothing.[18]

Appearance is a powerful mode of communication that should not be treated lightly. In fact, if a chaste woman walks around the Saudi capital in short sleeves and slacks, she will actually be sending a false message about herself. A wise and healthy public face is one that sends true messages about the inner person in a language others can understand.

WHAT WOMEN REALLY WANT

Women want to be seen in the eyes of a loving beholder, to be known for their true identities and respected. Appearance is a key to both. But there's more. Researchers from a variety of disciplines believe women want their love and respect in a very specific context: family security. Best-selling author and psychologist Warren Farrell thinks security and family are women's primary fantasy. He notes that year after year, the top-selling women's magazines are not *Glamour* or *Working Woman*, but *Better Homes and Gardens* and *Family Circle*. "*Better Homes and Gardens* outsells *Playboy* and *Penthouse*, [the two top-selling men's magazines], combined."[19]

How does a woman get family security? How does she get a man to marry her and stay with her through the raising of their children? We might not like what the answer often is: by being beautiful. In the next two chapters we are going to explore some controversial research. We want to let you make up your own mind about whether it explains part of beauty's power. When we first came across these studies, we found them at times thought-provoking and at times disturbing. Put on your seatbelt! You may experience some turbulence, but we think you'll find it worth your while.

A CLOSER LOOK

Next time you go to work or to church, notice how other women present themselves. What messages do you think they intend to send—through their makeup or lack of it, their hair, their clothing, and their accessories—about who they are and how concerned they are about respect? Also, notice how you present yourself in various contexts. What messages are you intending to send?

CHAPTER FOUR

BASIC INSTINCT

THE ETERNAL TRIANGLE

Richard sails into the party with Danielle on his arm. At thirty-three, Richard holds a Ph.D. in economics with some additional graduate study in psychology; he analyzes federal budgets for a large think tank. Surveying the room, he notes with satisfaction that all eyes are appraising Danielle. The twenty-eight-year-old actress knows little about psychology and less about economics, but what she lacks in education she makes up for in aesthetics; every man in the room is transparently thinking some version of "Wow."

Thirty-six-year-old Karla rolls her eyes. She has worked with Richard for four years, and while he often hangs out in her office to untangle some snarled idea (she, too, has a Ph.D.), likes to trade Congress jokes with her, and even concedes that she makes amazing lasagna, it has never occurred to him to ask her on a date. She doesn't need a Ph.D. to know why. Her wispy brown hair, long face, and angular body never turn heads the way Danielle does.

What is going on here? Why is this scene played out so often that it becomes cliché? Richard, Danielle, and Karla might be recent Latin American immigrants or Korean office workers, and the story would be the same. As Shakespeare mused,

Love looks with the eyes, not with the mind.
Therefore is winged Cupid painted blind.

Researchers in august-sounding fields like "evolutionary psychology" and "the psychophysics of beauty" think they have an
explanation for Cupid's visual bias. Magazines from *Newsweek* to
Mademoiselle have taken notice of this research. Both feminists and
evangelicals have protested the evolutionists' theory for different
reasons. The theory owes a lot to Charles Darwin, but even those
who think Darwin was more mythmaker than scientist can learn
a great deal from it if they read with critical eyes.

Over a century ago, Darwin speculated that animals develop
an instinct to prefer certain characteristics in a mate in part because
those characteristics are associated with higher success in reproduction. Every animal instinctively wants to pass on its genes to
a new generation, so it looks for a mate (or mates) with whom it
can conceive and raise as many offspring as possible who will in
turn reproduce successfully. Darwin viewed human beings as
highly evolved animals, so he proposed that this theory applied to
humans as well. Richard chooses Danielle over Karla because
instinct tells him she's the best bet for his genes.

For a century, this scenario remained just an untested theory.
It also left some big questions, such as, what is it about Danielle
that makes her seem a more likely baby factory?

Enter the evolutionary psychologists. In the 1980s, University
of Michigan psychologist David Buss, among others, set out to test
Darwin's theory. First Buss interviewed and administered questionnaires to 186 married adults and 100 unmarried college
students in the United States. That doesn't seem like a large sample to the layperson, but scientists consider it statistically
significant. However, it speaks only about Americans, not humans
in general.

Over a five-year period, Buss recruited "fifty collaborators from
thirty-seven cultures located on six continents and five islands,
from Australia to Zambia"[1] to aid in his research. Local residents
administered questionnaires in their native languages, in large cities
and rural areas, among the well educated and the poorly educated,

to capitalists, communists, and socialists from fourteen to seventy years of age. In all, they surveyed 10,047 people of every major ethnic, religious, and racial group. That study had such interesting results that Buss launched fifty more, involving thousands of persons. He also collected statistics from earlier decades. His published summary of findings is called *The Evolution of Desire: Strategies of Human Mating*. Others, such as Harvard neuropsychologist Nancy Etcoff and University of New Mexico biologist Randy Thornhill, have also added studies to the pile.

We aren't biologists and don't wish to debate here the theory of evolution. As will become clear, the fascinating data in these studies may or may not point to evolution. However, they do suggest that humans may have instinctive preferences for how a mate should look. Instinct may be one piece of the beauty puzzle. Furthermore, the data seem to mesh with what the Bible says about *the flesh*.

Let's look first at the research and then compare it to what the Bible says. Do Richards around the globe really prefer Danielles over Karlas? What do men want?

WHAT MEN WANT

Much has been made of different beauty standards in different cultures. Researchers do note some diversity in taste regarding skin color, plumpness, and most important features—such as eyes, ears, breasts, or genitals. However, for the most part, standards of beauty are remarkably consistent around the world. "Asian and American men, for example, agree with each other on which Asian and American women are most and least attractive. Consensus has also been found among the Chinese, Indian, and English; between South Africans and Americans; and between black and white Americans."[2]

Is this consistency merely evidence of television's hegemony? Maybe not. Even infants were found to look longer at photographs of people deemed attractive by adults, and year-old infants "showed more observable pleasure, more play involvement, less distress, and less withdrawal when interacting with strangers who wore attractive masks than when interacting with strangers who wore unattractive masks."[3] Nature/nurture studies are always open to debate, but these offer at least some evidence that standards of attractiveness may be more inborn than we might think.

Youth

Men in every one of the thirty-seven societies studied uniformly said they desire mates who are younger than they are. College men surveyed throughout the United States from 1939 through 1988 preferred women about 2.5 years younger. That figure turned out to be the average around the world. As men age, they prefer mates who are increasingly younger than they are.

Men also prefer women who appear to be young. Such signs of youth as smooth, clear skin, ungraying hair, and good muscle tone are considered attractive in a mate, even in cultures that revere the aged. Behavioral cues, such as high energy and a bouncy gait, are also desirable.

"When men and women rate a series of photographs of women differing in age, judgments of facial attractiveness decline with the increasing age of the woman. The decline in ratings of beauty occurs regardless of the age or sex of the judge. The value that men attach to women's faces, however, declines more rapidly than do women's ratings of other women's faces as the age of the woman depicted in the photograph increases."[4]

That's the first set of data: Men find youthfulness beautiful. You're probably thinking, "No kidding." It's no secret in our culture that youth rules.

Health

According to Buss & Co., clear skin, clear eyes, thick, lustrous hair, sound teeth, and an absence of sores and lesions are also beauty essentials. Disfigurement, disease, and pimples are as unappealing to the men of the Trobriand Islands as they are to men in the United Kingdom. Among fair-skinned peoples, color in the cheeks and lips denotes health and so is also considered attractive. Tiny flaws, such as Cindy Crawford's birthmark and the gap between Lauren Hutton's front teeth, add to a supermodel's appeal by giving her something unique; but in general, flawlessness is alluring.

Symmetry

"From zebra finches to scorpion flies, creatures scope out prospective mates by checking for at least one classic beauty benchmark: symmetry. Imagine a line drawn down the center of the face from forehead to chin. When eyebrows, eyes, ears and cheekbones match up perfectly, bang, you've got symmetry."[5]

According to Randy Thornhill, asymmetry in a scorpion fly or other animal (including humans) is a sign that the animal was injured or attacked by a parasite during development.[6] Asymmetry could also signal poor nutrition or a neurological problem. Consequently, symmetry is an excellent cue to an animal's health. Also, asymmetry (such as stretch marks and wrinkles) increases with age, so symmetry is also a measure of youth.

It's no surprise to Thornhill that male scorpion flies and swallows seek out symmetrical mates and avoid asymmetrical ones. What about humans? It turns out that most of us have feet that are slightly different in length—not enough that we can't buy shoes in pairs, but enough that the difference is measurable. The same goes for the breadth of our hands, the length of our ears, and so on. Further, some of us have feet that match better than others of us—that is, some of us are more symmetrical than others. So Thornhill and colleague Steve Gangestad measured people's foot breadth, hand breadth, ear length, and ear breadth and then independently had subjects rate them on attractiveness. The people with more symmetrical bodies were judged more attractive even by people who never saw their feet because symmetrical feet and ears tend to go with symmetrical facial features. (Take a moment now to measure your feet.)

Symmetry is so attractive to humans that we even prefer average faces over unique ones. In one study using computer graphics, composite faces were generated from sets of four, eight, sixteen, or thirty-two faces. People were asked to rate the attractiveness of each composite, as well as the attractiveness of the individual faces that made up the composites. "The composite faces were universally judged to be more physically attractive than any of the individual ones. The sixteen-face composite was more attractive than the four-face or eight-face composites, and the thirty-two face composite was the most attractive of all."[7] Superimposing faces tends to eliminate asymmetries, so the most "average" composites were the most symmetrical and hence, the most beautiful.

In nature, a composite face usually results from a broad gene pool, while extremely individual traits, such as misshapen limbs, tend to result from inbreeding, which can also cause serious inherited health problems. Symmetry, then, comes back again to health.

> "Smoothie®'s Waist Eliminator™. Get that desirable hourglass shape in a controlling nylon and spandex blend with flexible boning."[9]

Plastic surgeons know all this. An average nose is more attractive on a film star than her own, unique nose, even if every other actress in Hollywood has the same nose. Research even shows that "the size of a woman's breasts isn't as important as the firmness and sameness of the pair" (symmetry).[8]

The Chipmunk Look

The only thing better than average is an exaggeration of certain features. Computer-enhanced faces with unusually full lips, high foreheads, and small jaws were judged especially attractive by men, even when women thought they looked a bit "chipmunky."[10] Because of their very small jaws, like that of an eleven-year-old, these faces have relatively prominent eyes and cheekbones.[11] Large eyes, small jaw, high cheekbones — these are the salient features of a Renaissance madonna, a Gibson girl, or a contemporary model because they are agelessly popular with men.

Curves

We come finally to body shape. Preference for plumpness versus thinness varies the most around the world (and researchers have theories about why), but the range of preferred sizes is smaller than many American and Western European women think. In one study, "American men and women viewed nine female figures that varied from very thin to very plump. The women were asked to indicate their ideal for themselves, as well as their perception of what men's ideal female figure was. In both cases, women selected a figure slimmer than average. When men, however, were asked to select which female figure they preferred, they selected the figure of the average body size."[12] American women think men like women thinner than they actually do.

Don't believe it? Show a copy of *Vogue* to your favorite man. Ask him to rate the models as too heavy, too thin, or just right. Chances are you'll find that scrawny *Vogue* models make excellent clothes hangers, but they aren't a man's first preference. Most men like bodies that fit within a size range that denotes health.

Further, while size preferences vary, one aspect of body shape seems to be popular the world over: a certain ratio of waist size to hip size. It turns out that men around the world prefer a 0.7 waist-to-hip ratio (waist measurement divided by hip measurement). A perfect 0.7 woman would have a twenty-seven-inch waist and thirty-eight-inch hips — hourglass curves. A lower ratio means an even curvier woman. Researchers found that "although Miss America's weight has dropped steadily over the course of the last three decades, her waist-to-hip ratio has nonetheless remained steady at 0.7."[13] *Playboy* centerfolds showed a similar drop in weight yet the same steady waist-to-hip ratio. Supermodel Cindy Crawford is much taller and thinner than was actress Sophia Loren in her prime, yet both attained their fame as 0.7 women.

Why 0.7? And more broadly, why youth and health, full lips and tiny jaws? Here we shift from the hard data to the researchers' theories. We don't share their biases and so we think their theory has gaps, but we do believe the Bible supports their views in part. Instinct does seem to be one of several important influences upon men's taste in women.

WHY MEN WANT THAT

The Theory
Consider the plight of the ancestral male. In order to be reproductively successful, he had to mate with a woman who could bear many children who would live to adulthood. In many species, males don't need to guess which females are fertile: females go into heat and display obvious visual or olfactory signs. But human

females don't do this. Consequently, ancestral men had to look for indirect cues that a woman was likely to bear many strong children. Men who guessed right would be more likely to pass down their genes than men who guessed wrong, so those with the strongest accurate instincts would proliferate. What would these wise men look for?

First, women's ability to bear children declines steadily after the age of twenty. So it behooved an ancestral male to look for a mate as young as possible, with the most years for childbearing ahead of her. Instinct would tell him: find the ones that look young. Second, a healthy parent is most likely to bear a healthy child, so again instinct whispers: seek out the ones with signs of health, including symmetry.

What about that waist-hip ratio? Buss explains:

> Before puberty, boys and girls show a similar fat distribution. At puberty, however, a dramatic change occurs. Boys lose fat from their buttocks and thighs, while the release of estrogen in pubertal girls causes them to deposit fat in their lower trunk, primarily on their hips and upper thighs. Indeed, the volume of body fat in this region is 40 percent greater for women than for men. . . .
>
> Healthy, reproductively capable women have a waist-to-hip ratio between 0.67 and 0.80, while healthy men have a ratio in the range of 0.85 to 0.95. Abundant evidence now shows that the waist-to-hip ratio is an accurate indicator of women's reproductive status. Women with a lower ratio show earlier pubertal endocrine activity. Married women with a higher ratio have more difficulty becoming pregnant, and those who do become pregnant do so at a later age than women with a low ratio. The waist-to-hip ratio is also an accurate indication of long-term health status. Diseases such as diabetes, hypertension, heart problems, previous stroke, and gallbladder disorders have been shown to be linked with the distribution of fat, as reflected by the ratio, rather than with the total proportion of body fat. The link between the waist-to-hip ratio

and both health and reproductive status makes it a reliable cue for ancestral men's preferences in a mate.[14]

Further, a thickening waist is often a sign that a woman is either aging or pregnant, and in neither case available to make a new baby. And that anorectic model (who is probably missing periods because of her low body fat, which drives down estrogen levels) is less alluring to the average man than that luscious, curvaceous, high-estrogen baby machine in a men's magazine centerfold.

The "chipmunk" look — high forehead, tiny jaw, full lips, large eyes, and prominent cheekbones — is a composite and exaggeration of those facial features "that diverge in males and females during puberty."[15] Male hormones in teenage boys add bone to their jaws and lower their foreheads, while estrogen leaves jaws small and fills out girls' lips. Large eyes help de-emphasize women's jaws and so make them look more like women. Full lips and a small jaw are not certain indicators that a woman has high odds of getting pregnant, but they indicate on an instinctive level that estrogen has left its mark.

The appeal of large breasts also makes sense in terms of estrogen: since estrogen is what makes a girl's breasts fill out, then male instinct responds to bigger breasts as though they mean more estrogen — more of what it takes to be a woman. The fact that large-breasted women don't actually have higher estrogen levels or more frequent pregnancies than women with small breasts doesn't erase the instinctive reaction. Some evidence suggests that the obsession with large breasts is mainly an American fixation that dates only from the 1940s.[16] In earlier eras men liked breasts but were far more enthusiastic about voluptuous thighs. (Oh, for the good old days when big thighs were sexy!)

So according to evolutionary psychologists, one of the chief reasons Richard is drawn to Danielle over Karla is that his instincts observe her thick hair, curvaceous waist-to-hip ratio, symmetrical features, large eyes, petite jaw, and flawless complexion, and they signal to him: fertile. Instinct tells Richard that Karla's age, thin hair, and lack of curves make her a less likely candidate for bearing him a flock of children. She may be perfectly healthy and have plenty of estrogen, but Richard's instincts aren't refined enough to sense that. And even though modern-day Richard may not want to raise ten or even three children, his instincts were installed at a time when having as many children as possible was essential to the tribe's survival. Up until the industrial age, infant mortality was high and children were needed to manage farms, so men consciously chose wives for their ability to bear strong children. This urgent value ran right through Old Testament times, when barren women consistently suffered the shame their cultures attached to their failure at childbearing. Times may have changed, but instincts are hard-wired into human brains. Richard's are no different from Abraham's.

Thus, there is something to what Willard Harley said about a man's *need* for an attractive wife. To the degree that a man is ruled by instinct or desires to have children, he will be strongly motivated to mate with a woman who shows the signs of youth, health, and estrogen. However, we don't think that's necessarily something to cheer about. We are both glad not to be married to men controlled by such a perceived *need*. Even the researchers believe men can and should rise above mere instinct. "I don't know any scientist who thinks you can look to nature for moral guidelines," says Randy Thornhill. [17]

> American women spent more than half a billion dollars on shape-enhancing garments in 1995.[18]

While the Bible supports the notion that men often *do* allow instinct to rule them, it doesn't agree with Harley that men *should* do this, nor that their wives and girlfriends should encourage them to do so. Instead, the Bible calls this behavior, *living according to the flesh*.

The Flesh

It can be wearisome to read Darwinians talking about humans as though we were scorpion flies driven by DNA. Many readers will balk at the very mention of evolution. Yet, what's essential to this theory is not whether men's instinct for a certain type of woman has evolved over thousands of years or was created by God in an instant. What's essential is whether men have such an instinct at all. Granted that humans are not mere animals, are we animal-like in this way at all? We think the Bible says yes.

Consider how Genesis describes the making of men. "Now the LORD God had formed out of the ground all the beasts of the field and all the birds of the air."[19] In the same way, "the LORD God formed the man from the dust of the ground."[20] The terms are identical, suggesting that there is a sense in which humans are formed from the stuff of the earth in the way animals are and share certain key features with animals. No one disputes that our bodies are made of proteins and fats and minerals as animal bodies are, nor that our brains function through electrochemical reactions just as the brains of other mammals do. Human hormones affect us in much the same way that hormones affect other mammals. Scientists even call parts of our brain "the reptilian brain" and "the mammalian brain" because those parts of our brains are similar to what is found in reptiles and mammals.

One need not be a Darwinist to accept that some of our desires, thoughts, and preferences are ruled by animal-like instinct. Hunger for food, thirst for water, and the desire for sexual activity are all animal-like, instinctive drives that are part of being "formed from the dust of the ground." It's no surprise that mating is one of the prime arenas in which instinct is strong. God made us that way.

The Bible's term for the kind of instinctive desires we're talking about is "the flesh." Biblical writers occasionally use this word to mean "meat," a passive physical substance. But more often they use the word for "something *active*, a specific power or range of powers that is embedded in a body of a specific type."[21] When Isaiah says that the Egyptian "horses are flesh and not spirit,"[22] he means that horses have only the animal powers of horses, not the greater powers of spirit beings. When Paul contrasts Ishmael and Isaac, he says Ishmael was born of "the flesh"—of purely human biological powers and drives—while Isaac was born of God's spiritual promise.[23] Flesh in these instances is not inherently evil, but merely animal, mortal, and limited. There is also the subtle implication that flesh operates on its own, independent of God and therefore potentially in competition with God.

We should understand the flesh not as a man's sinful nature, but as his "lower" nature. Hunger, thirst, the desire for sleep, the ability to catch cold, the sex drive—all of these are features of the flesh, and none is inherently evil. In its proper place, thirst is a good thing; drinking water has value. Thirst becomes a problem only when it takes priority over something more important. A thirsty person who hoards water while someone else dies of thirst is violating love; at that point, thirst is not evil, but the thirsty person has directed his spirit toward evil.

Likewise, the animal-like instinct for a mate who will reproduce successfully is normal and valuable, but as a trait of a man's lower nature, it needs to be governed by a spirit submitted to God's Spirit. God commanded humans to "Be fruitful and multiply" and equipped them with a rough form of radar to identify mates with whom they could best carry out that command. But God intended humans to use love and wisdom to guide what they do with the information their radar gives them.

A fleshly drive becomes the cause of sin when it is allowed to run amok. Gluttony occurs when the normal desire for food becomes an obsession. Promiscuity occurs when the normal desire for sex is disconnected from the desire for relationship and given free rein. Even our longings for love and respect produce sin when they lead us to ignore God and trample others. The longings themselves are not sinful, but our responses to them may be. As the Russian philosopher Nicolas Berdyaev explained, evil is a question of the direction chosen by a person's spirit, not a matter of his natural drives.[24]

Thus, when a man's normal desire for a young, healthy, high-estrogen mate is blown out of proportion and ruled neither by reason nor wisdom from the Spirit of God, he gets into trouble. When a whole society of men behaves like this, a culture totters. Sadly, most cultures in human history have suffered from this ill.

SAMSON, THE ADOLESCENT MALE

If you want to see unruly flesh in all its glory, observe a group of high school boys checking out the girls on campus. At puberty, when adolescent girls' hormones are starting to resculpt their bodies into baby nurseries, adolescent boys' hormone-driven instincts are starting to tell them what should attract them. Their bodies tell them directly what instinct thinks of each girl who passes by. No matter what their spiritual background, they haven't had time to develop wisdom from the Spirit about mating, so instinct tends to be their sole criterion. Teenage boys tend to gravitate toward the girls with the most exaggerated display of fertility traits: the largest breasts, fullest red lips, most abundant hair, curviest hips, slimmest waist, biggest eyes, clearest skin.

Although endowed with supernatural strength from the Holy Spirit, Samson was a typical adolescent male ruled by fleshly instinct.

> Samson went down to Timnah and saw there a young Philistine woman. When he returned, he said to his father and mother, "I have seen a Philistine woman in Timnah; now get her for me as my wife."
>
> His father and mother replied, "Isn't there an acceptable woman among your relatives or among all our people? Must you go to the uncircumcised Philistines to get a wife?"
>
> But Samson said to his father, "Get her for me. She's the right one for me."[25]

Samson's top criteria for selecting women does not seem to have been kindness, loyalty, or spirituality. He was ruled by blind Cupid who sees only what his instinct-driven eyes tell him. Samson chose his bride based on sight alone. The literal Hebrew in the last sentence reads: "Get her for me, for she is *right in my eyes*" (our emphasis). The biblical writer records Samson's dialogue with the abrupt, demanding style all too familiar to parents of teenage boys.

Not surprisingly, choosing a wife by appearance alone proved foolish. Samson's nubile wife turned out to be controlled by her relatives and manipulative toward him. He bet her family they couldn't solve a riddle he gave them, and they coerced her into helping them cheat:

Then Samson's wife threw herself on him, sobbing, "You hate me! You don't really love me. You've given my people a riddle, but you haven't told me the answer." . . . She cried the whole seven days of the feast. So on the seventh day he finally told her, because she continued to press him. She in turn explained the riddle to her people.[26]

The marriage ended in disaster. Samson was furious at her betrayal and abandoned her; her father gave her to someone else.

But Samson didn't learn from his teenage sin. Sometime later he got into trouble by visiting a prostitute, and then came the Delilah fiasco. The text never mentions her looks, but it's clear Samson chose another manipulator loyal to her people rather than to him. The story is almost identical: her people want the secret of his strength (an even more important secret than the riddle at his wedding), and Delilah wears him down with statements like, "How can you say, 'I love you,' when you won't confide in me?"[27] This time the cost of choosing a wife by instinct rather than wisdom was that the Philistines captured him and gouged out his eyes. There would be no more choosing mates by sight; immature Cupid was blind indeed.

> ### SHAPELY DEFINITION FOR YOUR HIPS AND BOTTOM
> "The Buttbooster™'s multi-panel construction slims your hips as it lifts your bottom. Gravity-fighting construction miraculously accentuates your curves. . . ."[28]

Samson was not unusual. At thirty-three, Richard has a Ph.D. but still isn't wise enough to select a date who will be able to hold a conversation over the dinner table long after her looks have faded. And according to the research, plenty of forty-five and fifty-five-year-old men are still choosing mates largely by an instinct for a fertile woman, as well as by other fleshly drives that we'll get to in chapters 5 and 6. This is inevitable when men refuse to submit their flesh to the training of God's Spirit. The New English Bible uses the term "lower nature" to translate the Greek word for "flesh." In that rendering, Paul's contrast between the average man and the man of God reads like this:

Those who live on the level of our lower nature have their outlook formed by it, and that spells death; but those who live on the level of the spirit have the spiritual outlook, and that is life and peace.[29]

Make no mistake about this: God is not to be fooled; a man reaps what he sows. If he sows seed in the field of his lower nature, he will reap from it a harvest of corruption, but if he sows seed in the field of the Spirit, the Spirit will bring him a harvest of eternal life.[30]

WHAT ABOUT CHRISTIAN MEN?

So Willard Harley is partly right: If a woman is married to an emotional adolescent who lives primarily by his flesh, then she had better get that face lift. But after reading all this research, we badly wanted to know to what degree Christian men, married and single, are Samsons under the skin. I (Cinny) felt like rising to the defense of my husband and our friends. How typical are the men who end up in Harley's counseling office?

We found only one systematic survey among Christians that addressed this question. The National Institute for the Christian Single (NICS) gathered 611 extensive questionnaires from single persons, male and female, twenty-five to sixty-four years old in twenty denominations. In that study, the men rated a woman's appearance as the third most important quality they considered in seeking someone to date, behind the ability to communicate and personality, but ahead of her depth of faith, life experiences, and quality of heart. Instinct apparently governs the dating game to a substantial degree, even among Christian men. However, in choosing someone to marry, the men rated appearance only sixth. It seems that when these Christian men contemplated spending the rest of their lives with someone, their higher reasoning capacities overruled their hormones.

The survey also asked men to rate the minimum level of attractiveness they would consider in a potential wife. On a scale of 0 to 10, the men's average minimum standard was roughly 6.4. Interestingly, when the women rated their own attractiveness, the average score was also about 6.4. We highly doubt most single Christian women are only at the minimum level of attractiveness most Christian men would accept; we think this result reflects how critical women are of their own appearance. In fact, we think Christian single women can relax about trying to make themselves perfect 10s.

If this survey is relevant broadly, then it suggests that women seeking husbands can comfortably shoot for a 7 on the attractiveness scale and work harder on the areas that men rated as more important in a wife: the ability to communicate, depth of faith, personality, heart, and life experience. However, it's worth noting that the men still rated appearance as more important in a mate than intelligence![31] (By the way, the women in the survey rated intelligence ahead of a potential mate's appearance.) Further, the more willing a woman is to hold out for a man who sees beyond the obvious, the more free she is to disregard looks.

We also interviewed some men to see how their observations of other men stacked up with the research. Stan Thornburg, a Portland pastor who lectures on sexual ethics, definitely agrees that the men he knows possess the radar for young, healthy, high-estrogen women. He calls that radar "a screening device" that men use when assessing potential dates and mates. "I think it's extremely important to them," he says; "I think men really do put [beauty] pretty close to the top" of their priorities. "If a person falls below their minimum standard, then they don't get involved" in a dating relationship. On the other hand, he says, "Men want reasons to be attracted to a woman who may not meet their screening requirements. They know the ideal presented in the media is pretty inaccessible." I (Karen) feel annoyed to think that the men I meet may be *settling* for a normal woman because their ideals are inaccessible, but I suppose we are all settling for less than our fantasies when we commit to a spouse. I'm glad that, according to Stan, a woman who treats her own body with respect, who conveys an attitude that she likes her body and her appearance, and who knows how to be genuinely intimate stands a high chance of overriding the average man's beauty-screening device. In other words, the screening device is normal male wiring; only immature or unhealthy men are unable to override it when they meet a woman of rich soul.[32]

Dr. Tom Whiteman, a licensed psychologist with a Christian counseling practice in the Philadelphia area, agrees that the screening device operates in most of the men he knows. He asked men in a Bible study group of married couples, "What attracted you to your wife right away?" The universal answer was: "I liked the way she looked. I liked her smile." Tom says, "It was all based on looks. That initial attraction based on looks is there for men. That's what piques their interest. Beauty would be the first thing a man would notice. . . . We [Christian men] are no different than nonChristian men, but in church we pretend we are."[33] We women are probably no different in the way we initially evaluate people on appearance.

However, Tom also agrees that men often override the initial screening (positive or negative) when they get to know a woman. A man might at first be put off by a woman's weight, but over time he might be attracted to her character. Alternatively, he might initially be drawn to her appearance, but over time he might find her personality unlovely. As the NICS survey indicates, dating and mating are two entirely different matters for the typical Christian man.

Tom says single and divorced men in church singles groups he's observed tend to be very motivated by their desire for beauty. Typically, a beautiful woman might come once to a singles event, and the guys swarm around her, sit next to her, and toss out what Tom calls "pick-up lines: What do you do? Where do you work? Do you want to go out for coffee?" All this goal-directed attention generally drives these women away from the group. It is also common in Tom's experience for forty-five-year-old divorced men to go to the social events designed for men and women in their twenties, rather than to the ones for older singles. When the church objects, the man may ask, "Would you rather I go to a singles bar?" Just like the men in Buss's studies, these men want to date younger women.

What happens to a man's beauty radar after he marries? Tom thinks most married men turn off their beauty radar when it comes to their wives. A married man tends to find his wife attractive when she treats him as he likes to be treated and unattractive when she doesn't. Tom says, "Even when my wife gets dressed up, I may not even notice how she looks because I tend to take her for granted. But when we're out and another beautiful woman walks by, I tend to notice her!"

Biologists have documented that male rats, rams, cattle, sheep, and other mammals all show more arousal in the presence of a female with which they have never mated than one with which they have mated. Scientists call this "the Coolidge effect" after an off-color joke between President and Mrs. Calvin Coolidge about a rooster.[34] Male humans seem to possess this same mammalian instinct; it makes sense if the creature's goal is merely to spread genes. We're not suggesting that mammalian instinct is the only reason why some men have affairs, but it certainly seems to be one factor. It appears that throughout their lives, human males have to consciously choose to serve God rather than instinct in order to remain faithful to their wives. Many of the men we talked to said they have had to develop a lifestyle of rejecting the lie that some new, attractive woman will, as Tom put it, "make me feel young or special or give me what I'm lacking." The radar remains, but the mature man learns to override it so he can treat both his wife and other women with respect.

Cinny's husband Bob speaks frequently to men's groups and finds men quite willing to admit that instinct influences them profoundly. They don't experience instinct as a thought process. They're not thinking about having children — they're not thinking at all! However, he does not believe most of them are as juvenile as Harley suggests. "Most men will admit that they notice and look at attractive women," says Bob. "However, for most that is where it stops. There is a sense of attraction on one hand and yet a sense of respect for her on the other. Most realize the complications of following through on their basic instinct and aren't willing to jeopardize their marriages and families for a meaningless fling."

RESPECT

We have tried to make the case here that God may have had a good reason for wiring men with an attraction to certain physical features in women. As depressing as it sounds to us normal women, there may be a biological component to beauty standards. If men were sinless, this instinct might never be an occasion for heartache. Unfortunately, men are not sinless.

Further, the power behind these beauty standards doesn't end with an instinct for a fertile mate. We've talked about women's desire for respect—men want it just as badly. In fact, we sometimes wonder if men's respect instinct isn't even more powerful than their fertility instinct. Stan Thornburg thinks a man's peers strongly influence the degree to which he bows to or overrides his instinctive radar. If his friends express approval about his chosen woman, a man finds it easier to overlook her physical flaws. But if his friends joke that he could do a lot better than that, he loses confidence about choosing a less outwardly beautiful woman.

The fortunate woman is married to or dating a man with mature friends. Harley observed the same phenomenon, and the evolutionary psychologists have a theory about it: Fertility cues are not the only reason why Richard prefers Danielle; she also represents status.

A CLOSER LOOK

Show some photographs of women from magazines to a man you're close to. What does he like about the models in *Vogue* or *Cosmopolitan*? What doesn't he like? See if he thinks the models are too thin, and whether he goes for the women with the small chins.

To what degree do you think the men you know best are motivated by instinct? What makes you think so?

CHAPTER FIVE

MALE STATUS

THE ANCESTRAL PECKING ORDER

Remember when Richard arrived at the party with Danielle, and he noted with pleasure that the other male guests found her stunning? If finding a fertile mate had been Richard's only goal, we might have expected him to be jealous of his rivals' response. But just as important to Richard as her reproductive value is Danielle's ability to give him status. The theory works like this:

While ancestral men learned that young, healthy mates were most likely to bear them strong children, ancestral women learned that they needed mates with lots of material resources who could feed their children into adulthood. So while a woman's number one mating asset became her looks, a man's number one asset became his wealth. Sure enough, in all thirty-seven cultures Buss studied, men ranked beauty near the top of their list of desires in a mate, while women ranked a man's looks far lower. Women, however, consistently ranked a mate's good financial prospects about twice as high as men ranked women's.[1]

Our modern, Western phenomenon of high divorce rates and large numbers of women working to support children on their own is not the way our species is designed to function. Historically, women have been concerned to choose mates who not only have resources now but will have them consistently over the several decades when the couple is raising children. Consequently, instinct tells a woman to look for cues that a man will be economically reliable in the long term. Ambition and industriousness turned out to be very attractive to women in Buss's studies, probably because they are signs that a man will eventually get ahead. But social status proved even more attractive. As Henry Kissinger commented, "power is the ultimate aphrodisiac." Why? In most cultures, powerful men have the greatest consistent access to resources. Anthropologists observe that men in most societies arrange themselves in a pecking order, with the highest status men having the greatest access both to mates and to the resources to support them.

In a curious chicken-and-egg circle, high-status men tend to attract the most beautiful women, so having a beautiful mate tends to confer high status on a man. Other men and women view his mate as one of the resources he has been able to accumulate. (Translate: women are possessions.)

In several studies, people were asked to evaluate men for various characteristics, based on photographs of the men with "spouses" of differing physical beauty. "Unattractive men paired with attractive spouses are rated most favorably on criteria related to status, such as occupational prestige. . . . People suspect that a homely man must have high status if he can interest a stunning woman, presumably because people know that attractive women have high value as mates and hence usually can get what they want in a mate."[2]

In China, Poland, Guam, and Germany, men with attractive mates gained much more status than did women with attractive husbands. Likewise, men with unattractive mates lost much more status than did women with unattractive husbands. Beautiful wives are trophies around the world.

We have to hand it to David Buss and his friends for devising a plausible neo-Darwinian theory for why so many men are status-seekers. Still, we can think of an equally plausible reason: men, like women, want respect. It's possible to have a system of mutual respect among equals, but humans often treat respect as a limited resource that must be divided up: the more Joe gets, the less is left for Bob. Consequently, respect becomes a ladder, a pecking order, in which Joe has the highest status in the barnyard, then Bob, then George, and Frank is at the bottom looking up. To be at the bottom looking up is a fate worse than death, a respect famine, so life depends upon climbing. Being beautiful is just one of the ways women seek status, and having a beautiful mate is just one of the ways men do it. But in both cases, it's a powerful way.

CULTURAL SIGNS OF STATUS

Slim and Toned

The craving for status helps explain differences between the features men in various cultures deem attractive. For example, we've noted that 0.7 is the global ideal for the waist-to-hip ratio, but the preferred body size in the modern West is decidedly smaller than what is desired elsewhere in the world, or even in America and Europe a few decades ago. The difference is that while a plump wife displays a man's status in a society where food is scarce, a thin wife displays his status in societies where calories are abundantly available. When food is scarce, the man who can afford to feed his wife enough to make her plump must be a man of considerable resources. He therefore gains status and (in polygamous cultures) may even be in the market for a second wife. Also, a plump wife is probably one whose husband can afford to keep her away from hard labor in the fields.

A seminary professor told us that when he was a missionary in Africa, local men would reprove him for allowing his wife to get so thin. Her size reflected poorly on his willingness and ability to provide enough food for her. She made him look bad. But there was absolutely no way his American wife was going to give up her figure to "fit" in her temporary home if it meant she would then be too large to fit in the United States.

Clarissa Pinkola Estés, author of *Women Who Run with the Wolves*, heard the same concern from Native Americans who lived in the part of Mexico from which her ancestors came. Estés, who was big by U.S. standards, was too small in the eyes of those who shared her genes and thought women should be round like the Earth Mother.

The classical Greek statue of Aphrodite at the Getty Museum in Malibu is larger than life, standing at least nine feet tall. But even if she were scaled down to 5'8", she would still be massive—a cross between Xena: Warrior Princess and Roseanne Barr. The first time I (Karen) saw her, I was so surprised by the goddess's dimensions that I checked the sign to make sure that this was indeed supposed to be Aphrodite, the goddess of love, not Demeter, the mother goddess. Evidently, the Greeks had no trouble imagining the goddess of love as circumferentially gifted.

> "You're a woman of the 90's. Bold, self-assured and empowered. Climbing the ladder of success at work and the StairMaster™ at the gym. You're socially aware and politically correct. But you probably know all this already because every ad and magazine has told you a *zillion* times. No wonder you're thirsty. Obey Your Thirst."[3]

Unlike in Africa, Mexico, and ancient Greece, food is not scarce in developed countries today. All but the poorest people can afford enough high-fat, high-carbohydrate foods to gain weight. To stay slender in our culture, a woman has to pay for fruits and vegetables, lean meats, and even expensive diet shakes or food from weight-loss programs.

For the same reasons, it's not surprising that the high-status look is now not only thin but also toned. Fewer women today do hard labor, and many women sit all day in factories or offices. In order to have abs and buns of steel, a woman has to have the time and resources to exercise regularly, often in clubs and classes. The look that enabled Demi Moore to do the film *Striptease* reportedly required her to spend four hours a day working out, with the help of a personal trainer and $15,000 worth of gym equipment.[4] Only a rich professional beauty or a woman of leisure, supported by a very successful husband or father, has that kind of time and money for body sculpting. No wonder the look is associated with status.

In our food-rich society, eating has become a moral issue. A fat woman is not seen as well-provided-for; she is considered undisciplined. Jane R. Hirschmann and Carol H. Munter, psychotherapists who work with large women, tell horrific stories of how people of both sexes treat fat ladies in *When Women Stop Hating Their Bodies*. In their counseling practices they train women to recognize when another person's "bad body thought" is about that person rather than the woman being criticized. One of the most common critics is the lover or husband who claims to have lost interest in his large mate.

One woman named Harriet reported, "My husband said he couldn't stand how fat I've gotten. Fat, to him, is a sign of weakness and he can't stand weak people." From Hirschmann and Munter, Harriet had learned to suspect that his objection to her size might be more about him than about her. She questioned him:

> What was going on at that moment *inside of him* that he was repulsed by? . . . finally he was able to say that during a staff meeting that day, he felt he had not come across with his point of view strongly enough and, in fact, he was voted down on a very important issue. So it was *his* weakness that was bothering him and that provoked the bad body thought he directed at me.[5]

Harriet had looked the same way for months, but on a day when he was feeling insecure about his status in the male pecking order, her husband decided it was crucial for him to have a wife whom his culture told him looked high-status.

Harriet and her husband are caught in a cultural and instinctive bind. She needs his love and respect. But he also needs respect, both from her and from the men in his world. If the evolutionary psychologists are right, a man needs respect not just for his emotional health but for his access to a mate and the survival of his genes. The hunger for status is simply a swollen manifestation of the God-given longing for respect. Harriet's husband could benefit enormously from some help to understand his need for respect and put it in perspective. If he were Christian and had some friends to affirm what God says about his worth, he might find it a lot easier to live with a wife who can't make her body fit his ideal. But even if her husband never changes, Harriet may be able to come to terms with the pain of her husband's disrespect for her if she can understand that it comes from his own respect deficit.

Certainly, Harriet may have her own issues to deal with: she may be large because she's using food as a drug; her eating habits may be poor; or she may not be getting enough exercise. But if her husband were concerned for her spiritual or physical health, his response would be very different from revulsion. The complex causes of obesity tend to be obscured when people are lusting for status.

Increasingly, our cultural definition of the high-status body is colliding head-on with biological reality. The way girls are designed, a healthy adolescent "gains nearly 35 pounds of so-called reproductive fat around the hips and thighs. Those pounds contain roughly the 80,000 calories needed to sustain a pregnancy, and the curves they create provide a gauge of reproductive potential."[6] So men are designed to prefer women with those 80,000-calorie curves. However, the slim-and-toned mandate tells people to prefer girls who find some way (usually radical diet and exercise) to shed those thirty-five pounds. Because millions of dollars of advertising are currently supporting the status message, women seem to be hearing it much more clearly than the reproductive message. The Singh studies suggest that men find both messages compelling, and confusing, but still like shapely hips more than many women suspect.

> "A simple stroke of **Terracotta Bronzing Powders** imparts the healthy, radiant look of a tanned complexion, without exposing the skin to the sun's damaging rays."[7]

We will have more to say about fat in chapter 8. But as two women who have obsessed about fat for most of our lives, we have found it eye-opening to face the roots of our judgmental attitude towards fat women. I (Karen) was secretly arrogant about my skinniness for years—it was my proof of superior self-control. Yet reading and hearing large women discuss their pain has shown me that they deserve the same compassion I want for my areas of struggle. Compulsive undereating is certainly no less a sin than compulsive overeating, but it is a high-status sin in our society.

Tanned, but Not Born That Way

The curious phenomenon of the suntan is another status symbol that the evolutionists don't mention. A hundred years ago, the status messages of skin color around the world were clear: the lighter your skin, the higher your status. In Europe and America, very dark skin denoted African descent (very low status), moderately dark skin denoted either Mediterranean, Asian, or Latin American descent (low to moderate status), tanned northern European skin showed that one worked outdoors all day and was therefore from the working class, and fair skin suggested that one was of northern stock and well bred enough to stay indoors. Every woman wore gloves and a bonnet as much as possible in order to protect her fair complexion. Fascinatingly, the same system prevailed in faraway Japan, where the nobility powdered their faces and carried parasols, and the peasant women shielded their faces with bonnets while in the fields, just like their French and Italian sisters. This order of things — fairness equals leisure and therefore status — remained intact right into the twentieth century.

Then something momentous occurred — or rather, something momentous was finally noticed. Roaring Twenties style-setter Coco Chanel returned from a cruise on the Duke of Westminster's yacht with a tan. Suddenly, America and Europe woke up and realized that the Industrial Revolution had happened. Working-class women were no longer out in the fields but in the factories where their skin languished in sunless pallor, "a mottled, unappetizing grayish-yellowish-pinkish off-white threaded with blue veins."[8] Only the leisured class could afford to lounge on the Riviera, gaining a healthy-looking glow. At once it became fashionable for Caucasians of high and low status to sunbathe.[9]

We now have a confusing status system in which African-Americans know their children will fare better if they have lighter rather than very dark African skin, and Latinos still have low status in "white" society; yet "white" women feel compelled to visit tanning salons in order to darken their pale skin. There's no doubt that a little color in the skin looks healthier (and hence more attractive to instinct-minded mates), but the craving for a very dark tan can be explained only by the fact that it signals status. Even now that we know tanning ages the skin and multiplies by eight times the chance of deadly melanoma, people still lie out in the sun. Sometimes instinct — especially the instinct for status, which has as much to do with pride as with mating — produces results that don't serve the species well at all.

Euro-Beauty

Nonetheless, if the fair skin of Caucasian women is no longer coveted, most other Caucasian features are still considered to convey the highest status. Many black women express their identities through Afrocentric hairstyles such as braids, weaving, and close cropping. Still, many others continue to have their hair chemically straightened so that it can be styled in smooth shapes that resemble non-African looks. One never sees Oprah Winfrey in dreadlocks. A decade ago, Susan Brownmiller wrote, "'Good' hair is silken and soft to the touch; it is full, pliant, and yielding — the feminine ideal in matters of anatomy as well as in character and personality."[10] For persons of African descent, "good" hair by this definition is very hard to come by.

In her novel *Song of Solomon*, Nobel Prize–winning author Toni Morrison records the plaintive question of a young black woman, Hagar: "Mama . . . why don't he like my hair?"[11] "He" is the man she loves, and the hair he loves, according to Hagar, is "curly, wavy, silky hair." She has driven herself mad and pawned her mother's diamond ring to look good enough for him, but it's hopeless. Her hair is the same as his, and perhaps for that reason more than any other, he scorns it.

What else does he love? "Lemon-colored skin," says Hagar. "And gray-blue eyes. And thin nose."[12] Mercifully, the dangerous, caustic chemicals black women used to use in the attempt to lighten their skin are now mostly off the market. Yet if African-American women want and can afford plastic surgery, they almost always choose to replace their African noses with European ones. Likewise, Asian women tend to "Westernize" their eyes.

Among Latin women, beauty standards date back to the sixteenth century, when the Spanish invaded and began to intermarry with the native populations. Persons of Spanish descent had higher status than those of Mayan or other Indian descent, and even today, the Mexican upper classes, for example, look much more Spanish than do the rural poor. A Spanish look, especially the blond hair that suggests a pure strain of the Castilian bloodline, continues to carry higher status than an Indian appearance. Such biases are controversial among Latinos and vary from group to group in the Hispanic community, but they do feed the American sense that blond (or more recently, red) hair is more attractive than black hair. But blond hair on women has been worshiped around the world as evidence of Euro-American status, not least by men of darker ethnic groups who have struggled to climb the American social ladder.[13] Why do *Gentlemen Prefer Blondes*? Because they think having a blonde on their arm makes them look like gentlemen.

> "Confidence. Pride. Power. Nothing can help you get that feeling like the African Pride No-Lye Relaxer System. Its unique combination of ancient ingredients and advanced relaxer technology gives you the power to control your hair, your style, your world."[14]

XERXES, THE STATUS SEEKER

Certainly not all men feel driven to accumulate trophy women in order to enhance their status. Some men grow up enough to recognize and manage their inner urges for ever-younger, higher-status mates. Other men accept that they lack the resources to play the trophy game. But a man with the inner maturity of an adolescent and the resources to carry it off displays in technicolor the extremes to which instinct can carry a man.

Consider Xerxes (called Ahasuerus in most translations), the Persian king in the biblical book of Esther. Here is a man with absolute power in his empire, able to indulge his every whim. And what is his whim? The story opens as Xerxes is throwing a six-month-long party to show off "the vast wealth of his kingdom and the splendor and glory of his majesty."[15] At the end of the event he holds a week-long banquet for his noblemen and officials, while his wife, Queen Vashti, entertains their wives. On the seventh day, a blind-drunk Xerxes commands his servants "to bring before him

Queen Vashti, wearing her royal crown, in order to display her beauty to the people and nobles, for she was lovely to look at."[16] It's not clear from the text why Vashti refuses to display herself (some commentators speculate it was because she objected to appearing wearing *only* her crown), but she does. Xerxes throws a tantrum. The king's wise counselor advises him that her disobedience will set a bad example to the other women, so Xerxes agrees to depose Vashti and banish her to ignominy in his harem. That will teach all the Persian women a lesson.

The Greek historian Herodotus offers us information about Xerxes not mentioned in the biblical text. Herodotus's account portrays a monarch with the emotional maturity of a two-year-old. Once when Xerxes was having a bridge built over the body of water called the Hellespont, a tempest destroyed the bridge. Xerxes not only had the engineers executed, he actually had the sea flogged!

Herodotus also explains that the six-month display of splendor was preparation for a war against the Greeks. The Persians lost that war in the famous battle of Marathon. Chapter 2 of the book of Esther begins just after the Persian army has limped home in disgrace. His self-esteem and international status having taken a beating, Xerxes decides to divert himself by stocking his harem and conducting a beauty contest for a new queen. Soldiers are sent throughout the empire to snatch beautiful girls from the villages. Each is groomed in the capital and presented to the king for a night of royal pleasure. Those girls who fail to dazzle him are condemned to spend the rest of their lives in the cramped, stuffy isolation of the harem, cut off from family and probably childless. The one lucky winner will become queen. The Jewish girl Esther wins the contest. (The text implies, but does not state, that she has God's help.)

As in the case of Samson, God used the unbridled drives of Xerxes to achieve divine purposes. God used Samson's rage at his blinding to kill thousands of Philistines, and God placed Esther where she could influence Xerxes to prevent a massacre of Jews. Nevertheless, the biblical writers never gloss over the way both men made fools of themselves and hurt good people by letting their fleshly drives run wild. In both stories, women are portrayed as using any means at their disposal—their beauty and their wits—to out maneuver men who are not in control of their own inner worlds. Samson and Xerxes cannot be reasoned with, nor do they care to understand what drives them; they give the Holy Spirit no access to their hearts except through the resourcefulness of clever women. Delilah uses her manipulative skill to protect her (ungodly) people from Samson, while Esther uses her shrewdness to save thousands of lives. We may not admire Delilah as we admire Esther, but it's hard to blame her.

In the same way, it's hard to blame the actress Danielle for using what she's got. If she is simply a gold digger with a shallow soul, then we pity her; she may end up with an immature husband who treats her like a trophy. If she's insecure about having anything else to offer a man, then she deserves our compassion and our help in discovering what's inside her. But if her heart's desire is to marry well and raise terrific children, and she's using her looks as one of her chief assets, then perhaps she's just a realist.

Historically and around the world, Karla, the single career woman, is an anomaly. I (Karen) am profoundly grateful that I have access to education and work so that I need not depend upon a man for support. I am also grateful that my life is rich without a husband and children. In fact, I have no intention of playing the beauty game in order to net a husband who cares as much about status as Buss & Co. describe. But I don't think it's shameful to acknowledge that I and most women want husbands and children: God designed us that way. Nor do I think it demeans the noble efforts of single mothers if we say that it's a lot easier to raise kids with a man contributing substantially to the budget. If the evolutionists' research teaches us nothing else, it highlights the quandary women have found themselves in throughout history, as they seek to feed themselves and their children in a world too often run by men who live by the flesh rather than by the Spirit.

> "Even the most beautiful women have something to hide. Worrying about imperfections like birthmarks, varicose veins or scars can deflate your self-esteem. Well, fret no more! **DERMABLEND** Corrective Cosmetics is a line of opaque cosmetics designed to hide what you need to hide—simply, precisely."[17]

Even the researchers agree that the scramble for beauty and status is often counterproductive in modern society. The research shows not what should be, but what is in a world where people live too much by unexamined instinct. The more we encourage girls to acquire education and skills, the less they will be dependent upon looks for their economic well-being. But it's still a tough world out there, and beauty is still an advantage, especially if a woman wants a husband and children.

IS THAT ALL THERE IS?

After immersing ourselves in this research, we came up for air feeling that some balance was called for. The truth is that plenty of men are doing their part in relationships and are able to celebrate their wives for more than the number of status-points they win. Plenty of men, as Friday points out, are at least as interested in "warmth, kindness, a full heart, humor, initiative"[18] as they are in a woman's waist-to-hip ratio.

Christian psychologist Willard Harley encourages women just to accept the fact that they are status symbols for their husbands. "Juvenile as it may sound, people often *do* judge the ability and success of a man in terms of his wife's appearance. . . . When a man's wife lets herself become unattractive, the message comes across loud and clear that he probably couldn't get someone better, and probably he deserves her."[19] After all, shouldn't a woman who cares about her husband want to make him look good? We think Harley sells men short. Lots of men are able to discern where their appropriate desire for respect ends and a prideful craving for status begins. Still, the line between humility and pride is more blurry than we may be comfortable admitting. In 1996, a nationally known Christian leader addressed a gathering of the Evangelical Christian Publishers Association. In his remarks, he commented that his wife rarely passes a mirror in the car or beside an elevator without checking her appearance. He didn't mind that a bit, he said, because "she's my glory!" He was alluding to 1 Corinthians 11:7 — "the woman is the glory of man." That is, just as a man reflects the glory of God, or displays God's greatness to the world, so a wife displays to the world the glory of her husband. We're glad this man is proud of his beautiful wife, and maybe we're the only ones who detected the merest hint of boasting over a status trophy. But we question whether it was helpful to encourage the men in the audience to wonder whether their wives advertised a sufficient amount of their glory.

To accept that all men will struggle to some degree with their flesh may require us to pass through the normal stages of grieving in a fallen world: denial, frantic efforts to make it not so, anger, sadness, and eventually a courageous commitment to deal actively with what is. In a fallen world, symmetrical features and "good" hair are distributed unequally, like money and power, without regard to merit. This feels profoundly unjust, and one is moved to grief or anger for Morrison's Hagar who feels unloved because she lacks the high-status look that birth denied her. We will speak much more about constructive grieving in later chapters.

If instinct were the only power that drove men to pursue beautiful women, men might find it relatively easy to grow out of instinct's grip, and women might find it easier to respond well. What the evolutionists fail to acknowledge is that men may be animals, but they are not *just* animals. This is the chief gap in their theory. Men and women are spirit as well as flesh and so have spiritual yearnings as well as fleshly ones. In the next chapter, we will balance the fact that humans are flesh with the awesome truth that we are created in the image of God. Our longing for beauty is not just an instinctive drive, but also a yearning to return to paradise lost.

A CLOSER LOOK

Look at yourself in a full-length mirror. Which of your features are ones our society views as high-status? Which are low-status? What about somewhere in between? Do you tend to like the aspects of your body that are high-status and dislike those that are considered low-status? Why do you think that is?

Do you believe a man would be proud to walk into a room with you? Does it matter? Why?

SYMBOLS OF
LOST PARADISE

If humans were mere animals, just primates with extra-heavy-duty electrochemical powerhouses in our frontal lobes, then the evolutionary psychologists have the last word on men's attraction to beautiful women. However, the Bible affirms what even most scientists know: there is something about us that cannot be explained through biology alone. Thus, the mating instinct is not the only force in the human heart that gives physical beauty its power.

We read in Genesis that after God "formed the man from the dust of the ground," God "breathed into his nostrils the breath of life."[1] That Hebrew word for "breath," *ruach*, is the same word used in Genesis 1:1 for the Spirit of God. The story portrays God as a sculptor shaping a statue in clay, then breathing his own breath or spirit into the statue so that—as in the much later tales of Pinocchio and Pygmalion—the statue comes to life!

GOD'S REPRESENTATIVES
Sculptures of the human form were common in the ancient world, and all were religious works, intended as images of the gods or their representatives, the kings. In the Genesis story, God outdoes

all rival craftsmen by creating an image of Himself worthy of the name: not some static, lifeless statue, but a living, breathing, enfleshed spirit. In the previous chapter we find God describing His masterpiece thus: "Let us make man [*adam*] in our image [*selem*], in our likeness [*demuth*]."[2] *Adam* here is a collective noun, and the next verse makes clear that the term includes "male and female" as joint bearers of the divine image. *Selem* is a term "derived from the skills associated with handicrafts; it denotes something which has been cut out and carved and is therefore also applied to the images of idols."[3] *Demuth* denotes "similarity to" God in some way, but the text leaves the exact nature of the similarity vague.

When ancient kings had statues of themselves carved and erected in their domains, they did so in order to make themselves symbolically present to their people. The message was: Big Brother is watching you. This practice would have been familiar to the first Hebrew hearers of Genesis. Drawing upon this analogy, God explained to them that He was doing something similar when He formed His human images, set them up on earth, and said, "Let them rule over the fish of the sea and the birds of the air, over the livestock, over all the earth, and over all the creatures that move along the ground."[4] One of the chief elements of humans' likeness to God was that He conferred on them the responsibility of ruling earth as His representatives; they would be as God to the animals. However, unlike the all-too-familiar Near Eastern kings, who cared more for their subjects' obedience than their welfare, God charged humans with the job of tending and caring for His beautiful garden world.[5] Thus, the image of God in humans included sparks of God's authority, responsibility, and creativity.

After the accounts of Adam and Eve's rebellion, Cain's killing of Abel, the growth of corrupt human societies, the Flood, and Noah's rescue, Genesis 9:6 restates the fact that even the ragged remnant who stagger out of the ark are still made in God's image. Sin may have chipped some of the paint off the image and covered it with grime, but each human creature remains a disguised masterpiece.

BODY AND SOUL?

As a young Catholic girl, Mary Anne Tabor assumed the image of God was supposed to have something to do with her body. "Going to Catholic schools, and learning that I was made in the image and likeness of God, and learning that God created all things beautiful, left me in a quandary. At that time I was conditioned to believe I was not beautiful, yet if I was made in the image of God, either God was not beautiful or perhaps I was a mistake."[6] Chances are that Mary Anne never told the nuns who were her teachers about her confusion. Had she done so, more than likely the nuns, swathed head to foot

> "If I was made in the image of God, either God was not beautiful or perhaps I was a mistake."

because their tradition taught them to veil their feminine beauty, would have told Mary Anne that the image of God was imprinted on her soul and had nothing to do with her body.

Many Protestants today would say the same. However, this was not the view of the biblical writers. Our notions of human nature have been heavily influenced by the Greek idea that humans are immortal souls living temporarily in mortal bodies. By contrast, the Hebrews didn't think of soul and body as separable; they conceived of humans as enfleshed spirits, whole beings. When God breathed his divine spirit into lifeless clay, the result was a living *nephesh*.[7] *Nephesh* is often translated "soul," but in this verse modern versions prefer "living being." Body and spirit together comprise a living soul or being. Body and spirit together bear the image of God. Just as the lifeless earthen form cannot be called an image of God, nor can we isolate some part of the inner wiring of the living human and call it the "soul" if we mean something radically separate from the body. The breath or spirit of God infuses every cell, imprinting the whole person with the divine image. The living human reflects God's image as he or she breathes and moves and acts to rule, create, and love.[8]

In order to understand the power physical beauty has in the minds of men and women, we must grasp the fact that we carry the image of God in our whole selves: body and soul, outer and inner. Because this truth is so central and because it runs counter to many people's assumptions, we will take a moment to defend it.

Paul: A.D. 50

Greco-Roman converts to Judaism and Christianity struggled to come to terms with this Hebraic respect for the body. While classical Greek culture (around 450 B.C.) exalted the body, raising both sculpture and gymnastics to a status unparalleled until modern times, the philosophy of New Testament times reflected a culture weary of earthly life. Men of the Roman world favored those teachers who promised that one day their immortal souls would be freed from the prisonhouses of their bodies. Cults offering this kind of immortality flourished in the first century A.D. Consequently, a significant faction in Corinth simply refused to accept the apostle Paul's insistence that eternal life would be the resurrection of a whole human, body as well as soul:

> But someone may ask, "How are the dead raised? With what kind of body will they come?" How foolish! What you sow does not come to life unless it dies. . . .
>
> So will it be with the resurrection of the dead. The body that is sown is perishable, it is raised imperishable; it is sown in dishonor, it is raised in glory; it is sown in weakness, it is raised in power; it is sown a natural body, it is raised a spiritual body.
>
> If there is a natural body, there is also a spiritual body. So it is written: "The first man Adam became a living being"; the last Adam, a life-giving spirit.[9]

Christ was raised with a body capable of eating yet able to pass through the "solid" molecular structure of a wall;[10] His body was different—less limited—but still recognizably a body. In like manner, wrote Paul, resurrected humans would have "spiritual bodies"—bodies not limited by the many weaknesses of flesh, but under the pure rule of God's Spirit.

In another letter to Corinth, Paul reiterated,

Now we know that if the earthly tent we live in is
destroyed, we have a building from God, an eternal house
in heaven, not built by human hands. Meanwhile we groan,
longing to be clothed with our heavenly dwelling, because
when we are clothed, we will not be found naked. For
while we are in this tent, we groan and are burdened,
because we do not wish to be unclothed but to be clothed
with our heavenly dwelling, so that what is mortal may be
swallowed up by life.[11]

Paul did not long to be "unclothed" as a disembodied soul, but
clothed with a "heavenly dwelling"—a spiritual body.

The men of Corinth had been taught that because only their
souls mattered spiritually, they could do what they liked with their
bodies. Like some people today, they believed it was possible to have
enjoyable sexual contact body-to-body without that affecting their
souls at all. As a Hebrew, Paul knew this was nonsense. Paul said that
sexual intercourse unites two people at the core, that uniting the
bodies also unites the souls. Further, he insisted, "Do you not know
that your bodies are members of Christ himself?"[12] Our fleshly
bodies are indeed destined for death and decomposition, yet at the
same time, each cell of those same bodies is in some way part of
Christ. Not only that, "Do you not know that your body is a temple
of the Holy Spirit, who is in you?"[13] Limbs of Christ, temples of the
Holy Spirit—these terms go beyond the idea of God's image to
express a special holiness for the bodies of Christ's followers.

Ask any woman who has had a breast removed how that experience affected her. Very few will tell you it was simply the removal
of some diseased tissue that had no connection to their souls.
Most will describe the experience as a loss of part of *them*. Ellen
Lambert describes her shock when her doctor uttered the word
mastectomy: "I remember screaming over and over in my disbelief
as I sat in the doctor's office, feeling terribly alone. He couldn't
really be telling me I had to lose a breast when I had no sense of
anything at all being wrong."[14] Her lump had been discovered by
a mammogram before she could even feel it. "How could there be
something that 'bad' inside my body?" she asked herself, even

while knowing that cancer wasn't evidence of moral corruption.[15] In the same vein, writer Betty Rollins called her post-surgical appearance "this little Hiroshima of the torso."[16] Ellen concludes, "To lose a part of our body is to lose something more than a physical part of oneself; it threatens our essential sense of selfhood."[17]

Most women know without being told that our bodies are as much *us* as our thoughts are. This is why calls to ignore our outer appearance as spiritually irrelevant do not help us. Quite the contrary: the more we honor our bodies as *us*, as intertwined with our spirits, as limbs of Christ, temples of the Spirit, and bearers of God's image, the more we will understand and manage well the power of physical appearance in our lives.

Irenaeus: A.D. 200

About 150 years after Paul wrote to the believers at Corinth, a French church leader named Irenaeus was battling some slick religious marketers whom he called Gnostics, from the Greek word *gnosis*, "knowledge." The Gnostics said you could be saved only by receiving some secret knowledge, knowledge which they happened to possess and would be glad to pass on if you met their requirements. Gnostic systems varied and were tediously complex, but one core doctrine was that matter is evil while spirit is good; the body is the soul's prison, and we're all waiting to be set free from it at death.

In a training manual for persons who wanted to be baptized, Irenaeus interpreted Genesis 1–2 along the same lines as we have already done. He spoke of man as a compound of two elements, body and soul, for which God "took the purest and finest elements of the earth in order to mix his power with the earth in correct proportion . . . so that man should be like God *not only in his breath but also in his shaped flesh*."[18] Irenaeus insisted that the image of God infused all of man (and woman), both the inner and outer person.

To believe in Christ's incarnation is to believe it is possible for mortal flesh to carry God's image. God laughed in the faces of the Greek philosophers by doing what in their eyes was unthinkable for the pure, divine Spirit: God Himself took on flesh and was born as a human child. Jesus was the supreme "image of the invisible

God";[19] compared to Him, we are only dim flickers. Gnostic Christians claimed Christ only appeared to be embodied, but orthodox readers of the biblical text insisted that the divine Word indeed "became flesh and made his dwelling among us."[20] This text from John became a battleground of theological debate for more than a century, as so many men educated in Greek and Roman philosophy found the idea of a literal incarnation of

> *I have everything I had twenty years ago, only it's all a little bit lower.*
> —Gypsy Rose Lee [21]

God distasteful. And even some who accepted the incarnation, such as Origen and Cyril of Alexandria (Egypt), insisted that the image of God could be only in man's (or Christ's) rational soul. Whenever the Greek notion of the body's badness has reemerged, theologians have relegated the divine image to the soul.

THE MEMORY OF EVE

However, once we understand that humans cannot be neatly divided into body and soul, with one part a divine image-bearer and the other a mere shell, we can start to see how a man's response to a woman includes a spiritual dimension.

In Eden before her sin, Eve must have radiated the glory of God's image from her soul and spirit out through her body. Her body, untainted by aging or disease, would have been the perfect form Adam's flesh was designed to seek. She would have been a woman that we, if we saw her, would be tempted to call a goddess.

But she and her husband followed Satan in believing their almost-divine glory entitled them to set themselves up as actual god and goddess of their world. Ezekiel's words about the king of Tyre could apply to all three of them:

> Your heart became proud
> on account of your beauty,
> and you corrupted your wisdom
> because of your splendor.[22]

Consequently, God banished Eve and Adam from His garden and released upon them the ravages of death. First they became spiritually dead. We should not understand this to mean that they ceased to have spirits, ceased to have spiritual longings or a spiritual dimension to their lives. After the Fall, humankind's drive to worship something remained as powerful as their drive to mate. Rather, their spiritual death meant that their intimate connection with their Maker was over. Far from killing their drive to worship, this death merely blinded it, compelling them from one futile object of worship to the next. Just as the Cupid of man's flesh is blind, inclining him to select a mate for her looks, so also is his spirit blind, inclining him to set up gods and goddesses that symbolize or appear (deep inside him) to represent divinity.

As Eve's skin and waistline began to show the effects of time, Adam must have remembered how she looked in her glory days. And just as his sons inherited his fleshly instincts, so also they inherited, deeply buried, his memory of Eve. Today, when Richard looks at Danielle, his flesh responds to her as potential breeding stock, but his spirit responds to the way an ancient part of him remembers Eve.[23]

Danielle does not actually carry more of the image of God than Karla does, but to Richard's nearsighted spirit she represents the Eve who was created as a living sculpture of the Holy One. Danielle's physical beauty is a spiritual symbol of Paradise and resurrection, of all Richard most longs for. Hidden (in places Richard might fiercely deny exist) are his longing to be the strong governor of creation he was made to be, and his longing to be linked spirit to Spirit with the real God who could make sense of his world. The symbol is all the more potent because Richard has no idea what it triggers in the spiritual parts of his soul. In fact, the more committed he is to living as though he has no spiritual component, the more power these aromas of the divine will have over his untrained spiritual senses.

> "I could not have done this without you."—Nancy Sinatra's signed inscription of thanks to her plastic surgeon on a framed copy of her picture on the cover of *Playboy* magazine, May 1995[24]

PERELANDRA

C. S. Lewis was a leading scholar of medieval and Renaissance literature long before he converted to Christianity. Astute and widely read, he was well aware of how symbols in men's souls turn up in their religion, art, and literature. Memories of Eve turn up over and over in myths about goddesses. In fact, he knew, one of the reasons great stories affect us is that they tap into those symbols, so Lewis used them in his own books.

In his science fiction novel *Perelandra,* Lewis retells the story of Eve on another planet. An earth man named Ransom is kidnapped and transported to the planet Venus. The Roman goddess Venus was an Eve-substitute, and the Lady of planet Venus (or Perelandra, as Lewis calls it) is Lewis's Eve with green skin. Here Lewis describes her through Ransom's eyes:

> He had been expecting wonders, had been prepared for wonders, but not prepared for a goddess carved apparently out of green stone, yet alive.[25]

Notice the echoes of Genesis: the Lady appears at first as a living statue of a goddess. Knowing words could never capture Eve's beauty, Lewis suggests:

> Never had Ransom seen a face so calm, and so unearthly, despite the full humanity of every feature. He decided afterwards that the unearthly quality was due to the complete absence of that element of resignation which mixes, in however slight a degree, with all profound stillness in terrestrial faces. This was a calm which no storm had ever preceded.[26]

Lewis repeatedly mentions that Ransom "could not look long at her face."[27] At last he manages to do so unobserved, and muses,

> There was no category in the terrestrial mind which would fit her. Opposites met in her and were fused in a fashion

for which we have no images. One way of putting it would
be to say that neither our sacred nor our profane art could
make her portrait. Beautiful, naked, shameless, young—
she was obviously a goddess: but then the face, the face so
calm that it escaped insipidity by the very concentration of
its mildness, the face that was like the sudden coldness
and stillness of a church when we enter it from a hot
street—that made her a Madonna. The alert, inner silence
which looked out from those eyes overawed him; yet at
any moment she might laugh like a child, or run like
Artemis or dance like a Maenad.[28]

Her body expresses the beauty of a young woman's flesh and
her face the beauty of a young woman's spirit; she is at once Eve
and Mary, a holy Venus.

She also bears the image of God in her noble rule of her subjects:

She had stood up amidst a throng of beasts and birds as a
tall sapling stands among bushes—big pigeon-coloured
birds and flame-colored birds, and dragons, and beaver-like
creatures about the size of rats, and heraldic-looking fish in
the sea at her feet. . . . They surrounded her ten or twenty
deep, all facing her, most of them motionless, but some of
them finding their places, as at a ceremony, with delicate
noiseless movements.[29]

And later,

She turned as they approached her and welcomed them,
and once again the picture was half like many earthly
scenes but in its total effect unlike them all. It was not
really like a woman making much of a horse, nor yet like a
child playing with a puppy. There was in her face an
authority, in her caresses a condescension, which by taking
seriously the inferiority of her adorers made them somehow less inferior—raised them from the status of pets to
that of slaves.[30]

This serene, pure, chaste, yet regal Madonna-goddess is the woman every man's spirit desperately wants to see when he looks at a beautiful woman.

THE CALL OF ROMANCE

The Face

A sixteen-year-old boy looks across a classroom on the first day of school and sees her. Not just any girl, but Her. He is used to his flesh responding to a girl's red lips or curves; he knows how it feels for his body to kick into gear and let him know he is ready to be sexual. But this is different. This Face! The sight of her suggests scents and sounds he half remembers, though he has never smelled or heard them: scents of fruit trees and birds singing in a garden he has never seen. He knows She is a goddess. For weeks he watches her every day in class—what she wears, how she moves, who she speaks to, how her voice sounds. He thinks of her all day and dreams of her at night. He imagines her as powerful, invulnerable, inaccessible in her beauty.

Perhaps he never speaks to her. Or perhaps he musters the courage first to speak to her, then to ask her out. Maybe they date for a few months, and gradually he grows disappointed. She is easy, weak, vulnerable, even ordinary—not the goddess he thought she was. They break up. She is hurt: she has no idea what she represented in his head, and even if she does, she's frustrated that he can't care for her and see her as beautiful in herself, a real flesh-and-blood girl. She is torn between her desire to be loved for who she is and her desire to be the Madonna-goddess of his imagination, and hers. For she, too, has memories of Eve buried in her soul. She devours romantic books and movies, recognizing in the heroines the almost-goddess she was made to be, as well as the goddess her lost boyfriend thought she should be.

Nearly every man and woman has been the boy or the girl in this story—maybe many times. Some men fall into a cycle of seeing a Face, then dropping the woman they're with to pursue her passionately, obsessively, until they discover she is not the goddess, and finally drop her to pursue another Face. Some women, like

Danielle, may find themselves playing the Face over and over with different men who are repeatedly disappointed when the Face doesn't turn out to be the Eve of the men's dreams. Marilyn Monroe was one of these women, and the anguish—the pressure, rejection, and loneliness—of being worshiped and dropped over and over drove her to drug abuse and possibly suicide.

> "He said the first thing he noticed was your great personality. He lied."[31]

Other women, like Karla or Alison, who have not been born with faces and bodies that allow them to play this role, are spared the trap but nevertheless watch the game unfold, enviously wishing just once they could be queen for a day. It doesn't help to tell them the game is no fun.

The Research

If this notion of the Face in men's fantasies sounds far-fetched to some readers, it doesn't sound that way to Robert M. Schindler of Rutgers University and Morris B. Holbrook of Columbia University. Their research into this subject made it into the *Journal of Psychology and Marketing*, a periodical that publishes academic research into how best to sell products. In "Critical Periods in the Development of Men's and Women's Tastes in Personal Appearance," Schindler and Holbrook set out to disprove the notion that there's no accounting for taste. They showed forty fashion ads to people sixteen to ninety years old. The ads depicted women from *Vogue* or men from *Esquire* that reflected distinctive styles for each three-year interval from 1933 to 1990. After crunching numerical results through a statistical analysis, Schindler and Holbrook found that women's tastes for how both genders should look tended to stay current, updating as fashions changed. Men's tastes in women, however, tended to reflect preferences for the look that was current when they were in their late teens and early twenties, peaking when they were about twenty-four years old. Men seemed to feel nostalgic for a past look in women, while they didn't show the same nostalgia for earlier men's looks. Women didn't seem to show much nostalgia at all.

Why do men carry a torch for how women looked when the

men were in their late teens and early twenties? Schindler and Holbrook attribute the nostalgia to "heavy exposure . . . with strong positive affect."[32] That is, in their late teens men first become fascinated with how women look, so they are heavily exposed to women's looks during that period. Heavy exposure leaves its mark on their memory circuits. But the decisive factor is "strong positive affect" ("affect" is psychobabble for "emotional response"). In other words, for the first time in their lives men have really great emotional experiences connected with how women look. Many become sexually active during this period; most fall in love for the first time. Those great memories stick with a man even into his eighties, according to this research.

Subscribers to the *Journal of Psychology and Marketing* don't read the magazine out of mere curiosity. The article ends with a section called "Implications for Marketing." Schindler and Holbrook advise marketing managers to carefully select "female images designed to appeal to men" when creating ads or product packaging. If a product is aimed at older men, the model should look not contemporary, but vintage. "Colloquially, selling Oldsmobiles might benefit from the use of a Marilyn Monroe look-alike."[33] Likewise, "the 'retro' look might appeal to older men and therefore to women wanting to attract older men." Denim clothing, "natural-look makeup, [and] products for the care of longer hair" should continue to sell strongly because of the large number of people born between 1947 and 1962. Advertisers can bank on men's vulnerability to a Face.

> *Age is something that doesn't matter unless you're a cheese.*
> —Billie Burke[34]

The Hymn

The romantic fantasy that allures so many men and women really is something we were made for. At the center of our English Bible (near the culmination in the Hebrew order of books) lies a wedding hymn called the Song of Songs. It was probably composed for a royal wedding, but the story consists of a youth and a maiden playing at king and queen, shepherd and shepherdess, and—in another echo of Genesis—garden visitor and owner of the garden.

There is no talk of the practical goals (children, social alliance, and economic success) that dominated marriage decisions in the ancient world. Instead, a great deal is said about passionate love and sensual beauty. Both lover and friend call the bride "most beautiful of women" again and again. She is "lovely as Jerusalem, majestic as troops with banners,"[35] a strong, regal beauty. With a lover's eye for every feature, he describes her hair, teeth, temples, eyes, cheeks, neck, lips, and breasts.

> How beautiful you are, my darling!
> Oh, how beautiful!
>   Your eyes behind your veil are doves.
> Your hair is like a flock of goats
>   descending from Mount Gilead. . . .
> Your lips are like a scarlet ribbon;
>   your mouth is lovely. . . .
> Your two breasts are like two fawns,
>   like twin fawns of a gazelle
>   that browse among the lilies.[36]

The poem is a feast of senses: sight, sound, scent, touch, and taste. Kisses and caresses can be spoken of, but other intimate things may only be hinted at in the language of fragrance: "beds of spices,"[37] entering the beloved's garden, eating her honey, and drinking her wine.[38]

So erotic is this hymn that some people used to wonder why it was in the Hebrew Scriptures. Around A.D. 100 Rabbi Aqiba offered the first allegorical interpretation: that the poem really symbolized the love between God and His people. The celibate Origen enthusiastically embraced Aqiba's idea, and it still reigns supreme in most popular studies of the book. However, "No poet who intended to express something else—namely Yhwh's love for his people—would have written in so totally profane and areligious a fashion and with such wholehearted abandon to the joys of the senses."[39] God is never even mentioned in the Song.

However, the allegorizers are not really wrong: the Song does point beyond itself to divine love. But the reason an erotic poem can do this at all is because the erotic attraction between a man and a woman is intensely spiritual. (Or, conversely, the attraction between a man and a woman is spiritual because God made it a symbol of His love for us.) In the Song of Songs, physical beauty is the supreme symbol of all that is desirable in a woman, even in the Bride of God. As a spiritual symbol, then, beauty is as potent as they come.

The lover in the Song is captivated by his beloved's beauty as the young teenager of our story is captivated by the Face of the girl in his class, as Richard is captivated by Danielle, and above all, as Adam was captivated by Eve. The Song describes human love as it was meant to be had there been no rebellion and we still lived in the garden. It portrays a man's spiritual response to a woman's beauty in a world where flesh has not run amok. It describes the beauty Danielle and Karla both know they were meant to have, and the response they know they were meant to evoke in men who would not drop them in a few months.

In the real world romance rarely if ever works out this way. Therefore, the Song ultimately points ahead to the end of the Bible, where at the resurrection God renews what was shattered and unveils "the new Jerusalem, coming down out of heaven from God, prepared as a bride beautifully dressed for her husband."[40] So just as Richard's heart is tugged by deeply buried memories of Eve, so it also leaps forward blindly toward that image of the bride. Knowing nothing consciously about Christ, and certainly not about Genesis or Revelation, Richard's spirit sees only well enough to be entranced by a woman's Face.

To Richard's spiritually clouded eyes, Danielle symbolizes Eve, the Beloved, the bearer of the divine image. Never mind that to discerning spiritual eyes Karla or some other plain woman might reflect God's image much more faithfully than Danielle does. Never mind that *every woman*, of whatever age or size, carries the divine image. And never mind that there is far more to the image of God than how a woman looks to a man. For Richard, Danielle is a symbol of what he yearns for: Paradise. Just as a photograph of a sizzling steak may trigger our hunger for lunch, so a symbol need not be the real thing to affect us powerfully.

In fact, men are not the only ones who respond to women like Danielle as icons of divinity. Women, too, know we were made to be as pure and lovely as Eve, and we stare at models with a mixture of awe and envy. They represent the beautiful creature we know lives somewhere inside each of us, the beautiful Us who is too little expressed, recognized, honored, and loved.

What happens when fallen humans confront an incarnate symbol of our deepest longings and identity? Too often, we worship. Humans generally feel more comfortable adoring a concrete symbol of the divine than the God of whom all created beauty is mere reflection. Like all of Eve's children, we prefer graven images over real ones. We turn to idolatry.

Let's look at how we idolize beauty and in doing so wreak havoc for ourselves and others.

A CLOSER LOOK

Some actresses represent the Face for a while in the public imagination until another face takes their place. In 1995, Julia Ormond was the Face for many men. Uma Thurman has held the position, too. These women's images seem more ethereal than that of earthier sex symbols. Then came 1996's Liv Tyler and Gwyneth Paltrow—girls next door. Ask some men whether any actresses' faces stick in their minds as especially captivating. Who are those actresses, and what is it about them that seems so powerful? Ask your women friends as well. Do they come up with the same names?

How easy is it for you to think of yourself as carrying the image of God within you, your whole body and soul? Try looking at yourself in a mirror and saying, "Behold the image of God!" Do you want to laugh or cry? Why?

PART TWO

WHERE WE GO WRONG

CHAPTER SEVEN

THE GODDESS OF BEAUTY

GETTING WHAT WE WANT

Women want love, respect, and family security. We don't just want these; most of us hunger for them ravenously. Some of us may silence the hunger by keeping busy, but if we take time to become still and silent, we can hear it gnawing inside us. A few of us get enough love and respect from the people in our lives that we are unaware of any hunger.

Several strategies for satisfying our hunger are available to us. A few women pursue God passionately until the sustenance they get from the Holy Spirit enables them to be content with whatever they do or don't get from people. Others seek fulfillment through an artistic, athletic, or business endeavor. Women of our generation have more access to this option than at any other time in history, and some choose it. Still others find solace in addictions to food or chemicals. Many women pin their hopes on relationships with other women, but for whatever reason, this, like the other strategies, normally ranks behind women's primary strategy for getting what they want: pursuing a man.

If the sales of women's magazines, romance novels, romantic films, and books about relationships are any indication, women's chief strategy is to conform as much as possible to the image of the ideal woman embedded in a man's brain. "Romance novels comprise 40 percent of *all* paperback book sales." After *Better Homes and Gardens* and *Family Circle,* four of the next nine top-selling magazines are women's magazines that focus on beauty and relationships with men.[1] While men's mental image varies from culture to culture and from man to man, we've seen that it also remains remarkably constant. Even though some men insist that depth of faith and quality of heart are more important to them than a potential wife's looks, most women still act as though beauty were the key to a man's heart. This focus may be linked to our sense that beauty is our birthright as bearers of God's image, that our beauty of body and soul would be perfect if only we lived in a perfect world.

For their part, men also hunger for love, respect, and children. It seems that men are wired to seek all of these, at least in part, through women who conform to an ideal standard of beauty that lives in men's minds. So, like women, men have a choice: they can either look to God as the provider of love and respect, or they can demand their ideal.

For most men, of course, this is not a one-time, either/or choice, but a gradual process of growing either toward God as the focus of their hopes or toward alternatives. In the same way, women may sample various strategies for getting what we want and grow gradually toward or away from God. But this gradual process boils down to a long string of mini-choices.

Numbers 1 and 2 of God's Top Ten Commandments are: "You shall have no other gods before me" and "You shall not make for yourself an idol in the form of anything in heaven above or on the earth beneath or in the waters below. You shall not bow down to them or worship them; for I, the LORD your God, am a jealous God."[2] The word for "idol" here is *selem,* "image." God had already made an image to represent Himself on earth; anything less than a living, breathing, creating, and loving human was a disgrace. Further, the image that God made was not supposed to be worshiped. God's human images were supposed to draw all eyes toward the Source of their beauty: God Himself. Sadly, men and women prefer to worship something we can control, so we make our own idols and provoke our divine Lover to jealousy.

WHAT IS IDOLATRY?

Idolatry is a choice not to worship the real God who deserves authority in our lives, but instead to worship other things (money, work, food, beauty) that seem to offer us what we most long for. Historically, feminine beauty has ranked at or near the top of the list of idols for both men and women. Men worship the beautiful woman of their imaginations, and women worship her, too, aspiring to become her.

The modern term for idolatry and bondage is *addiction*. Psychiatrist Gerald May explains,

> Spiritually, addiction is a deep-seated form of idolatry. The objects of our addictions become our false gods. These are what we worship, what we attend to, where we give our time and energy instead of love. Addiction, then, displaces and supplants God's love as the source and object of our deepest true desire.[3]

In writing to the Christians in Rome about the behaviors he witnessed in Corinth and elsewhere, the apostle Paul eloquently explained how idolatry came about. He said every human culture had enough information about God to respond with gratitude and worship, but humans preferred not to give God that much power in their lives. This decision to ignore the Creator actually clouded their perception of reality: "Their thinking became futile and their foolish hearts were darkened. Although they claimed to be wise [the Greeks were famous for their pursuit of wisdom], they became fools and exchanged the glory of the immortal God for images made to look like mortal man and birds and animals and reptiles."[4]

Humans choose to worship the created beauty of women rather than the original beauty of God. We choose to worship neither God nor even the living women whom God made as His image-bearers. Instead, we prefer to worship images of images: statues or billboard goddesses. Why? Because both God and real women are hard to control. They frighten us, both women and men, by their unpredictability. They have the power to say no to our hungers. But statues, models, women on pedestals, and ideal women in our own minds are easy to control. What men and women rarely realize, however, is that while the images are easily controlled, when we worship them we become enslaved to fleshly drives, the demands of "the world" or culture, and even the Evil One. We become addicted and driven. When we worship false gods, we lose more control over our lives than we gain; hence, Paul calls idolators "fools."

Because all human beings are spirit as well as flesh, all have a built-in drive to worship something. Humans tend to worship things that innately carry or offer power, such as wealth, the forces of nature, a woman's power to bear children, a man's power to make war, or physical beauty. If a beautiful woman represents Par-

> "I'm the messenger of beauty."
> —Avon Lady Rodriguez, who sells perfume and powder to native women in the Amazon jungle[6]

adise lost, sexual fulfillment, and plenty of children, it's not surprising that men throughout history have put beautiful women "on a pedestal" as representations of the goddess of beauty. Likewise, since beauty seems to promise women a husband, children, financial security, love, respect, and influence over others, it's no wonder women "idolize" models who seem to embody beauty's power to give them what they crave.

Consider the term *model*. The dictionary's last definition is "a person employed to display clothes in a shop etc. by wearing them." However, the first definition is "a three-dimensional reproduction of something, usually on a smaller scale."[5] Fundamentally, the models we see in magazines and on runways are reproductions of the goddess of beauty. They are not intended to look like normal women, nor are they intended to be portraits of unique women with names and personal identities. They are surgically enhanced, photographically enhanced, computer-enhanced goddess images. We know the names of several supermodels, but these women still represent the goddess for us. They are "celebrities"; we rarely view them as individuals. In this way they resemble the many portrayals of the Blessed Virgin Mary that can be found across Europe and Latin America; Mary looks different in each painting and statue, but all of these representations have certain features in common and are meant to symbolize the same holy woman.

THE GODDESS

Germany, Crete, and Babylon

Living surrounded by images of the beauty goddess is nothing new. The earliest known goddess figurine, the so-called Venus of Willendorf, dates from the Stone Age. Her large breasts and belly, as well as her pronged feet designed to be plunged into the earth, suggest a pregnant earth mother goddess representing the potency of the land's and woman's fertility. To honor the earth mother was to honor the source of all life.

If the evolutionary psychologists are at all correct, feminine beauty and fertility are linked in men's instincts. Long before the biblical Abraham was born, sculptors of clay goddesses from Cyprus and stone ones from Crete were putting most of their effort into detailing the vaginal area and breasts with nipples. These body parts carried their erotic charge for men precisely because they represented a woman's ability to bear children. They represented the essence of femininity that fascinated, allured, and even frightened men.

The snake goddesses sculpted in Crete around 1600 B.C. (after the biblical Jacob and before Moses) are buxom but slim, not unlike Barbie dolls but definitely made for religious worship. Without written evidence archaeologists cannot be certain what worshipers sought from these snake goddesses, but fertile fields, herds, and women are likely probabilities. Ishtar, the Babylonian moon goddess of love and fertility, was painted with flowing hair and large breasts. Crete and Babylon were not worshiping pregnant goddesses, but deities who possessed eternally youthful strength, beauty, and potential for fertility, not unlike the models on our television screens.

Greece

We know relatively little about the religions of Crete and Babylon, but the great deal we know about Greece tells us that the cult of beauty was flourishing there as early as the ninth century B.C. At about the time the prophet Elisha was shaking things up in Israel, Homer wrote his magnificent poem *The Iliad* about the war between Greece and Troy. While some historians believe the real Trojan War was probably motivated by economics (competition over grain trade in the Black Sea), Homer says Greece and Troy went to war over a beautiful woman. The Trojan prince Paris had run off with the wife of the Greek (Achaian) king Menelaus. At one point in the poem, the old men of Troy sit gazing up at Helen high above them and comment,

> Surely there is no blame on Trojans and strong-greaved
> Achaians
> If for long time they suffer hardship for a woman like
> this one![7]

Four hundred years after Homer, the Greek playwright Euripides wrote in *The Trojan Woman* his version of how Paris won Helen. According to Euripides, Greece's three greatest goddesses were quarreling over a golden apple marked "For the Fairest," and they went to Paris to judge among them. They didn't ask him to judge their radiant divinities but to choose which of their bribes was most desirable to him. The queen of the gods offered him political power; the goddess of war offered him military victory; and Aphrodite, goddess of love and beauty, offered him the most beautiful woman in the world. Paris chose the latter and thereby showed that he worshiped and desired feminine beauty above all else.

While Helen was the epitome of human beauty to the Greeks, Aphrodite was the essence of beauty itself. According to Homer, even the gods were

> amazed by the beauty
> Of violet crowned Cythera[8]

when they first beheld her. Historian Nancy Qualls-Corbett described Aphrodite this way:

> Aphrodite was not associated with fertility . . . Aphrodite
> reigned over love and passion, and her image is perhaps
> the most renowned for these attributes today. Regardless of
> her name or locale, the goddess of love is associated with
> springtime, with nature in bloom, the time when dormant
> seeds burst forth in splendor. *Beauty* [emphasis ours] is
> the quintessential component; Aphrodite's nakedness is
> glorified. She is the only goddess to be portrayed nude in
> classical sculptures. The loveliness of her feminine body is
> adored and adorned.[9]

The most famous image of Aphrodite is the Venus de Milo, the Latin name for a statue found on the Greek island of Milos. Today the Aphrodite of Milos lacks head and arms and looks serene in white marble, but originally she had all her limbs and was brightly painted. She was not sculpted as a work of art to be admired but as an object of worship. Her sinuous shape accents her hourglass curves, just as models often pose today, and her creator gave great attention to properly detailing her breasts and pelvis. She reigned over a culture that understood the intimate connection between sexuality and spirituality and saw physical beauty as an essential component of both.

Aphrodite was often called "the golden one" because of her radiance and freedom from corruption (gold does not corrode like other metals). She was beautiful "through an unself-conscious radiant presence."[10] We might use similar language to talk about Eve before the Fall but even more of the God whose radiance she only reflected. The Greeks understood that there was something divine about feminine beauty, but as the apostle Paul said of them and the other nations, they "worshiped and served created things rather than the Creator."[11]

THE SACRED PROSTITUTE

Paul wrote those words from Corinth, a city renowned in the ancient world for its temple to Aphrodite. This prime attraction for sailors and tourists boasted at least a thousand sacred prostitutes, both male and female. Paul probably would not have been comfortable with

Homer's Aphrodite, but the Aphrodite he encountered in Corinth was even more raw a deification of the mating instinct. The classical Greek goddess had been submerged by the Syrian fertility goddess Astarte, whose worship the Old Testament prophets had heartily condemned. Corinth's Aphrodite bore only a Greek veneer.[12]

Sacred prostitutes represented the goddess and enabled worshipers to unite with her physically and spiritually. These lovely young women would take men into their inner sanctuaries, draped in veils and lit with candles, to kneel before an image of Aphrodite. The priestess/prostitute would pray that the goddess would receive their love offering. Qualls-Corbett described how the man was supposed to be transformed by the sexual encounter:

> The qualities of the receptive feminine nature, so opposite from his own, are embedded deep within his soul; the image of the sacred prostitute is viable within him. He is fully aware of the deep emotions within the sanctuary of his heart. He makes no specific claims on the woman herself, but carries her image, the personification of love and sexual joy, into the world. His experience of the mysteries of sex and religion opens the door to the potential of ongoing life; it accompanies the regeneration of the soul.[13]

Wow! We can understand why more than an appreciation for Greek architecture drew thousands of tourists to Corinth's temple each year. When the mating instinct and the worship instinct met in the cult of the beauty goddess, the result was explosive. And while the particular young woman who was playing the role of Aphrodite in this drama may or may not have been objectively beautiful, to the male worshiper she embodied the golden goddess. Her clothing, makeup, perfume, and physical surroundings were all designed to send the man forth with a memory, a mental image, of having been with the divine beauty. He could then continue to worship that image in his heart and draw strength from the fantasy.

Imagine what most modern men would give to make love to the embodiment of a goddess, whose image they could then carry within them forever. Imagine if a man could feel his soul reborn by uniting with a woman. In fact, these are very close to the feelings of men today who feel compelled to risk their marriages and careers for pornography or prostitutes.[14] Anonymous sex tastes momentarily like a sip of the water of life because the partner is a fantasy woman who offers an illusion of intimacy without rejection. A prostitute, even one an objective person would call unattractive, offers a willing backdrop against which a man can project his imaginary ideal. Porn queens even more closely embody the fantasy goddess; many pornographic actresses and models have literally been sculpted by a surgeon's knife into supremely effective graven images.

Hollywood makes a lot of money telling stories about the almost religious ecstacy people feel when they unite with a gorgeous lover. Audiences identify with the characters and experience the ecstacy right along with them, as the music swells and the lighting softens to reproduce the aura of Aphrodite's temple. Even our words *ecstacy* and *catharsis* are Greek words that originally described the spiritual experience worshipers had when they viewed sacred drama or participated in rites that drew them out of their earthbound lives and gave them a taste of untamed divinity.

> "**Les Météorites Finishing Powder** unites the most beautiful colors in the universe in six different pastel-colored spheres that, when combined, create a heavenly veil of perfection for the face. A swirl of the Météorites Brush over the powder pearls collects haloes of tint from each color, all creating a divine finish for the face."[15]

Of course, lovers generally feel ecstacy in sexual union even when their partners are not gorgeous. Why, then, does Hollywood invariably use beautiful actors? Because filmmakers understand the power of symbol and imagination. Beauty is in the eye of the loving beholder. Real lovers generally perceive each other as beautiful, so people imagine the ideal lover as beautiful. The lovers of Eden were beautiful, so the lovers of our imagination are beautiful. We, the audience, vote with our purses that we want to see beautiful people in movies.

Even men who don't go so far as to have affairs admit to carrying an ideal image of a beautiful woman in their heads, concocted from some blend of real women they have known, movie stars, and centerfolds. For our part, most of us women carry our own internal image of the perfect beauty. We compare ourselves and each other to this ideal and are sometimes harsh when we or others don't measure up. We may even tape a picture of our favorite image on our refrigerators to remind us that looking like her is more important to us than eating.

THE GODDESS TODAY

Journalist Naomi Wolf observed that the best thing one can say today about a woman is that she looks "divine."[16] Wolf understood that beauty is an object of worship in our culture, just as it has been for centuries.

A whole book could be written about manifestations of the beauty goddess in contemporary culture. We will look at three manifestations: models, who are the goddess incarnate; Barbie, her preeminent sculpted image; and Disney, one of the many distributors of her mythology.

A Day in the Life

In many ways women today are under more pressure from the beauty cult than in Paul's day. Until the advent of mass media and transportation in the twentieth century, most men and women lived in a village or small town and were exposed to perhaps a hundred women in their entire lives. Most were peasants who might occasionally glimpse a bejeweled noblewoman, but she was not held up as a model whom peasant women should imitate or peasant men should hope for. Even aristocrats were far more limited in their experience than we are today.

Now each woman is compared not to a hundred other women of her own class and income level but to the roughly 600 most beautiful women in the world. That's about how many models and movie stars we see in a lifetime, and they are selected from among thousands. They are selected for possessing the clearest skin, the firmest breasts and muscles, the most perfect waist-to-hip ratio, the most symmetrical features. Then they are subjected to the kind of beauty treatments that put Xerxes' six-month regimen to shame.

How common is the model body? The Nina Blanchard Talent Agency ran a beauty contest at a local television station in search of promising new models. Approximately 40,000 pictures were submitted, of which ten were judged suitable as semi-finalists. Four of those were finally approved as having modeling potential.[17]

A *Mademoiselle* reporter followed top model Manon for a week. Thursday Manon's hair was orangish for a commercial, but after three and a half days in a salon, her hair was pale blonde for the cover of the "Sand" shade of Clairol's Glints™ line of hair color. (We, too, could look this good if a professional colorist spent three and a half days using Glints and a lot of other stuff on our hair. But we're supposed to believe we can look this good just by using what's in the package at home.)

It took four hours for the photographer to shoot 300 frames, only one of which was chosen for the Glints box. For a single picture used, photographers typically shoot seventy to 360 frames. Manon is a pro—she knows "how to show her face at its best angles . . . with the light coming from the right in order to offset the tilt of a nose broken in a handball accident nine years ago."[18] (Too bad we can't make sure we're always seen from our best angle.)

On another morning, Manon is up at 4 A.M., breakfasts on herbal tea and fruit (no caffeine; it's bad for skin), and is at a shoot by 5 A.M. for prep. It takes several professionals an hour and a half to style her hair and paint her face. From 6:30 A.M. until 5 P.M. she poses for fifteen photos in a department store catalog. Those clothes will never look that good on us unless we have her body, her colorist, stylist, and cosmetician—and 300 tries to get it right!

Many models have nose jobs, breast jobs, or other surgeries. And even after all that, these perfect women aren't perfect enough, but require photographing through frosted filters and thousands of dollars worth of computerized airbrushing before they are fit for us to behold them as goddess surrogates.

Who can compete with this? Ancient men knew that no real woman looked like the Aphrodite of Milos, and no sexual experience at home was supposed to be like sex with a sacred prostitute; but modern men are bombarded with the message that they should expect their mates to look like models. The ads drill women with the doctrine that we can and should be cellulite-free goddesses if only we invest the proper money and effort. Mature men and women laugh off this propaganda, but its relentless barrage takes its toll on all but the best of us.

> Shelley Michelle stood in for Julia Roberts in the nude scenes in *Pretty Woman* because Roberts's body wasn't "good" enough.[19]

Barbie

For many of us, the barrage started early when we received our first Barbie dolls. According to M. G. Lord, journalist and author of *Forever Barbie: The Unauthorized Biography of a Real Doll*, "Barbie may be the most potent icon of American popular culture in the late twentieth century."[20] She has an advantage over movie stars and models that contributes to her staying power in the marketplace: "She can never bloat. She has no children to betray her. Nor can she rot, wrinkle, overdose, or go out of style."[21]

Ruth Handler, co-founder of Mattel, created Barbie in the late 1950s. She had observed her daughter, Barbara, playing with paper dolls that came with various outfits. Handler had noticed how girls fantasized about their adult life through their play with paper dolls. She came up with the idea of developing a grownup doll that came with her own real clothes. However, she had a tough time selling Mattel on the idea of a doll with breasts.

Baby dolls had been in vogue for fifty years, but Barbie was modeled on the Bild Lilli doll, a lascivious German plaything for adult men. Lilli was herself based on a cartoon character from a tabloid newspaper and was marketed as a sort of three-dimensional pinup. "She was a pornographic caricature, a gag gift for men, or even more curious, for men to give to their girlfriends in lieu of, say, flowers."[22] Lilli had an extensive wardrobe fitting for a high-class call girl. "Gentlemen prefer Lilli," said a brochure promoting her outfits. It continued, "Whether more or less naked, Lilli is always discreet." As Lord put it, "Lilli isn't just a symbol of sex, she is a symbol of illicit sex."[23] Further, the Lilli of the cartoons was not just a male fantasy, she was an Aryan male fantasy: a fair-skinned, blue-eyed German doxy to the core.

No wonder the folks at Mattel doubted whether the ice-blonde bombshell Handler came up with was appropriate for little girls. Handler knew nothing about the Lilli cartoons or what she represented in Germany; Handler had simply noticed a grownup doll with her own wardrobe in a Swiss shop while on a family vacation and brought some back to show her colleagues. But while Handler could imagine her as a wholesome, all-American girl, Lilli's (and hence Barbie's) body spoke louder than any ad copy.

Mattel hired Ernest Dichter, director of the Institute for Motivational Research and brilliant pioneer of research into how to manipulate women's emotional needs in order to sell products, to research and plan a marketing strategy for the Barbie doll. Dichter's research showed that while little girls would love Barbie, their mothers would hate her and the image she projected. The job of the advertising campaign was to overcome these parental objections. Dichter "urged Mattel to exploit mothers' dark, unarticulatable fear that without a stern tug in the right direction, their boyish daughters would grow up into unmarriageable brutes."[24] Barbie would teach their daughters how to dress and become attractive to a man, a mother's subtle and unspoken prime directive.

From the beginning, then, Barbie was designed to appeal to the female mating instinct, the female drive to become the male sexual fantasy in order to secure home and family. Barbie was perfectly shaped to teach girls how to appeal to men's flesh.

Mattel introduced Barbie as a fashion model. If models are the goddess's modern sacred women, Barbie is a little graven image of them. Her promoters

> strategically ignored the fact that Barbie was a thing; they imagined her as a living teenager and invented a life for her that was as glamorous and American as Lilli's had been tawdry and foreign. "The positioning from the very first commercial was that she was a person," [said Handler.] "We never mentioned the fact that she was a doll."[25]

Just as models were persons-turned-into-statues, so Barbie was a statue-turned-into-a-person.

Despite the hype, Barbie's promotional debut to toy stores in 1959 appeared to be a failure. She was dressed only in a black-and-white bathing suit. Store owners felt she was too sexy and wouldn't sell. However, the stores that purchased Barbie found their stock disappeared off the shelves. She became a revelation of the meaning of femaleness to a generation of girls. "She didn't teach us to nurture, like our clinging, dependent Betsy Wetsys and Chatty Cathys. She taught us independence. Barbie was her own woman. She could invent herself with a costume change: sing a solo in the spotlight one minute, pilot a starship the next."[26]

Barbie had no husband or children and projected a message foreign to the 1950s: that her identity was not defined within the context of her relationships to family or her responsibilities to men. Ken was a mere accessory, a boyfriend deemed necessary because mid-century Americans believed a woman was a failure without a male companion.

Yet it is her body shape that interests us here. Her biographer, M. G. Lord, reveled in Barbie's symbolism:

> Narrow of waist, slender of hip, and generous of bosom, she was the ideal of postwar feminine beauty when Mattel, Inc., introduced her in 1959 — one year before the founding of Overeaters Anonymous, two years before Weight Watchers, and many years before Carol Doda pioneered a new use for silicone. . . . Barbie has, in fact, a drag queen's body: broad shoulders and narrow hips, which are quintessentially male, and exaggerated breasts, which aren't. . . . Barbie is a space-age fertility symbol: a narrow-hipped mother goddess for the epoch of cesarean sections.[27]

One can get carried away with this rhetoric, but Lord has a point. Barbie's body is the stuff of fantasy; no real woman is proportioned like her without the help of extensive "plastic" surgery. (With great difficulty we remind ourselves that Barbie is plastic and real women aren't.) Yet the broad-shouldered, long-legged, large-breasted, narrow-hipped look has become the one sought far and wide for the cover of the *Sports Illustrated* swimsuit issue. Her features are those of the high-fashion model, the role model for all girls of what a beautiful woman looks like: high cheekbones; large, round eyes with no heavy Asian lids; the perfect blemish-free, apricot skin of a Euro-American; wide forehead and tiny chin; and long, swinging hair. Even now that Mattel makes Black Barbies, the dolls are still Euro-Barbies with darker skin. No real woman of purely African or Asian descent has either form or features even close to Barbie's.

> Barbie's measurements if she were a full-sized human: 36-18-33.[28]

Barbie's body is not that of real women, but the body of fantasy, even of quasi-religious myth. *Religion* is the system of thought by which a group of people lives. *Myths* are the sacred stories people tell to convey the core beliefs of their religion. *Religious objects* such as statues and masks are used when people act out these sacred stories. The Cretan snake goddesses whom Barbie remarkably resembles were probably used in this kind of sacred drama. In a similar way, as they play with dolls, children act out the stories that will become the beliefs they live by. Playing with Barbie has taught two generations of girls how to be women.

Watch a couple of girls play with their Barbies, and see how they set up scenarios in which this strong, beautiful, independent young woman goes forth into her world to get what she wants: love, respect, material comfort, and pleasure. While we may laugh, Lord comes dangerously close to the truth when she says, "Forget trying to be Barbie; even gorgeous grown people would be hard-pressed to pass for an eleven-and-a-half-inch thing. But maybe they should build a shrine to the doll and light some incense."[29]

Girls loved her in 1959 and they still love her today. After celebrating her thirty-fifth anniversary, "Barbie is sold in 140 countries at the rate of two dolls every second. Every year, sales of Barbie and her paraphernalia total more than a billion dollars."[30]

The Wonderful World of Disney

And then there's Disney. While many women recognize how Barbie tempts girls to grow up as beauty worshipers, Disney seems harmless at first glance. But Disney is our culture's premier purveyor of mythology about what's important in life. No religion indoctrinates children more powerfully than Disney, and Disney teaches girls to value beauty above any other feminine quality.

Lilli/Barbie pioneered the business of turning cartoons into dolls, but nobody plays in the cartoon/toy big leagues like Disney. A century ago children learned the central cultural myths in fairy tales told to them by grandparents or read from the annals of the Brothers Grimm. Today you'll be hard-pressed to find a child who has read the Grimm's version of Snow White or Cinderella, but almost everyone on the planet has seen the Disney versions.

Susan J. Douglas, professor of media and American studies at Hampshire College, deconstructs the gospel according to Disney with tongue firmly implanted in cheek:

> First, there were the good and wonderful girls, the true princesses, the ones we were supposed to emulate. They were beautiful, of course, usually much more beautiful than anyone else, but completely unself-conscious about it—you never saw Snow White or Cinderella preening in front of some mirror. They were so virtuous, so warm and welcoming, so in tune with nature, that bluebirds couldn't resist alighting on their heads or shoulders and surrounding them with birdsong. (I remember playing in the woods as a kid and feeling completely rejected when birds would only run away from me.) . . .
>
> Because they were so beautiful and kind and young, they were detested by older, vindictive, murderous stepmothers or queens wearing too much eyeliner and eyeshadow, usually blue or purple. These women had way too much power for their own good, embodying the age-old truism that any power at all completely corrupted women and turned them into monsters. In their hands, power was lethal: it was used only to bolster their own over-weening

vanity, and to destroy what was pure and good in the world. In the ensuing battle between the innocent, deserving, self-sacrificing girl and the vain, black-hearted, covetous woman, the girl won in the end, rescued from female power run amok by some handsome prince she had met only once. She lay there, in a coma, or was locked in some garret, waiting, powerlessly, for some cipher of a guy she barely knew to give her her life back through a kiss so powerful it could raise Lazarus from the grave.

The only good women besides the princess were the chubby, postmenopausal fairy godmothers, asexual grandmas well beyond the age of successfully competing in the contest over "who's the fairest of them all." Except for them, all females were in competition, over who was the prettiest, who was most appealing to men, who the birds and dogs liked best, or who had the smallest feet.[31]

Part of the power of these stories comes from age-old symbols that recur throughout most known cultures: the good, beautiful virgin; the power-hungry villain; the hero. These symbols echo throughout the biblical story, in which the Hero (God) strives through trial after trial to rescue his beautiful Bride from the clutches of her evil Enemy. There is something profoundly true about this story that permeates myths and fairy tales around the world.

But when Disney tweaks stories to fit its mythology, it flattens heroines into empty-headed Barbie dolls. In the original *Peter Pan*, for instance, Tinker Bell is largely a flash of light. In Disney's version, she is pretty but vain, always admiring herself in mirrors and pools, scheming and possessive of Peter. In *Pocahontas*, Disney completely rewrites history in order to make the film's heroine sweet and pretty instead of strong, wise, shrewd, tragic, and ordinary-looking. And it's astonishing how much Tinker Bell, and even more the recent heroines of *Beauty and the Beast*, *The Little Mermaid*, *Aladdin*, and *Pocahontas*, look like Barbie. Of course they're drawn to be easily reproduced as dolls and mass marketed, but must the mermaid, Ariel, have a "waist the diameter of a chive"?[32] Must Pocahontas and *Aladdin*'s Jasmine have D-cup breasts filling out low-cut dresses, along with that same chive waist? Why are their breasts much more prominent than their hips, when nearly every woman born is built just the opposite? Must every children's cartoon heroine look like Lilli?

It's true that Ariel is "brave, curious, feisty, and defiant"[33] and Belle of *Beauty and the Beast* is at first more interested in books than in boys. But their most noticeable trait is their beauty, not their character; and in the end, in the gospel according to Disney, both characters are saved from death and boredom through marriage alone. Raise your daughter on these movies, and don't expect her to like her body when she's fifteen.

THE FRUIT OF IDOLATRY

How has the worship of Aphrodite and Barbie affected us? The goal of idolatry is to gain control over our lives, to guarantee that we will have what we want. For men that might be many children, status, or sexual ecstacy that "opens the door to the potential of on-going life." For women it might be love, financial security, and respect. In both cases the deepest yearning is for the perfection of Paradise: the eternal youth and beauty of Eve, constant access to sublime sex without hassles or rejection, perfect love and honor. God doesn't guarantee us those things, so we pursue a way to guarantee them without God.

Tragically, idolatry is a fraud. In the next several chapters we'll survey what the worship of beauty has actually guaranteed. The ugly story includes ways in which women have scarred themselves by going to life-threatening lengths to get or retain beauty. Proud women have tried to use beauty to manipulate men and have hurt each other through competition and envy. Idolatrous women look upon neither themselves nor other women with the kind of love that confers beauty. The story also includes men's determination to control women's beauty, a determination that has produced gilded and not-so-gilded cages, lust, coercion, and violence. Idolatrous men look upon women not with the face of love but with the face of control. The worship of beauty defaces everyone involved.

A CLOSER LOOK

Find a magazine ad with a scantily clad model selling some product. Ask yourself how it affects you. Do you have to consciously reject the message that you should look like her, that your failure to look like her is a failure that could cost you something precious? Or, does the image make you mad, make you laugh, or not affect you at all?

Next, ask a man in your life how the image affects him. Ask for a straight response. Does he have to consciously reject the message that he should want her, or do those images have no effect on him whatsoever?

CHAPTER EIGHT

AGE, FAT, AND OTHER SINS

Nothing gives one the feeling of control better than knowing the rules. In a confusing world, it feels great to believe that if we do this and this and this, then we'll get what we want. Most religious systems appeal to this feeling by stating the rites one must perform and the laws one must follow in order to get the god to do what one wants.

Obligingly, the beauty goddess has a set of rules about which she says, "Do this, and you will live." Those rules vary somewhat from culture to culture, but they largely conform to the standards the evolutionary psychologists identified: youth, health, high estrogen, sexual readiness, and status. "Do this," the goddess whispers, "and you will be Eve. Men will adore you and women will respect you; money and children will be yours." We will examine three commandments for women that dominate our culture:

Thou shalt not age.
Thou shalt be thin.
Thou shalt have perfectly symmetrical, large, firm breasts.

Girls learn these rules early. To the degree that they don't learn to find their value elsewhere, they pursue the rules with religious zeal.

THE TERROR OF AGING

After fourteen years as *the* Lancôme model, Isabella Rossellini saw her career with the cosmetics giant end in 1996. When the news of the impending divorce was announced in 1994, James Kaplan of *New Woman* asked, "Could the decision, just possibly, have anything to do with her age?" Rossellini was forty-one at the time, forty-three when her last advertising spread was shot. She confided to Kaplan: "Officially they don't admit it, but in our private encounters, they tell me they're concerned. So I don't know what to say—they've kind of left me with a hot potato."[1] One wouldn't want an old lady of forty-three modeling in ads for anti-wrinkle and skin-firming creams.

The signs of aging signal to men everywhere that a woman is losing her reproductive usefulness. They also remind both women and men of their mortality. Thus, the yearning for perfection, the fear of becoming invisible and dispensable to men, and the fear of death all conspire to make women rage against crow's-feet. While it is healthy for a woman to think her body is as much her as her mind is and to believe that it carries some of her identity, when a woman identifies too much with the pretty young face she sees in the mirror she'll feel her identity crumbling as that face ages. It's devastating to feel that the self she knew and loved has died and been replaced by a stranger, a Wicked Old Witch, or a pathetic old has-been. The temptation to attack that alien visage with a scalpel and turn it back into the familiar self can be overwhelming. Cosmetic surgeons make a lot of money from women too attached to the mask of youth.

While studying for her master's degree, Mary Anne Tabor worked behind a cosmetics counter in a department store. There she served more than a few desperate clients who wanted her to do something, anything, to restore the good feelings they'd had about themselves when they were young.

A chic, fortyish woman showed up one day, inquiring about

newer, better products. Since she was already investing heavily in one of the world's premier cosmetic lines, Mary Anne decided the woman, whom she called Mrs. D., needed compassion more than cosmetics, so she approached the ritual of the makeover more like a minister than a saleswoman. She gently removed Mrs. D.'s makeup and tenderly applied "anti-stress" eye cream.

> "Notice how very little of the product I am using," I said to Mrs. D. as I put the creme on her fingertips. "I would like you to apply it, Mrs. D.," I said, "so you can feel the fine texture of this creme." What I was really doing was taking notice of how she applied the product. She used hard and jerky movements, rubbing the creme in as if her face were furniture and the creme furniture polish. She hurried as if she were in a great rush. I asked her if she still had time and she looked confused and said she had all day.[2]

Mary Anne chose to care for her client as a human being and paid attention to signs that the woman did not care for herself in that way. But she pretended she was purely professional, explaining that the product did not have to be rubbed in. "Then I applied it to her face very tenderly, thinking that it would probably feel good to touch her face gently."[3] Mrs. D.'s eyes filled with tears; Tabor wondered how long it had been since anyone had touched her with compassion.

Before long Mrs. D. broke down completely and sobbed her whole story:

> She said she felt worthless. She had received lots of attention when she was younger; in fact her husband had been one of her many suitors who competed for her affections. . . . Life had been fine until her mother died several years ago, and then her world began to fall apart. Her mother had been her major support system and had always assured her of her beauty.
>
> One day she realized that her mother was gone, her children were grown, her husband was enmeshed in his

work, and she was older. She no longer felt beautiful and her husband was no longer attentive to her. . . .

Mrs. D. felt that her days were numbered and she would be discarded just like those Barbies who had been handled so much they ended up on thrift shop racks in the used toy section.[4]

Having been born with Snow White's face, Mrs. D. had invested all her sense of self in that image that gave her men's attention and her mother's approval. Everyone in her world had agreed that her looks were her most valuable asset. Her husband and her mother were like the magical mirror of Snow White's stepmother: Every day she asked who was the fairest, and every day they gave the right answer. But when Mrs. D.'s mirror inevitably reflected a different answer one day, she shattered. Losing one's mother is painful for most people, but it's far worse when she is one's sole source of nurture, the sole person who gives one the face of love.

Aging tests all our relationships: Does he love me for my looks or for all of me? Has he grown up spiritually, or is he just older? But most of all it tests us: How hard is it for us to drop the mask of youth and take up another mask, that of a mature woman? Is this an insignificant loss, a sad one, or one that shatters the soul?

Accepting our aging bodies is all the harder when our livelihood seems at stake. One woman we know, obliged to return to work after her husband died, had a face lift. She said she needed it to compete in real estate because clients don't respect a wrinkled face. She may be one of many career women who see plastic surgery "as a professional, rather than a personal, obligation."[5]

Researcher Danette Carol McEntee found that married women in her study feared aging less than single women did. She theorized that married women felt more secure. But many of the married women said their husbands considered them less attractive as they aged, and that response from their husbands made them feel less secure and less comfortable with aging. McEntee also studied husbands and found that the older the wife, the more the husband's reported loss of sexual interest and greater unfaithfulness. Happily married women were more able to identify with being the age they really were, while divorced and widowed women reported the greatest difference between their real age and the age they felt they were. Insecurely married women fell somewhere in between.[6] It's harder to accept oneself as aging if aging may mean being alone.

A study of the elderly found that people's fear of aging grew from their fears of dying, of being ill or handicapped, of being alone, and from being unattractive and therefore unwanted. Unattractiveness was strongly linked in elderly people's minds with being unwanted and alone.[7]

Mary Anne's story about Mrs. D. also highlights the priestly role we give to beautifiers in our culture. It only makes sense that if we worship beauty, then cosmetologists will be our clergy. Women go to salespeople like Mary Anne not just for makeup but for reassurance, self-respect, self-knowledge, hope. Am I lovable? They want to know. Who am I, an Autumn or a Spring? Am I a bright person or a subtle person? Should I be soft and delicate, or bold and striking? Can you make me into a person men will want? Can you make me the person I was when I was happy?

In "The Frosting of the American Woman," J. Greg Getz and Hanne K. Klein documented their research into the functions that hairstylists serve in women's lives. Their studies revealed exactly the same dynamic as we saw between Mary Anne and Mrs. D.: the stylist as therapist, mother, sister, priest.[8] A stylist told us she actually took a course in psychology for her cosmetology degree and has used that knowledge for years. People learn to love and trust the person who makes them beautiful.

I (Cinny) am old enough to know that losing my youthful beauty requires an adjustment. It's a death of one identity and a birth of a new one. But the degree to which that death feels like a disaster is the degree to which a woman is worshiping the beauty goddess, treating her anti-aging rule as the source of life and hope.

There is no denying I enjoyed being the focus of attention and admiration as a younger woman. However, I have found middle age often to be accompanied by a new and welcomed anonymity.

To move through my world unnoticed and invisible is a surprisingly positive experience. Relying on youth for love, respect, and security is like building one's house on sand: the storm is bound to come sooner or later to wash everything away.

THE CULT OF THINNESS

Young Victims
Youth is important in all human societies, but thinness, as we saw in Chapter 5, relates to status. The pursuit of youth breaks hearts and budgets, but increasingly, the quest for thinness kills.

Mary Pipher, a clinical psychologist who specializes in the treatment of adolescent girls, writes in *Reviving Ophelia: Saving the Selves of Adolescent Girls* that it's normal for teenage girls to pay more attention to their bodies than younger girls or older women because at that age,

> The body is changing in size, shape and hormonal structure. Just as pregnant women focus on their bodies, so adolescent girls focus on their changing bodies. They feel, look and move differently. These changes must be absorbed, the new body must become part of the self.
>
> The preoccupation with bodies at this age cannot be overstated. The body is a compelling mystery, a constant focus of attention. At thirteen, I thought more about my acne than I did about God or world peace. At thirteen, many girls spend more time in front of a mirror than they do on their studies. Small flaws become obsessions. Bad hair can ruin a day. A broken fingernail can feel tragic.[9]

Mary Pipher's comments can reassure mothers who worry about their daughters' new appearance obsession: this is a normal phase that, in the normal course of things, a girl will outgrow. Sadly, we do not live in the normal course of things.

Page after page of women's magazines, especially those aimed at teenagers, depict models who are far below a healthy body weight. According to *People*, the height and weight of the average American woman in 1996 was 5'4" and 142 pounds, while the height and weight of the average fashion model was 5'9" and 110 pounds.[10] There is no way the average American girl is going to make her body like that of those goddess surrogates, yet girls' magazines churn out the goddess's propaganda: Your salvation—your entire hope for love and respect in this world—depends upon being beautiful/thin enough to attract boys. In our study of these magazines we found nothing about politics, careers, athletics, academics, or religious faith—only the beauty commandments.

Girls who devour these magazines get a double message: "Be beautiful, but beauty is only skin deep. Be sexy, but not sexual."[11] This sounds a lot like the double message we noted from the church in Chapter One. We learn to be beautiful enough to gain attention, but also not to want too much attention or we'll appear vain and maybe even be "asking for it."

Mary Pipher laments:

> Generally girls have strong bodies when they enter puberty. But these bodies soften and spread out in ways that our culture calls fat. Just at the point that their bodies are becoming rounder, girls are told that thin is beautiful, even imperative. Girls hate the required gym classes in which other girls talk about their fat thighs and stomachs. One girl told me of showering next to an eighty-five-pound dancer who was on a radical diet. For the first time in her life she looked at her body and was displeased.[12]

And where did the 85-pound dancer get the idea of going on a radical diet, just when she should have extra nutrition for a growth spurt and plenty of fuel for her physically demanding workouts? She probably got it from her instructor, just as gymnasts get this message from their coaches: successful dancers and gymnasts are elfin, airy waifs, flying through the air with nothing to weigh them down. People (that's us, the audience) don't like looking at dancers and gymnasts who jiggle.

Like actresses and models, whose livelihood depends on their thinness, gymnasts and dancers are at high risk for anorexia (addiction to not eating) and bulimia (addiction to bingeing on food and then making oneself throw up, or abusing laxatives or exercise). Persistent vomiting damages tooth enamel and the esophagus with stomach acid, induces digestive problems, and sometimes causes heart attacks because of imbalanced electrolytes. Anorexia can cause heart attack and even death from starvation. Women with eating disorders are the kamikazes of the beauty cult, willing to die for their goddess's rules.

> "She's too fat to make the Olympic gymnastics team."— Judge at gymnastics competition, speaking of 93-pound Christy Henrich, who later died from anorexia nervosa at 47 pounds[13]

As the addiction progresses, they become secretive about bingeing or dieting, feel driven and guilty, and gradually distance themselves from other people. Anorectic women tend to be "perfectionistic and controlled," while bulimics are often "impulsive and . . . experience themselves as chronically out of control."[14] In both cases, control is the central issue. Both anorectics and bulimics are generally people-pleasers who try to meet the standards set for them by society and, if they are Christians, by the church. They are most common at suburban, middle to upper middle-class white schools where girls avoid glasses, do their hair, have straightened teeth, and try in all ways to be perfect as the people around them are perfect.[15]

But more and more they are turning up in all strata of society. "Estimates of bulimia run as high as one-fifth of all college-age women."[16] "A survey in San Francisco found that eighty percent of fourth-grade girls (around age nine) were dieting."[17] A Vermont survey found two-thirds of thirteen to eighteen-year-old girls were trying to shrink back to that pre-pubescent look.[18]

Now, the causes of eating disorders are complex and extend far beyond the desire to look good. For example, girls who were sexually abused or who have chaotic family backgrounds seem to be at greater risk for bulimia.[19] I (Karen) grew up feeling that my family was out of control with rage and with sexual behaviors that frightened me, so I latched upon food as a way of feeling I had some control over my life. I couldn't control my parents' and others' behavior, but I could control my weight. In a sense, then, beauty had nothing to do with my anorexia. However, the fact that I chose weight out of all the other hundreds of things I could have tried to control has a lot to do with what weight symbolizes in our society. To me, weight (not grades or hours spent in prayer) was the ultimate symbol of a woman in control of her life. Fat was the ultimate symbol of weakness and failure. I did not come up with these ideas on my own; I picked them up from the people around me.

> "BATMAN AND FATGIRL"
> —Tabloid headline mocking nineteen-year-old Alicia Silverstone, who was about to star in the next *Batman* sequel and who dared to attend the 1995 Academy Awards weighing 10 pounds more than when she starred in *Clueless*.[20]

Mary Pipher also notes that because of the way in which human brains develop, most early adolescents think concretely and literally; adolescents develop abstract thinking later if encouraged to do so in a relatively low-stress environment. Hence, both teenage boys and teenage girls have difficulty appreciating inner beauty. The symbol is the reality. Girls also tend to take literally insults to their bodies, such as the common, "move your fat [rear]" and the label "Thunder Thighs." Girls do not say to themselves, "This person has said something negative about my body, but the comment really says more about that person than about me. Moreover, whether he likes my body or not does not affect my soul." To girls, even more than the rest of us, their bodies are them, and they have not developed the skill of evaluating what is said to them. So they shrivel inside.

Girls learn a large vocabulary for talking about their looks but little about how to verbalize feelings. Even eleven-year-olds waiting in the wings on the opening night of a play can be heard to say, "I feel so fat," and, "No . . . You look great, but look how big my stomach is."[21] They have learned from their elders not to say, "I'm afraid of failing, so I feel anxious about being seen in this play tonight," but rather to say, "There's something wrong with my body that makes me unworthy of being seen." Their bodies are metaphors for their negative feelings about what is currently happening. Girls like this may have difficulty confessing to God, "Lord, I am struggling with anxiety about failing tonight; please help me trust You," because according to the goddess their "sin" is body size rather than lack of trust. They have learned from their culture to fear sinning against the goddess more than ignoring the real God.

Thinness and Christians

Because fat represents low status in our food-rich society, fat women face some of the worst prejudice our culture dishes out. People stereotype fat women as self-indulgent, undisciplined, aggressive, stupid, lazy, morally weak, and above all, out of control. In fact, we said so to a thin Christian woman, and she retorted that sometimes fat women *are* that way to some degree. Of course. But the same could be said of us. No stereotype is entirely false, but because it is a blanket condemnation, a stereotype is almost always spiritually destructive. Jean Kilbourne, a watchdog of destructive advertising, says our society is "increasingly obsessed with being in control,"[22] and therefore, fat people represent the lack

> "OH what SELF CONTROL"
> —ad for Light n' Lively® Free™ Nonfat Yogurt

of control we fear. It can be argued that our society is increasingly obsessed with self-indulgence, not self-control, but even so, in the church we are often obsessed with control of both self and others. True self-control is a result of consistently focusing one's trust on God's Spirit,[23] but many of us substitute imitation lite self-control generated by pride.

Remember the story about the overweight Christian speaker in Chapter One who was told she lacked self-discipline? This is a common Christian judgment of fat women. Although overweight men seem to have no trouble being taken seriously as pastors and speakers, heavy women lose respect. The church rarely denounces overeating as a sin like drinking or adultery, but instead quietly ostracizes the transgressors. Instead of providing a safe environment in which an overeater can admit and explore the reasons for her sin, we simply shame and dismiss her.

For instance, Sally was a leader in a local branch of a national Christian women's Bible study organization in the 1980s. When she had to move from the area, she recommended a successor. "There was a particular woman I felt would be a wonderful Bible lecturer and teacher. She was the wife of an attorney, deeply loved by the women around her, and was my first choice for my replacement. However, she was rejected as a teacher by the area leadership because of her weight. They felt she was overweight and therefore had a problem. The leadership associated overweight with sin, so weight becomes a moral issue."

Sally is deeply troubled by this apparent double standard of a Christian organization. She said, "This event really shaped my message and my life as to what organizations and churches I choose to be part of. I wanted to be part of a group that showed more grace and acceptance toward others, rather than just talked about grace."

We asked Sally why she thought some heavier women today are accepted as Christian humorists. She pointed out, "It's okay for a woman to be fat if she's funny. That seems to work. However, if you're heavier and not funny, that doesn't seem to work."

Along the same lines, a woman whom we'll call Jill told us,

> I was involved with [a major parachurch organization] as a college student. The staff stressed the importance of presenting a good image if one wanted to be a student leader. As the music leader, I was told I needed to dress a certain way and project a certain attractive and well-put-together image when I was up front in the meetings.
>
> Two of my friends who wanted to go on staff with [this organization] were denied this position based on their being overweight. I think they were only twenty-five to thirty pounds overweight, which didn't seem like much to me. They were told they had to work on their "weight issues." As a result, another friend, before applying for a staff position, went on a diet and exercise program to make sure that this rejection didn't happen to her.

This weight issue seemed to be an unspoken policy, frustrating to Jill and her friends.

The leaders of these two organizations evidently assumed that any overweight woman must be overeating and therefore lacked self-discipline. While overweight is often the result of overeating, it's noteworthy that the leaders called the sin "weight issues" rather than "gluttony issues" or "lack of self-control." We also wonder whether they scrutinized slim candidates for other signs of lack of self-control, such as overwork, overspending, a sharp tongue, or watching too much television. Perhaps overeating seems more sinful than those excesses today because our society calls it sin. Further, overeaters can't hide their impulsiveness the way workaholics, overspenders, and TV addicts can. Too often, the standard of gluttony is not what or how much one eats, but whether it shows in one's waist size.

It's true that gluttony is a sin—the worship of food rather than God as the source of happiness and comfort, and the determination to eat too much while others go hungry. Gluttony is a form of greed. But not every woman who eats more than 1,800 calories per day is a glutton. Many simply lack the genes to be svelte or are physically active enough to require more calories.

More importantly, as C. S. Lewis astutely recognized, gluttony consists not simply in the quantity of food eaten but in the attitude of eating. In his shrewd satire of temptation, *The Screwtape Letters*, Lewis's demonic main character says picky eating, the precise insistence on toast done just so, is as gluttonous as overeating:

> One of the great achievements of the last hundred years has been to deaden the human conscience on that subject [of gluttony]. . . . This has largely been effected by concentrating all our efforts on gluttony of Delicacy, not gluttony of Excess. Your patient's mother . . . is a good example. She would be astonished—one day, I hope, *will* be—to learn that her whole life is enslaved to this kind of sensuality, which is quite concealed from her by the fact that the quantities involved are small. But what do quantities matter when we can use a human belly and palate to produce querulousness, impatience, uncharitableness, and self-concern? . . . She is always turning from what has been

offered her to say with a demure little sigh and a smile "Oh please, please . . . *all* I want is a cup of tea, weak but not too weak, and the teeniest weeniest bit of really crisp toast." . . .

The real value of the quiet, unobtrusive work which Glubose has been doing for years on this old woman can be gauged by the way in which her belly now dominates her whole life. The woman is in what may be called the "All-I-want" state of mind. . . .[24]

The "All-I-want" state of mind might for some of us express itself in the demand for fat-free cookies, ice cream, and salad dressing; for sugar-free soft drinks with our fast-food sandwiches; and for protein diet drinks that cost as much as a full meal. Requesting healthful food is laudable, but when the demands that food be done "just so" come from our compulsion to obey the beauty goddess, when our bellies dominate our lives, we have crossed the line into gluttony.

> A recent study found that 11 percent of Americans would abort a fetus if they were told it had a tendency to obesity.[25]

The Bible encourages us to fast periodically in order to remind ourselves that we live not by bread alone but by God's life-giving words. Fasting and dieting are not at all the same thing. Fasting is an act of humility and dependence upon God; dieting, except for health reasons, can be a proud act ("I can make my body look however I want it to") whose goal is pleasing people rather than God. Dieters rarely gain more compassion for the hungry as a result of their self-deprivation, while fasters often report growing more generous. In fact, dieting can often make a person angry at being deprived, envious of those who don't need to diet, judgmental toward those who are larger than the dieter but don't watch their weight, and obsessed with food. Obsessive thinking is a common sign of an idolatrous heart.

Dieting can reflect a commitment to become perfect through flesh-driven willpower, rather than a commitment to become like Christ through the Holy Spirit. Paul saw this at work in Galatia: "I would like to learn just one thing from you: Did you receive the Spirit by observing the law, or by believing what you heard? Are you so foolish? After beginning with the Spirit, are you now try-ing to attain your goal through human effort?"[26]

Unless it is part of repentance from gluttony or a concern for one's health, dieting is a spiritual discipline for disciples of the beauty goddess. Worshiping thinness is not better than worship-ing food. We lack space to treat adequately the causes and cures of weight gain, but the woman who knows she is overweight might seek answers to questions like these:

&Do I eat to feed soul hunger as well as body hunger? That is, do I use food for emotional comfort? If so, why do I do this? How can I learn more appropriate ways to handle emotions and find comfort?

&Am I greedy about the pleasure of having something tasty in my mouth? Do I have difficulty saying no to pleasure? If so, why is that?

&Am I genetically predisposed to be large or gain weight? Do I come from a long line of big women? If so, is this a medical problem that requires a medical solution? Should I simply ask for help in learning to love the body God gave me?

&Have I damaged my body's metabolism through past diet-ing? If so, how can I learn to live with the consequences?

&Is my metabolism slowing as I age, while I continue to eat as I have always done? If so, how do I learn to pay attention to my body's signals about how much food it really needs? How can I come to accept the loss of my youthful metabolism?

&Am I in the habit of eating as much as the people I live with? Since men, active children, and adolescents require more food than the average woman, how can I learn to eat according to my body's needs, rather than keeping up with everyone else?

&Do I get enough exercise? How can I build that into my routine?

These are just a few of the many questions that might apply to this complex issue, which has physical, spiritual, emotional, and social dimensions. Not every large woman is gluttonous, and not every glutton is large. A woman's repentance from gluttony involves asking herself probing questions about why she eats and seeking God's grace to eat no more—and no more demandingly—than she needs.

We question whether barring overweight women from positions of responsibility is the most helpful way for the Church to encourage them to examine their hearts honestly and see if they need to address gluttony as a spiritual issue. Shame and rejection rarely encourage people to do the hard work of pursuing the grace of God. Many women rejected in this way will simply become more committed to

> YOU'RE TOO FAT TO BE MY FRIEND
> —topic of *The Ricki Lake Show*,
> 6 February 1996

the belief that their value rests in their appearance, more committed to serving the beauty goddess rather than the Creator. We might take our cue from Paul:

> My friends, if anyone is detected in a transgression, you who have received the Spirit should restore such a one in a spirit of gentleness. Take care that you yourselves are not tempted [to worship the beauty goddess]. Bear one another's burdens, and in this way you will fulfill the law of Christ. For if those who are nothing think they are something [because they are slimmer], they deceive themselves.[27]

Perhaps a better way to fight our culture's fat obsession is to make fun of it. An article in *People*, "How the Stars Fight Fat," unleashed a flood of angry letters like this one:

> Oh, how wonderful. Gaggles of supermodels and super-hunks who can afford personal trainers and their own live-in cooks tell me how to fight fat! How about doing it on a budget with a *real* job?[28]

BREASTS: HOW MUCH IS ENOUGH?

A 1996 ABC poll found that 23 percent of respondents have wanted a different breast size.[29] As we talked to women, we found large-breasted women who wanted to be smaller and small-breasted women who wanted to be larger.

The evolutionary psychologists say men care more about symmetry and firmness than size, but most women today believe men think bigger is better when it comes to breasts. Certainly men who are fed a steady diet of models and actresses with implants get used to the idea that a normal, healthy woman has D-cup breasts that never sag. Compared to surgically perfected goddess surrogates, ordinary women look deformed. Young people in particular, who never knew a time when all actresses didn't have perfect breasts, can think the ones girls grow naturally are inferior. Boys call girls flat or tomboys at school, or ignore them until they grow breasts. One woman's father actually offered her breast surgery or $1,000 on her twenty-first birthday.[30] Small-breasted women complain that clothing often bags or gapes at the neck because they have nothing to fill it out.

From a well-endowed woman's point of view, small-breasted women at least have the advantage of being able to appear modest in any top. Those with large busts report having to wear oppressive bras to hold their breasts in place and having to work hard to cover their busts discreetly. One woman says businessmen associate big breasts with promiscuity and don't take her seriously.[31]

One young woman, Stacy, told us,

I wore a 36C throughout high school and was bigger than most of my friends. The standard comment from the guys was, "What size are you?" When I reacted they would say, "Why are you so upset? That's a compliment."

As I got older, I got larger. Basically, I felt like a freak of nature. It wasn't like a big butt which is behind you so you can't see it. My breasts were right out in front and one would see them when they looked at my face.

I experienced comments from my teachers, peers, employers, and strangers. Their comments about my breasts seemed different than comments about some other part of my body. Breasts are viewed from a sexual perspective and make a girl feel even more uncomfortable. When you're young it's hard to understand why a grown man is looking at an eighth-grader.

Curiously, Stacy thinks small-breasted women look fine in bikinis, while she would look immodest; but another woman told us she didn't have the "right" proportions to look "right" in a two-piece swimsuit because her breasts were too small. "Right" for her was defined by models whose bust and hip size were equal. The fact that models are atypical (most women have bigger hips than busts) doesn't change the fact that to this woman they are the yardsticks of perfection. Maybe these two women could compromise and agree that a firm C-cup is ideal, but that ideal excludes most women.

> "You'd be in really good shape if you had breasts."[32]

Large-busted women may also suffer back pain because they carry a pound or more strapped to their chests. Stacy said she asked her doctor about reduction surgery, and he recommended it, but her insurance company dismissed it as not medically necessary. "My doctor said that insurance companies are run by men who don't understand the physical and psychological pain large breasts can cause a woman," she said.

SURGERY: NO LONGER A LAST RESORT

Meanwhile, heedless of back pain, women continue to ask doctors to insert up to a pound of saline and plastic into their chests. Silicone is less popular now that we know its hazards, but some women continue to ignore the dangers of surgery itself: the potential for painful and ugly scars that never heal, loss of breast sensitivity, blood loss, infection, allergic response to anesthesia—the list is frightening.[33] Medical problems caused by elective cosmetic surgery are rarely covered by insurance.

Despite the risks and costs—or perhaps because of the risks and costs—the public remain fascinated by women who have resculpted themselves surgically. This willingness to undergo blood sacrifice in devotion to the goddess inspires awe. Forget the Hollywood stars—our personal favorite is Cindy Jackson, who has outspent them all with twenty-plus operations to reinvent herself as Barbie. Really. Surgery has made Ivana Trump rather Barbie-esque, but for Jackson, it's a mission. She founded the London-based Cosmetic Surgery Network to assist other women in becoming part of what she calls her "bionic army."[34] Besides making her own operations tax-deductible, her consumer watchdog network informs women about the risks and rewards of each type of surgery. Jackson has been on every known talk show, but when she speaks of her sister—"she has the perfect life and I have the perfect face and body"—we hear echoes of the rivalry between Leah and Rachel.

> "She has the perfect life and I have the perfect face and body."[35]

In 1992 alone, 365,000 Americans chose cosmetic surgery not for medical reasons, but solely to improve their appearance so they would feel better about themselves. The operations included, among others, face lifts to erase the signs of aging, liposuction to reduce fat, breast augmentation, and chin, eyelid, and nose alterations to improve facial symmetry and make one look more European. (Breast reconstruction for cancer patients and breast reduction for women in pain are considered medical procedures and so are not included in the 365,000.)

Almost 70 percent of cosmetic surgery patients had incomes of less than $25,000. This is no longer a luxury of the rich. Eighty-seven percent were women (which leaves a striking 13 percent who were men seeking the knife to improve their looks). Roughly 4 percent were under eighteen years old; children received 11 percent of all "nose jobs." Twenty percent were minorities, mostly African-American, Asian, or Latino.[36]

The number of cosmetic surgeries climbs each year; the total for 1994 (including surgeries for medical reasons) was almost two million.[37]

Cindy Jackson's friend, British plastic surgeon Dr. Edward Latimer-Sayer, believes he's in the business of helping average people:

The majority of my patients are housewives, nurses, hairdressers, secretaries—ordinary people. They don't want to be out of the ordinary, but they just feel that one particular part lets them down. An attractive young girl with a big hooky nose doesn't feel normal.[38]

The surgeon thinks having ethnic distinctives Europeanized is simply pragmatic:

> If you have the double fold—what they call the European eyelid—you are considered more trustworthy, higher class, and you're more likely to do well in life. . . . If you have the Oriental eyelid with the thick upper lid with no fold, it's like being a second-class citizen. . . . Now if there's a little simple cosmetic operation to make somebody go from a second-class citizen on appearance to a first-class citizen on appearance, no wonder it's popular.[39]

No wonder indeed. It's much simpler to get an operation than to combat anti-Asian sentiment in Western countries. Race relations would be far simpler if we all made ourselves over as Barbie. Dr. Latimer-Sayer mused on:

> If for instance, someone had developed a technique to make black people white . . . they would have been swamped, wouldn't they? Not because there's anything wrong with being black, but it's nicer to be white in a white society.[40]

On the other hand, maybe black people would find it nicer to make white society into a black-and-brown-and-white society. Maybe it would be less simple, but more scriptural, to do plastic surgery on the culture!

DISCERNING IDOLATRY

Plastic surgery is the ultimate way to seize beauty's blessings: love, respect, and financial security. Is it always sin to go under the knife? Is a face lift always idolatrous? What about breast reduction? And what about using anti-wrinkle creams, hair coloring, and Slim-Fast? Does every effort to minimize one's age and size amount to worship of the goddess and her rules?

As we've searched the Scriptures for principles by which women can discern when their thoughts and actions cross the line into idolatry, we have made a surprising discovery: Like money, status, and physical strength, beauty is a source of power.

"GO CURVY!"
—*Mademoiselle* cover article on plastic surgery[41]

Power is not necessarily evil, and the Bible offers a way to tell when we're using power in evil ways and when we're using it appropriately. We can judge how our use of power affects other people: are we loving them or controlling them? And just as important, we can go to the root and test the spirit with which we are using power. Behind virtually every abuse of beauty's power is pride.

A CLOSER LOOK

Inventory your bathroom and your daily schedule. How much time, money, and emotion do you spend in a given month on efforts to look younger or thinner? Why do you suppose you do this? Do you think you spend too much time and money on yourself, or possibly not enough? Which items on your inventory do you think reflect idolatry?

Examine your breasts in the mirror. (Your doctor told you to do this, anyway.) What do you feel when you look at them? Do you like them, or do they seem unacceptable in some way? What do they say about you: your age, your genetic inheritance, the children you've nursed or haven't nursed? If you or someone you love has had breast cancer, how does that affect what you see when you look at yourself? How easy is it for you to be grateful for the breasts God has given you?

CHAPTER NINE

PRIDE

THE ALLURE: POWER FOR THE POWERLESS

Beauty offers power, and power is not in itself evil. Esther, for example, is praised for wielding beauty's power to save lives. People use power to run churches, corporations, and countries. Sometimes they use that power well; at other times they abuse it.

Historically, the less comfortable a society has been with women using power forthrightly—at home, at work, or in politics—the more women like Esther or Delilah have resorted to indirect sources of power, such as appearance, to get things done. Beauty often allures women who otherwise feel powerless to get what they want from life.

For example, medieval law declared even a noblewoman to be her father's or husband's property. She had no rights of inheritance, authority over her children, protection from domestic violence, political voice, or access to higher education. Consequently, when the cult of courtly love (an aspect of chivalry) came into fashion in the late Middle Ages, noblewomen embraced it eagerly.

The great romances of courtly love, such as *Tristan and Iseult*, taught knights to adore beautiful and nobly born women

147

as symbols of the peaceful virtues of truth, love, and charity. Many of the romances described knights who pledged their undying love for beautiful but married noblewomen whom they could never touch but had to worship from afar. Knights carried their ladies' handkerchiefs into battle; the ladies' husbands weren't jealous because the worship was never supposed to lead to anything carnal. It was like (and often compared to) adoration of the pure, virginal Mother of God.

Women far preferred being put on pedestals in this way to being treated as mere sex objects, son-bearers, and political pawns. Courtly love offered noblewomen the power to gain respect and influence. Not surprisingly, the money paid to monks to spend years copying and illustrating a single manuscript of a medieval romance often came from wealthy women who liked being treated as goddess surrogates.

Women are still the chief consumers of romance books, and romances with pretty girls on the covers pour out of Christian bookstores. A part of each of us likes to imagine ourselves on a pedestal, adored by a good and rich man, especially if we doubt our power to win love and respect just for who we are. Even though our society gives women unprecedented access to education, political influence, and jobs, we still know that beauty wins attention and respect. In fact, a woman whose intelligence or strong character might intimidate men can use the trappings of beauty—attractive clothes, hair, makeup, and nails—to appear less forceful so she can achieve her ends in a less threatening manner.

What makes the difference between a righteous Esther and a woman who is using beauty's power in an idolatrous manner? One measure is the difference between humility and pride.

The apostle Paul told the Philippians, "Do nothing out of selfish ambition or vain conceit, but in humility consider others better than yourselves. Each of you should look not only to your own interests, but also to the interests of others."[1] Pride looks to her own interests; humility weighs her longings for love and respect alongside others' needs. Pride determines to be on top at any price; humility refuses to climb at others' expense. Pride believes she can do what she likes with her own body; humility knows Christ bought her body with His blood.[2] Pride controls; humility loves.

Let's look at some ways in which proud women respond when they detect the heady aroma of beauty's power.

JEZEBEL

Jezebel, the Phoenician queen of ancient Israel, was the Bible's Wicked Witch of the West. Once she got her husband under her thumb, she tried to convert Israel to fertility religion and systematically murder the Lord's prophets. She plotted Elijah's death and killed common people in order to steal their property. In her last appearance in his account, the writer of 2 Kings described the aging queen preparing to face the man who would have her assassinated: "When Jezebel heard [that Jehu had arrived], she painted her eyes, arranged her hair and looked out of a window."[3] Unafraid and unremorseful, she nonetheless would not be seen without her beauty mask. The deliberate care she gave her appearance with death at the door would have been regal in a finer woman, but in the case of this power-hungry queen it was merely a chilling display of pride.

> "Makeovers are *the* official art form of the 1990s, you know."
> —Douglas Coupland, *Microserfs*

Compare Jezebel's arrogance to Esther's three days of humble fasting before she adorned herself to face Xerxes. Esther wasn't interested in exalting herself above other women or triumphing over anyone but the evil Haman, but Jezebel craved her own aggrandizement at everyone else's expense. Esther knew she merely reflected God's glory; Jezebel lusted for her own glory. Pride is the normal human desire for respect swollen to an obsession with status, the normal human longing for love bloated into a demand for worship.

Jezebel's father was a Phoenician king. Recall these words addressed to another Phoenician ruler, the king of Tyre:

> Your heart became proud
>   on account of your beauty,

and you corrupted your wisdom
>   because of your splendor.
So I threw you to the earth;
>   I made a spectacle of you before kings.[4]

These words could easily apply to women who let their God-given beauty move them to pride rather than humble gratitude.

GOD'S ARROGANT BRIDE

In fact, the proud, adulterous beauty became a metaphor for idolatrous Israel in the Old Testament. God likened Jerusalem to an abandoned baby whom he rescued and raised. Over the years, he said, "You grew up and developed and became the most beautiful of jewels. Your breasts were formed and your hair grew, you who were naked and bare."[5] When she was old enough, God married her and arrayed her like a queen:

> I bathed you with water and washed the blood from you and put ointments on you. I clothed you with an embroidered dress and put leather sandals on you. I dressed you in fine linen and covered you with costly garments. I adorned you with jewelry: I put bracelets on your arms and a necklace around your neck, and I put a ring on your nose, earrings on your ears and a beautiful crown on your head. So you were adorned with gold and silver; your clothes were of fine linen and costly fabric and embroidered cloth. Your food was fine flour, honey and olive oil. You became very beautiful and rose to be a queen. And your fame spread among the nations on account of your beauty, because the splendor I had given you made your beauty perfect, declares the Sovereign LORD.
>
> But you trusted in your beauty and used your fame to become a prostitute. You lavished your favors on anyone who passed by and your beauty became his. You took some of your garments to make gaudy high places, where

you carried on your prostitution. . . . You also took the fine
jewelry I gave you, the jewelry made of my gold and silver,
and you made for yourself male idols and engaged in prostitution with them. And you took your embroidered
clothes to put on them, and you offered my oil and
incense before them. . . .

At the head of every street you built your lofty shrines
and degraded your beauty, offering your body with
increasing promiscuity to anyone who passed by.[6]

Ezekiel blushed at nothing in detailing both the beauty and the
adultery of God's Bride. This passage wonderfully illustrates the
double-edged quality of beauty as the Bible portrays it. On the one
hand, Jerusalem's beauty was good: God made her beautiful and
even adorned her for the nations to admire. On the other hand,
Jerusalem made several fatal mistakes in handling her beauty.
First, she forgot that God deserved the credit for it; she was arrogant instead of grateful. Second, she trusted in her beauty to get
what she wanted, rather than trusting God to give her what was
good for her. She sought control by worshiping a false god. And
third, she degraded her beauty by giving it—this gift from God—
away to other lovers. She thought she was selling her beauty to buy
love, but she was only being used:

You adulterous wife! You prefer strangers to your own
husband! Every prostitute receives a fee, but you give gifts
to all your lovers, bribing them to come to you from everywhere for your illicit favors. So in your prostitution you
are the opposite of others; no one runs after you for your
favors. You are the very opposite, for you give payment
and none is given to you.[7]

Ezekiel's adulterous queen is a metaphor for Jerusalem, but we
can all learn from her error. Jerusalem thought she was smart in
declaring independence from God and marketing her charms in
order to get what God wouldn't give; but she ended up bereft,
helpless under her idols' control.

THE PRIDE OF RICHES

More often than not, the pursuit of beauty for prideful reasons is associated with wealth and indifference to the poor. Isaiah warned Jerusalem's women:

The LORD says,
    "The women of Zion are haughty,
walking along with outstretched necks,
    flirting with their eyes,
tripping along with mincing steps,
    with ornaments jingling on their ankles.
Therefore the Lord will bring sores on the heads of the
        women of Zion;
    the LORD will make their scalps bald."

In that day the Lord will snatch away their finery: the bangles and headbands and crescent necklaces, the earrings and bracelets and veils, the headdresses and ankle chains and sashes, the perfume bottles and charms, the signet rings and nose rings, the fine robes and the capes and cloaks, the purses and mirrors, and the linen garments and tiaras and shawls.

Instead of fragrance there will be a stench;
    instead of a sash, a rope;
instead of well-dressed hair, baldness;
    instead of fine clothing, sackcloth;
    instead of beauty, branding.[8]

Here we see a much different view of beauty and ornamentation than we saw in the Song of Songs. This is beauty abused by proud women, ornamentation collected by rich women who care more for exalting themselves than for helping their poorer neighbors. The prideful lust for one's own power and glory now takes on social and political dimensions. Money idolatry and beauty idolatry are closely linked as twin sources of pride and power. Eventually, though, God promises that the proud will be shamed and the power-hungry enslaved. Addiction always ends there.

Toward the end of his diatribe against whoring Jerusalem, Ezekiel warned her about her sister Sodom's sin. "Now this was the sin of your sister Sodom: She and her daughters were arrogant, overfed and unconcerned; they did not help the poor and needy."[9] Isaiah and Ezekiel condemned not women's beauty, but their abuse of it as idolatry, pride, and lack of compassion. Clothes and jewelry were means by which wealthy women flaunted their superiority over the poor in Isaiah's day, just as today one can often tell a woman's income by how much she is able to spend on her clothes, hair, nails, facials, jewelry, and exercise. To adjust Helena Rubinstein's line, we might say there are no ugly women, only women with limited budgets.

> "New shoes. Belgian chocolates. And now. Maybelline Revitalizing Lip Indulgence. Just the latest of life's little indulgences."[10]

Although she deserves applause for standing up to her less-than-princely husband, the Princess of Wales might have sat for Isaiah's portrait of rich women who revel in their power as though it will never end. *Vogue* detailed her 1994 expenses: $1,500 for highlights; $12,000 for haircuts; $300 for makeup; $2,100 for facials; $6,000 for manicures and pedicures; $3,200 for body-care products; $6,000 for personal exercise trainer; $7,400 for gym memberships—the list goes on. Princess Diana is no actress or model whose livelihood depends on her looks, but she spends $38,000 per year (not counting her huge designer wardrobe) for something as vital to her as food and shelter: the adulation of millions. Her expensive, perfect appearance props up her pride and accords her astonishing power: attention, lovers, public forgiveness for her infidelities, and the popularity that forced the royals to give her favorable divorce terms. In fact, when it came down to the battle royal, beauty bought by money was virtually the only power Diana had.

Some beauty worshipers even use the language of religion. Irena, a Latvian model, describes one of her many costly beauty rituals like a convert reporting a spiritual experience:

"You know how all those old movie stars looked like
movie stars?" Irena speaks with passion, conviction. "It's
the brows." Then, lowering her voice to a reverent whisper: "Go see Anastasia. She will change your life."[11]

Can perfect brows change your life? Are they your ticket to a
better job, a fabulous husband, your mother's approval, and your
peers' respect? If so, then maybe the brow-priestess Anastasia is
worth her fee.

In *The Power of Beauty*, Nancy Friday champions the worship
of beauty in such graphic terms that we struggle to find a passage
to quote that won't offend our readers. Men, she says, love to worship women's bodies if we let them; Friday has been glad to let
them.[12] She admits to feeling overwhelmed by her closets bulging
with designer clothes, but still insists, "Before women can enjoy
the rewards that come with the beauty we now work so hard to
purchase, we must learn to see our beauty as power."[13] She offers
herself as a role model of a woman who began using this power
in her youth and still does so:

> There was nothing reckless in my new exhibitionism [in
> the 1960s], the exhilaration of walking along on a summer
> evening in a sea-green Pucci dress, a wisp of a garment
> you could hold on the tip of a pinkie nail and under which
> I wore only stockings and a garter belt. If men hadn't
> looked, I would have been disappointed. Choosing to be
> visually appraised, drawing eyes to my body, and by my
> choice, gave me a surge of control. I knew exactly what I
> had put on and why; I accepted that it was my job to be
> responsible for the waves I had set in motion.[14]

Even setting Friday's sexual morals aside, this is the boast
of a woman proud of her ability to control men's responses,
proud to have the right kind of body and the money to adorn
it. Money oozes through every page of her memoir: as a teen she
tanned on the beaches of the world; in her twenties she wore
Pucci; and now she says there is no reason a woman in her

fifties needs to give up the power of her beauty because she can simply buy "synthetic estrogen, testosterone, amazing beauty creams, revolutionary bodybuilding machinery, cosmetic surgery," as well as designer clothing and anything else necessary to catch the eye.[15] Traveling in her circles, she has neither awareness nor patience for women who can't afford to remain priestesses of beauty, nor does she think

> "So much of what goes into my closets is there to make up for what I didn't get back then [as a child], to disguise the ugly child who wasn't really all that bad."[16]

there is anything more important on which to spend her wealth.

TREND-SETTERS

Money finances beauty and beauty earns money. The link between money, power, pride, and beauty idolatry is clearest among those who get rich and receive acclaim for setting the trends the masses are supposed to follow. Queen Catherine de Medici of France (1519-1589) and Queen Elizabeth I of England (1533-1603) were the first to wear the iron corset: a hinged bodice of iron bands that tightened a woman's waist to thirteen inches.[17] They were the most powerful women of their day—men called their thirst for power "unnatural" in the fair sex—yet while men of their rank wore iron armor over their clothes to make them look like soldiers, Catherine and Elizabeth wore it under their dresses to discipline their bodies into unnatural curves. These queens who would bow to no man coveted that divinely feminine waist-to-hip ratio. Soon every woman in Europe was copying their iron discipline, crushing their internal organs to achieve high-status figures.

Girls today don't have to reckon with queens setting iron corsets as the fashion trend, but they are bombarded with messages from fashion magazines and other media that tell them how women should look. Fashion magazines illustrate the insidious way in which women cooperate with worldly propaganda they know is damaging. The magazines are largely staffed and even owned by women, and their financing comes from big cosmetic and clothing companies that place advertising in them. Those companies, in turn, have many women on their payrolls and even their boards. More and more major designers, such as Liz Claiborne and Donna Karan, are women. So in the end, lots of women as well as men are benefiting from the beauty propaganda: they are not only making lots of money, but they also receive the status our society accords to major players in this all-important industry. If the beauty goddess gives them the financial security and respect they long for, why shouldn't they evangelize for her?

Still, many women on magazine staffs feel ambivalent about the goddess they serve. Consequently, they also run articles that make great show of biting the hand that feeds them. *Elle* warns against "The Real Waif Look," when fourth-grade girls go on diets because their culture tells them that the perfect body is that of an eight-year-old.[18] *Cooking Light* interviews "a supreme court of looks"—including, among others, designer Donna Karan; Grace Mirabella, founder and editor-at-large of *Mirabella* and former editor at *Vogue*; and Andi Matheny, "a stand-up comic and actress who recently appeared in an Oil of Olay ad campaign about how to have younger-looking skin"—about reinventing the concept of beauty.[19] "Today's beauty is beauty from the inside out," says Karan, who markets thousand-dollar jackets. "Individual women are less focused on our looks," says Matheny. And,

> "Hey, Coke, want 17½ million very interested women to think Diet? Better than one out of three *Ladies' Home Journal* readers buy and drink diet soft drinks. That's more than any other women's service magazine. . . . We not only offer you a greater proportion of diet-conscious readers, but we give you a very healthy environment for your ads, too. . . ."[21]

Mirabella is optimistic that things are about to change: "Today a 24-year-old model is considered old. We're all in the habit of working with teenagers; that's what we push, and that's what people see. But the world has evolved, and we're going to have to figure out how to present women of other ages."[20]

The world has certainly evolved: the population is aging, including Grace Mirabella. But we think these ladies protest way too much. They're all making big money from the beauty cult, and so is *Cooking Light*. They're also spending big money on their own appearance, and they glory in their status as trend-setters. Whether they cry crocodile tears about the tyranny of beauty worship or trumpet the new fall fashions, these women know that their pride and power come from the goddess.

ORDINARY FOLKS

The fashion gurus have the resources to be extreme beauty worshipers, just as rich drug addicts can carry their habits to extremes. Still, even many middle-class women are willing to invest large percentages of their incomes into a look that will win them respect. A medical secretary turning fifty told us she was saving for an eighty-five-dollar haircut at an exclusive Beverly Hills salon. She said this salon is worth it because the stylists know how to shape a style to a woman's unique features and age.

Who are we to say no haircut is worth eighty-five dollars? Likewise, who are we to say that what a businesswoman, a speaker, the wife of a prominent pastor, or just an average churchgoer spends on clothes and grooming is excessive? In each case, the spiritual standard is less the price tag than the degree of pride motivating the buyer.

At whatever age or income level, pride moves the haves to lord over the have-nots. In *Reviving Ophelia*, Mary Pipher says this attitude starts when girls are young:

> While peers can be satisfying and growth-producing, they can also be growth-destroying, especially in early adolescence. Many girls can describe . . . the scapegoating of girls by one another. Many girls become good haters of those who do not conform sufficiently to our cultural ideas about femininity.
>
> Like any recent converts to an ideology [beauty idolatry], girls are at risk of becoming the biggest enforcers and proselytizers for the culture. . . . They punish by walking up to girls with insults about their clothes or bodies. They

punish by nicknames and derogatory labels. They punish
by picking a certain girl, usually one who is relatively
happy, and making her life miserable. . . .

My classmate Patty was obese and slow-moving. She
suffered the most. Her nickname was "Mammoth," and
girls called her this to her face.[22]

To shame another woman because she lacks either the natural
gifts, the financial resources, or the skill to beautify herself to our
standards is an inexcusable expression of pride.

THE LUST FOR CONTROL

How do we know when our use of power is prideful? Paul used
the term "selfish ambition," the clash between others' interests
and our own.

Pride moves some women to seek power over men without
regard to the interests of the men or anyone else. The pretty
teenager who enjoys the boys' puppy eyes when they look at her
can easily become a manipulative tease. At first she just basks in
the attention that comes when she arches her back a certain way,
or sits on a table and swings a bare leg. Eventually she learns to
use body language to manipulate boys into catering to her every
whim. Manipulation is loveless, treating others as objects to meet
one's own needs. Control strategies are a sure sign of a pride that
considers oneself more important than anyone else.

A young woman named Kelly admitted to us that as a waitress
in a restaurant chain she always knew how to get permission to
leave early or how to get the best section where she could earn the
most tips. Normally she hated being known as "the blonde with the
really big boobs," but when she wanted something from her manager,
she knew how to mesmerize him by standing or walking in a certain
way. Kelly's strategy was not much different from the way Esther
maneuvered Xerxes, but when the motive is to control a man for our
own ends, we have to ask ourselves what God would think.

When a woman feels like Esther, powerless to take care of herself by any means other than her body and her wits, fear can take
over. Fear says, "I can't survive without love, respect, and money.

If I don't have control over those, I'll die!" When Esther felt powerless, she humbly put all her chips on God's number. Humility enabled her to act shrewdly without lowering herself to the same hateful level as her enemy. But women who lack that ingrained trust often feel driven by fear into strategies to control their own bodies and/or others through their bodies. Fear often lies behind decisions as minor as the crash diet before the high school reunion and as major as breast implants or bulimia. It's not easy to get to the place where we can say, with Esther, "If I perish, I perish."[23]

In order to get to that place, Esther needed to fast for three days and know that her people were backing her up. She needed to sense herself lovingly connected to a community of faith. But too often, we find pride and the fear of not being in control lead women to damage their sisterhood with envy and competition. Instead of cheering each other on to Esther-like courage, women too often reinforce one another's feelings of being locked in a battle to get what they want from men by beating each other in a beauty contest. This beauty competition born of women's fear and envy has harmed us immeasurably.

A CLOSER LOOK

It's easiest to see pride in others. Which women at your workplace or church seem motivated by pride in the way they present themselves in public? How can you tell?

Set aside some time for quiet prayer. Ask God to expose any ways in which pride drives your choices about your appearance. Is your craving for respect excessive?

Fasting helps a person acknowledge the things that drive her and submit them to God's Spirit. Nothing exposes our dependence on food quicker than going hungry. Try a fast from makeup. How hard would it be for you to go a day, a week, or a month without makeup? How hard would it be to go to the office or church just once with your face bare? Explore your emotions around this thought.

Chapter Ten

COMPETITION

WINNERS AND LOSERS

A person can view power in either a win-win or a win-lose way. A woman who is able to celebrate both her own and another's beauty has a win-win view; she feels so connected to her sister that she feels honored when her sister is honored.[1] She feels empowered when her friend has power. When friends help each other shop or bustle around a bride to adorn her for the big day, beauty rituals bring them together. The whole group gains when one member is glorified.

By contrast, a beauty idolator sees love, respect, and wealth as win-lose commodities. She feels her pride threatened when people enjoy another woman's beauty. To her, humility is no option; there is either the pride of the winner or the humiliation of the loser. She also feels her value threatened: the more others enjoy her rival's beauty, the less attention is left for her. Consequently, contentment is no option for her either: she either has the power to get what she wants, or she envies those who have it. This win-lose attitude condemns her to constant fear of loss and shame.

Good husbands and good jobs really are in limited supply. There is a sense in which women who want to marry are all competing for the best available men, and women who want to be promoted at work are all competing for the position. And like power, competition is not inherently bad. A little healthy rivalry can spur everyone on to be the best she can be. However, when pride and fear fuel the competition for the man or the promotion, things get ugly. When they fuel a battle to be chief hen in the church coop, they grieve the Holy Spirit.

ENVY IN ACTION

Stranger Versus Stranger

At its coolest, envy is the frosty green glance two women give each other in the ladies' room, supposedly surveying their own appearance but subtly evaluating one another's. Sometimes a ladies-room glance is merely curious and appreciative: "Oooh, that color is really striking on her!" But sometimes it is the "controlling gaze" of one who claims the right to judge.[2] Men are wont to frankly stare at a woman when they size her up, but competitive women look sidelong, alert to whether they have won or lost the silent contest.

Wolf describes the envious woman's attitude:

> The unknown woman . . . is unapproachable, under suspi-
> cion before she opens her mouth because she's Another
> Woman, and beauty thinking urges women to approach
> one another as possible adversaries until they know they
> are friends. . . . Women can tend to resent each other if
> they look too "good" and dismiss one another if they look
> too "bad."[3]

Advertisers play on women's envious tendencies. A milk ad features slim and busty Naomi Campbell saying, "You're probably going to hate me, but I've never dieted a day in my life. Being so busy, I usually just grab something real quick. Which is why I love milk. One percent lowfat. With all the same nutrients as whole milk, it's just what my body needs. Well, that and a closet full of ultrashort, supertight, little black dresses."[4] This ad copy and her milky-sweet smile are calculated to raise the blood pressure in any woman over a size six.

Envy is part of the reason why the respect game is such a minefield, both at work and at church. Once, when I (Cinny) arrived in a town so my husband could take a new pastoral position, the women of the church greeted me with humor: they were glad I had finally arrived because they were "so tired of hearing about the new pastor and his beautiful wife." Apparently the senior pastor had remarked upon Bob's "beautiful wife" more than once, oblivious to the subtle dynamics of women's envy. I tried to play along with a self-deprecating joke ("I'm sorry I can't quite live up to that billing"), but even though we were all laughing, I wondered if some women in the church were unamused. My insecurity alarms went off: Were some people here already resenting me before they even knew me? Were they going to gossip about my appearance? I was hyper-vigilant about what I wore at that church for a long time, careful to look the part of a humble pastor's wife, whether I was actually humble or not.

I had discovered envy in myself years earlier. When Bob was in seminary, one of his classmates was married to a beautiful woman, whom I knew casually and would have liked to have known better. But I was too intimidated by and envious of her sophisticated look; she came from a wealthy East Coast family. I would occasionally see her across a room at church or at the seminary, but although I had friends who knew her, I never approached her.

At the end of our four years there, this woman's husband invited Bob and me to their home for dinner. I was nervous and excited. However, my envy crumpled as this couple described the four years of depression, family problems, and loneliness they had suffered, and the lessons God had taught them. Now I was impressed, and humbled. We laughed and cried together, and I told her about my envy and yet my deep desire to get to know her. But it was too late: school was over and we were moving. I had lost the possibility of a friendship with a wonderful person because I couldn't get past her beautiful exterior.

Friend Versus Friend

This competitive spirit starts as soon as girls are aware that boys are desirable and limited merchandise. In a scene from the critically acclaimed television series *My So-Called Life*, sixteen-year-old Angela reviles her small bust and envies her childhood friend, Sharon, for being voted the "most globally endowed" sophomore girl by the boys in their class. Sharon, however, can't imagine being envied for what she regards as a curse. She's convinced her boyfriend is dating her only for her breasts, although he denies it. After some sniping, Angela and Sharon finally come to terms with each other in the girl's restroom. "Why do girls have to tear each other down?" asks Sharon. "Because they're jealous," Angela replies.

> What you have is God's gift to you. What you do with it is your gift to God.

Beauty idolatry feeds jealousy. Desirable boys are in scarce supply, so the competition is fierce. One must worship the beauty goddess in order to win the power struggle. However, it is possible for girls to overcome idolatry with love. The scene concludes with a surprising spiritual reference from the Girl Scouts, ironic when applied to breast size: "What you have is God's gift to you. What you do with it is your gift to God."

Sister Versus Sister

When women are locked into competition for the same man's affection, the win-lose approach heats envy white-hot. For Leah and Rachel, the yearning to be loved and respected was inextricably intertwined with the reality of who was fairer than whom. Their rivalry blazed as fiercely as anything in a prime-time soap opera. Leah had "weak" eyes, "but Rachel was beautiful of form and face." That is, Rachel's figure and facial symmetry suggested good breeding stock, while Leah's weak eyes made one suspect sickliness. Not surprisingly, Jacob loved the pretty one. However, polygamy was in vogue, and the girls' father tricked Jacob into marrying Leah as well as Rachel. While Jacob fulfilled his duty toward his plain-faced wife, "he loved Rachel more than Leah."[5]

The woman who has lost a man's love because she lacks the signs of youth and health has reason for grief. It was not idolatrous for Leah to feel stricken and long to win her husband's love by giving him children.

Out of compassion, God turned the tables on instinct and made the homely woman more fertile than the comely one. But in an era when fertility was supposedly a woman's highest value, not even Leah's proof that her weak eyes did not represent sickliness won Jacob's affection. Yet while Leah envied Rachel for Jacob's love, Rachel envied Leah for her children. The story depicts the pretty wife as competitive and conniving:

> When Rachel saw that she was not bearing Jacob any children, she became jealous of her sister. So she said to Jacob, "Give me children, or I'll die!"
>
> Jacob became angry with her and said, "Am I in the place of God, who has kept you from having children?"[6]

Since nagging Jacob achieved nothing, Rachel resorted to demanding that he impregnate her maidservant and designate the child as Rachel's. When the scheme worked, she crowed: "I have had a great struggle with my sister, and I have won."[7] Later, the sisters bargained over Jacob as though he were a stallion; Rachel agreed that Leah could spend a night with him in exchange for some mandrake plants that Leah's son Reuben had found (mandrakes were supposed to increase fertility). Rachel was hardly a saint, but apparently her looks kept Jacob interested even after she failed to prove herself as a baby factory.

We wonder what the evolutionary psychologists would do with this story. For some men at least, even in cultures that prize women almost exclusively for their childbearing ability, the instinctive attraction to a well-formed woman overcomes even the objective evidence of her poor fertility. Moreover, God seems more than able to turn the fertility rules on their heads. Rachel may have looked outwardly like the most likely mother, but in the long run Leah bore children sooner and twice as often.

Most women have found themselves at some time in the place

either of plain Leah, envying a rival for winning a man's love, or of pretty Rachel, alternately lording over her competitor and raging that attractiveness doesn't give her everything she wants. It is terribly hard not to envy a sister who has what we yearn for.

Leah and Rachel's story illustrates how complex forces from many directions press in on women, pushing them to compete. It's difficult to isolate these forces because all work together, but other than the Evil One (who doubtless has a hand in all temptations), the strongest forces seem to be men, mothers, and society—including peers and the media. We've already said quite a bit about social pressures and we'll speak of men at length in Chapter Eleven. Here we'll address their role briefly in order to set the stage for the fascinating role mothers play in passing on their own love-hate relationships with the beauty goddess.

MEN AND THE REST OF SOCIETY

In *The Beauty Myth*, Naomi Wolf blames men entirely for setting up the competition, asserting that the beauty myth promulgated by men "encourages women's wariness of one another on the basis of their appearance."[8] There is some truth to this charge; historically, men's obsessive tastes have sometimes set ghastly standards for women to meet. For example, tiny feet were the premier sign of femininity to Chinese men for a thousand years, so for a millennium mothers started binding their daughters' feet when they were between five and eight years old. The four small toes were tied under the foot with a binding cloth, while the heel was pulled under tightly toward the big toe. Every two weeks the bindings were tightened and the foot squeezed into a smaller shoe. One Chinese woman reported that it took three years to achieve a three-inch "golden lotus," the Chinese term for a sexy little foot.[9] Footbinding caused bleeding and infections, as well as pain and sometimes gangrene, but men loved the result. Not the least of its merits was that footbinding made it nearly impossible for a woman to walk, let alone run away from her husband.

In our day, many men continue to find little feet crammed into pumps with pointed toes and stiletto heels sexy. Men love the way high heels increase the tilt of a woman's behind and force her pelvis to sway more when she minces along. But today, at least, plenty of men are willing to be seen with a woman in flat shoes. That was not the case in medieval China, where a girl with unbound feet was unmarriageable except to a peasant. Heeled pumps are still considered more professional than flats, but it's difficult to prove that men are entirely responsible for this lingering code. Women have a way of latching onto these standards of femininity and turning them into contests that lose sight of men altogether.

Laura Sinderbrand, director of the Edward C. Blum Design Laboratory of the Fashion Institute of Technology in New York City, has traced how fluctuations in women's economic and social freedoms have often matched fluctuations in their mode of dress.[10] Tight corsets, constricting skirts, and hobbling footwear seem to have been in fashion during periods when women have been most socially confined. By contrast, styles have been freest — as in the 1920s — when women's freedoms in other arenas have been expanding. Clothing has always been a potent form of communication, and one thing it has communicated about women is the degree to which society thought the wearer had to be controlled. After reading Sinderbrad's findings, we wondered exactly who this "society" is that decides how much women need to be controlled. Men have certainly had a lot to do with society's decisions, but women from Catherine de Medici to Grace Mirabella have done more than their share of damage.

We don't think that in general blaming men gets women very far. Women do better to take responsibility for their own feelings and disappointments, rather than ascribing all the power to men. When a woman has lost a lover to a rival, anger may be a stage in her process of grieving and coming to terms with the loss. If she stays in the stage of blaming others, however, she is not likely to become a more beautiful person.

MOTHERS' CONFLICTING ROLES

Helping Their Daughters Conform

As we studied women's growth into beauty competitors, we found that one of the most tragic roles in the process belongs to mothers. Footbinding highlights the way that society has given mothers the task of shaping their daughters into obedient servants of the beauty goddess. How would it have felt to wrap one's daughter's feet, to press them into smaller shoes, and to force the little girl to walk on them despite the pain? Every mother knew the agony her daughter was suffering, for her own mother had done the same to her.

Perhaps the feeling resembled the grief with which the mother of the twentysomething waitress Callie described to us how she used to scold her daughter about her weight and urge her to squeeze into a girdle. She never wanted to hurt her daughter; she gave her the girdle "for her own good," so she would be acceptable in American society. "Society" consisted both of prospective husbands and of those ladies who served as the unofficial police of propriety.

"My mother had a very traditional view of beauty," Callie told us. "It seemed to be a restrictive one, very binding, illustrated by the girdles she wore and always wanted me to wear. Comfort was not an issue; appearance and acceptance were. During the sixties when women were burning their bras, my mom didn't burn her bra. She wanted a better bra to make her look bigger and firmer.

"I wasn't encouraged to develop my own style of dressing. I think daughters feel they need to be a cookie cutter of their mom and copy her style, her colors, and her clothes. When I left home to go to college, I was free from Mom's scrutiny and began to experiment with fashion. Finally, at the age of twenty-three, I realized I didn't have to dress like Mom and really began to develop my own style. I found this to be very freeing.

"My mom always had a lipstick thing. She always had her lipstick on and I didn't like wearing lipstick. Mom had a uniform that I would describe as a girdle holding her butt in, a tight bra, pressed clothes, and lipstick." Callie hated it when her mother pressured her to wear the same uniform.

"Weight was always an issue to Mom. It was my biggest source of frustration because now I know it became an issue for her and for me long before it really had to be. Now I look at my high school pictures and realize I had a great body. However, it was a confusing time for me. In high school, when I looked in the mirror I saw a firm and shapely body, but I got messages from my mother and others that it wasn't. The message was that I was fat and too busty. Now I look back at my youth and feel I was robbed of feeling good about how I looked.

"This led to two years of abusing diet pills and throwing up. It really messed up my metabolism. I had a distorted view of my body and couldn't trust the scale or the mirror. I thought the message they gave was good, but apparently others didn't agree. I thought, 'What I see isn't what others see.' When you think you look fine and others, your mom and your peers, say you look fat—and then you say you look fat and others say you look fine—it's very confusing. All I kept thinking was, 'Why does everyone think I'm so big?' Throughout my high school years I was a size ten."

Callie continues to struggle with her weight because compulsive dieting has lowered her metabolism to the point where losing weight is difficult. However, her mother's willingness to admit the ways she has hurt her daughter is no small help. While this change of heart can't change the past, at least it gives Callie an ally rather than a critic as she deals with her body in the present.

A hundred years earlier, this 1960s mother pouring her daughter into a girdle would have been lacing her little girl into a corset. The iron of Elizabethan days was out of vogue, but the *Englishwoman's Domestic Magazine* printed a young woman's letter in May of 1867 inquiring "if it is possible for girls to have a waist of fashionable size and yet preserve their health."[11] She herself said, "After the first few minutes [of being corseted] every morning I felt no pain, and the only ill effects apparently were occasional headaches and loss of appetite." However, doctors protested that tight corsets displaced organs. "The clergy spoke from their pulpits against the contraptions, noting that, when pregnant women laced themselves tightly in order to look socially respectable, abortions were frequently the result."[12] But neither good Christian mothers nor their daughters paid any attention. They seemed resigned to the pain and fainting spells if those were the price of looking marriageable and fashionable.

Fashion historian Laura Sinderbrand marvels at what women once put up with from corsets:

> Strangely enough . . . it was the women who championed this fashion feature in their lives much more strenuously than is understandable. You would have thought they wouldn't have wanted the discomfort, that they would have seen it as another repression in their lives. But since the only commodity they had was their physical attractiveness, this was the one part of their lives they could control.[13]

Victorian mothers believed their daughters' welfare depended upon winning good husbands, and winning a good husband depended upon having a tiny waist. It's a sad state of affairs when one has to risk her health to get a man.

Adolescent counselor Mary Pipher laments, "Nowhere are the messages to mothers so contradictory as with their adolescent daughters. Mothers are expected to protect their daughters from the culture even as they help them fit into it. . . . They want their daughters to be relaxed about their appearance, but know that girls suffer socially if they aren't attractive."[14] Callie's mother felt she was protecting her daughter from social rejection by schooling her to worry about her weight. Today she fears she made things worse rather than better.

It seems that many good-hearted mothers teach their daughters to worship the beauty goddess not because they like the goddess, but because they recognize her power. As long as she holds the key to men's hearts, she reigns over both work and marriage. These mothers are pragmatists rather than true believers. If they thought there were a way to stand against the goddess without subjecting their daughters to her wrath (the loss of love and respect in society), they would embrace it enthusiastically.

In *When Women Stop Hating Their Bodies*, Jane Hirschmann and Carol Munter describe Ruth, whose mother was

> inordinately concerned about appearances and accept-
> ability. "How did he like you?" her mother asks on the
> phone the day after a date, never, "How did *you* like
> him?" Inquiring about her work, Ruth's mother will ask,
> "How do they feel about you at work? Are you making a
> good impression?" never "How do *you* like your job
> these days?"[15]

Ruth's mother knows how much of her daughter's happiness rests on whether men and employers approve of her, but she likely does not know how much of her daughter's spiritual health and maturity rests on being able to relax in God's approval, no matter what people think.

Setting an Example

In addition to being active trainers of their daughters, mothers are also role models, often unaware of how much their daughters pick up. A woman named Julia recounts what she learned in a teachable moment:

> When I was very young, I thought that my mother was
> beautiful. . . . Then one day, I saw her look in the mirror
> and grimace at her reflection. I was confused. I asked her
> what was the matter and she said she looked "ghastly"
> without her makeup. I also remember her complaining that
> she had nothing to wear even though I thought her
> wardrobe was vast and magical. By the time I was six or
> seven, I realized that my beautiful mother did not think she
> was beautiful at all. That made me sad—and it made me
> sad to see her not eating in order to get thinner.
>   I remember wondering why someone as beautiful as my
> mother would think she was ugly. And then why did she tell
> me I was so pretty? What did it mean to be pretty? Was *I*
> pretty enough to look in the mirror and like what I see?[16]

With just a look and an offhand comment, Julia's mother taught her fear and the twin poles of pride and shame. Many people think pride and shame are opposites, when really they are just two poles of the same self-absorption. Pride says, "I should be winning the beauty contest!" But when we fail to measure up to such an impossible standard, we swing from pride to shame, feeling ugly, unworthy to be seen. From this sense of humiliation well up thoughts like "I haven't a thing to wear" and "I look ghastly without my makeup." Julia's mother could have moved from humiliation to humility before God by admitting that winning the beauty contest was probably not a very smart goal to bet her life on. However, God may have been no more than an abstraction to Julia's mother, and humility an unknown concept. In any case, she seems to have moved from humiliation not to humility, but to envy, believing if only she had money for better clothes (or perhaps if God had been decent enough to endow her with better features) then she would be a winner instead of a loser.

Envy Between Mothers and Daughters

Mothers agonize over how to set a good example for their daughters and to what degree they should help their girls conform to society's norms. But mothers are horrified if they find themselves feeling envious toward their daughters, while their daughters are envying them. When *My So-Called Life*'s Angela obsesses over a pimple, her mom, Patty, is long on advice for getting rid of the pimple but short on understanding why it bothers Angela so much. Patty is preoccupied by her aging, so she presses Angela to join a mother-daughter fashion show to compete with a friend and her daughter. Patty takes Angela to a cosmetic counter ostensibly to get Angela a makeover, but she ends up buying an eye cream for herself. Eventually a quarrel erupts. "Who am I looking my best *for*?" demands Angela. *For her mother* is the unspoken answer. Angela assumes her mom must think she's ugly because Patty keeps trying to train her how to look good. Angela feels inferior to her beautiful mom, who seems reluctant to voice her fears about losing her beauty.

Patty finally realizes why she put so much pressure on Angela to be in the fashion show: she needs to bolster her own sense of being approved by the world. To her husband she says, "I, like all women, am becoming less attractive and more expendable while you are becoming more attractive." She fears losing her looks may mean losing him. "Do you think there's anybody in the world who thinks they're attractive?" she asks.

In the end, Patty and Angela talk. "Did you love being pretty?" Angela inquires. "I dunno," says Patty. "I don't think I ever really let myself know I was. I just wish I had been able to enjoy it."

This episode highlights the complex interplay between mothers and daughters regarding something so central to their identity as appearance. Patty genuinely wants Angela to be beautiful and feel beautiful, yet part of her envies her daughter's youth. She knows she is passing the torch of sexual attractiveness to a new generation, and she wishes she had been given some say in the matter. She hopes the loss of beauty won't cost her too dearly. She understands how much may be at stake: her husband's love and her peers' respect. She also worries about how much is at stake for Angela and can't imagine why Angela takes her advice as criticism.

For her part, Angela believes in her mother's beauty but has trouble believing in her own. She reads every offer of help as confirmation that she is ugly. It never occurs to her that her mother is as envious of her as she is of her mother. The show's conclusion makes it clear that it is up to the adult, who should have more experience facing and articulating her feelings, to open up honest dialogue.

This story illustrates what is possible between mothers and daughters when both are willing to sort out their confusing emotions and come clean with each other. When this doesn't happen, mothers (or stepmothers) and daughters can play out a Snow White scenario. The aging beauty lets her grief over losing her looks and her fear over what else she might lose drive her to fierce jealousy. She feels in competition with the younger woman for a man's affection: the Queen's husband, who is Snow White's father. In the fairy tale, jealousy moves the Queen to seek her rival's death. In real life the older woman rarely attempts murder, but she may nurse a secret resentment. She may even be unwilling to admit she feels such unacceptable feelings as resentment or envy, especially if she is a

Christian. But feelings have a way of breeding when locked in dark closets and told to be quiet. An older woman who doesn't admit, understand, and deal with her own mixed feelings about aging will find it hard to love a young woman well.

Battling Peer Pressure

Still, while mothers often feed their daughters' anxiety over looks in ways they aren't aware of, many mothers feel they fight a lonely battle to protect their daughters from the ravages of beauty worship. In *Reviving Ophelia*, Mary Pipher records story after story of mothers striving to teach their daughters to believe in their own beauty in the face of negative messages from the media and their peers:

> My cousin's common sense told her that her daughter shouldn't have a two-hundred-dollar low-cut dress for her eighth-grade graduation. But all her daughter's friends had such dresses. Her daughter begged her to buy it because she was afraid that she would feel like a geek at her graduation party.[17]

This cousin sounds like the Christian mother we talked to whose twelve-year-old came home from school one day announcing that she was going on a diet. She was bigger than her fourteen-year-old sister, she complained, requesting SlimFast for lunch from now on. In vain this mother tried to explain that her older daughter had smaller bones, and that her younger daughter favored her husband's side of the family. Such reasoning meant nothing to a young girl who was being teased by boys at school.

> "Twenty years of feminist politics and here I am, with a daughter who wants nothing more in the whole wide world than to buy Rollerblade Barbie."
> —Susan J. Douglas[18]

Mothers strongly influence their daughters' sense of self, but television starts dishing out its relentless message early. When peers seem to become all-important in adolescence, many mothers find themselves in all-out war against the beauty cult that is brainwashing their kids.

QUITTING THE CONTEST

The biblical writers unanimously applaud team playing and unanimously condemn competition fueled by envy. The tenth commandment forbids men to covet others' wives because such secret thoughts tear communities apart. Coveting another woman's breasts, youth, waistline, outfit, or boyfriend does the same damage. It is impossible to love our neighbor as ourselves if we hate her for her looks and hate ourselves for ours.

Many women we talked with claimed to feel little competition with other women. They tended to be spiritually mature, not given to pride nor driven for power. They also tended either to have been more nourished in relationships with women than with men, or to be securely married and over forty. The former group valued female relationships to such an extent that they would not sacrifice those ties for male attention. The latter group felt secure enough emotionally and economically that there was nothing to compete over. Security—financially, relationally, and spiritually—seems to significantly reduce envy and competitiveness over beauty.

By contrast, it appears that the less sense of control women feel in their lives, the more likely they are to get hooked on ways of controlling their own bodies, whether by lacing, girdling, footbinding, vomiting, exercising, or starving. The competitive instinct, which could be channeled productively into ways to advance God's kingdom, is wasted on the drive to catch men's and other women's eyes. *"What do you think would happen if all women stopped hating their bodies?"* Jane Hirschmann and Carol Munter routinely ask participants in their workshops for large women. "No question about it," answered one woman, "We would take over the world."[19]

The beauty contest is about control and power. Contestants depend on looks rather than God to get what they want; this is the essence of the idolatry that sets them on a relentless seesaw between pride and humiliation. How ironic it is that this effort to grab power through idolatry actually saps women's power to achieve constructive goals. As Isaiah promised, idolatry always leads to slavery.

We have spent several chapters detailing women's efforts to get control through beauty. We have emphasized women's responsibility because we believe too much literature encourages women to blame somebody else for their slavery. But our treatment would not be complete without a look at what happens to women when men worship the beauty goddess.

A Closer Look

Do you scrutinize other women's appearance when you're at a party, a restaurant, or church? Do you look with the curious gaze that enjoys others' beauty, or the controlling gaze that judges and either dismisses or envies? Do you think you compete with other women to look the best?

Have you ever been in Leah's position, losing a man to a rival? If so, how has that experience affected you? If you're accustomed to being the winner in beauty contests, how has that experience affected you?

CHAPTER ELEVEN

WHEN MEN WORSHIP BEAUTY

We have to stand up like women and take responsibility for our part in the oppression we, our daughters, and our friends feel from the beauty goddess. But at the same time, we know we've had help from the other side of the gene pool. In both women and men, controlling behavior—the unloving exercise of power—is the chief evidence of beauty idolatry. While women have sought power *through* beauty to win the love and respect we yearn for, men have sought power *over* beauty in order to taste Paradise apart from God.

Idolatry comes in degrees. Each person worships idols to the degree that he or she is not passionately pursuing God. Some of us are deeply dependent upon God and have only minor flirtations with idols; others of us ignore God completely and are devoted to one or more idols. And a great many of us live somewhere in between, or move back and forth between God and our idol(s) of choice.

Likewise, most of us have our own personal prioritized list of idols. The one at the top of our list is the one we think about the most, the one to which we give most of our time, energy, and money. Feminine beauty might top one man's list because he believes a beautiful woman has the most power to offer him what he yearns for. For another man, work might top the list, then money, then people's opinion, and then maybe a beautiful fantasy woman. We might say the man in the first category is addicted to sex or lust—he fantasizes, pores over pornography, frequents prostitutes, or has affairs. For the man in the second category, his fantasy woman is a little idol he keeps on his shelf to be worshiped now and then in his mind. He would never risk his job or his reputation in order to act out his fantasy because he values them ahead of his fantasy. He may be no closer to God than the first man, but his worship of beauty is less intense.

Among the men we know well, few are worshiping beauty in the extreme ways we will describe in this chapter. By contrast, we know many good men who have learned to value God and the real women in their lives more than fantasy beauties. It's worth underscoring this: *Every* man notices attractive women. *Not* every man worships or fantasizes about them. In this chapter we will not speak much about the men who are winning the battle against idolatry. Instead, we will examine what happens when men treat feminine beauty as an idol that promises pleasure, status, or reproductive success.

Our main focus in this book is on women's choices, but we address men's idolatry because often a woman's choice to worship beauty is grounded in a belief that she must do so in order to get what she wants from men. To the degree that a woman lives (or believes she lives) with a man or a culture of men who worship beauty, to that degree she will feel pressure to worship beauty as well.

What do men do when they worship women's beauty? For the most part, they try to control it—at least in their minds, if not through outright possession of the beautiful woman. Let's look briefly at why they long for control, and then explore how they act out that desire for control.

WHY MEN DESIRE CONTROL

To Guarantee Respect and Reproduction

Remember, the goal of any idolatry is to control our ability to get what we want, rather than trusting God for it. We've seen that most societies accord a man more respect the more attractive his wife is. We've also seen that at an instinctive level, a young, healthy-looking, curvaceous, large-eyed, small-chinned beauty seems to promise the greatest chance of passing a man's genes to the next generation. For many men, respect and reproduction are too important to entrust to a God who might do anything. A man will keep those matters firmly in his own grip unless he has compelling reasons to believe that trusting God is a better bet.

To Protect Themselves from Rejection

The mind of a fourteen-year-old boy teems with images of fantasy women; they well up from his own mind and blend with the media concoctions that bombard him. Magazines and movies feed his fleshly desire for the fourteen-to-twenty-nine-year-old-model woman. These fantasy women become for him idols that promise his heart's desire. As Warren Farrell puts it in *Why Men Are the Way They Are*, "This socialization is so powerful that the genetic celebrities in his [high school] class can influence boys like a drug. He becomes addicted to an image; anything less feels like an inferior fix."[2]

> "Among Secretary General Boutros Boutros-Ghali's suggestions for achieving greater U.N. recognition in its 50th anniversary year was an advertisement featuring a beautiful woman in an expensive car driving by the U.N. building and exclaiming, 'Ah, the United Nations!'"[1]

The boy projects the goddess's image onto the girls around him, but he soon finds that winning their affection is not easy. Marketing researchers have found that the most dependable way to sell a product to a man of any class in our society is to appeal to his anxiety about being rejected by beautiful women.[3] The young boy feels powerless to win acceptance from the pretty girls around him simply by the quality of who he is, and the stunning models and pornographic goddess-surrogates he sees in magazines are entirely out of reach.

Unless he's making serious progress toward spiritual maturity, a human being generally responds to powerlessness by looking for a way to take control of his situation. Many men try to take control by changing themselves: they strive to become athletic or military heroes to impress the girls, or they strive to succeed financially in order to appeal to women's desire for financial security, or they may even strive to develop their character. But their fear of being rejected by women lingers, sparking what is often called "locker room talk." In their private male domain, boys banter about girls' body parts and about their prowess at "scoring." Their goal isn't so much to denigrate girls as it is to gain status in a masculine society.

Is it possible that construction workers whistle at a pretty woman passing them in the street not to put her down, but to build themselves up in their own eyes and those of their coworkers? These behaviors may be men's efforts to grasp at self-respect and a feeling of being in control of the situation. Whistling may be the only way they can avoid the helpless feeling of being totally ignored by this seeming goddess.

Taken to an extreme, these attitudes can produce sexual addiction. Dr. Harry Schaumburg, a specialist in sexual addiction especially among pastors, writes,

> "What I need and want," the typical sex addict thinks, "I have to have. My desires need to be fulfilled if my life is going to be worth living. I don't want to feel rejection. I want to be appreciated. Life should deliver the benefits I desire." . . . The addict comes to believe that "if the situation I set up happens [the encounter with a prostitute or fantasy woman], I'll be fulfilled. I'm the one who can define what will bring me fulfillment or prevent pain."[4]

Men yearn for the Paradise where perfect intimacy was possible. Idolatry offers the illusion of being with Eve.

To Protect Themselves from Women's Control

A former youth worker named Jim offered us another explanation for why men feel the need to control women's beauty. To some men, Jim says, the powerful attraction they feel for a woman seems like a force emanating from her. They are not in control of their attraction to her, so she must be. A venerable male myth says that a beautiful woman actually has the power to cloud a man's mind so he can't help having sex with her or even throwing his life away for her.

These men feel they must either control the beautiful woman or be controlled by her, so they choose the former. I (Karen) have a friend who spent two years in Kuwait studying Kuwaiti culture. Kuwaitis believe that men are helpless against the lust they feel when viewing an uncovered woman, so they are within their rights to assault any woman who goes out in public without her *abiyeh* (black polyester shroud) and *hijab* (headscarf that covers both head and face, and sometimes eyes). Even a Western woman with arms and legs covered is repeatedly subjected to obscene gestures and comments, as though she were a prostitute deliberately trying to tempt the men.

This tendency to feel that temptations come from outside us when really they come from with-in us is called *projection*. As C. S. Lewis wrote, "men call a woman voluptuous when she arouses voluptuous feelings in them."[5] Men may feel that temptation comes from women when really, as the apostle James wrote, "each one is tempted when, by his own evil desire, he is dragged away and enticed."[6]

Finally, in men's minds feminine physical appearance symbolizes femininity in general. It's what makes a woman a woman. Some men who feel their mothers controlled them when they were young may well carry a lingering desire to control a woman before she has a chance to control them. This desire to control women may spill over into a desire to control their appearance.

HOW MEN TRY TO CONTROL BEAUTY

Just as idolatry comes in degrees, so does control. At its lowest level, a man's inclination to control women's beauty begins when he starts thinking of them as objects rather than human beings. In its more severe forms, the drive to control may produce oppressive and even violent words and actions. The progression looks something like this:

Viewing Women as Objects
In his mind, an idolatrous man may reduce a woman to a thing, a graven image. Farrell explains,

> The male's feelings of powerlessness before a genetic celebrity—the feeling of having to beg like a puppy for every morsel of her attention and sexuality by performing, paying, risking rejection, and being told he's dirty or akin to a rapist—makes his ego fragile and his self-concept vulnerable. *Vulnerability creates defenses.*
>
> How does he defend against this vulnerability? In the sexual arena he discovers the *first defense* of stage 3: *It hurts a lot less to be rejected by a sex object than it does to be rejected by a full human being.* So if a male can turn women into objects and sex into a game (and call it "scoring"), he will be able to treat rejection less seriously. He will hurt less.[7]

We asked some men whether this theory made sense to them. Yes, they told us, treating women like objects makes a guy feel safer from rejection, more in control. One man told us about the mental process he went through as a teenager to turn a certain girl into an object in his mind, but he couldn't articulate why he did it.

Many men objectify strikingly beautiful women, especially models and actresses. These are our culture's goddess surrogates. Some men also objectify women when they are with other men in social or work situations. However, these same men don't seem to seek their idols for personal companionship, possibly because they believe those women are inaccessible or because they find them intimidating. Object-women are useful as fantasies and trophies, but not for closeness. Most men we know want to marry a woman who knows how to be intimate and can help them overcome their inner barriers to intimacy.

To explain the difference between appreciating and objectifying someone, literature professor Ellen Lambert contrasts two ways in which a person may look at another person: the "curious" gaze and the "controlling" gaze.[8] The curious gaze is that of a child just discovering that girls' bodies are different from boys'. It is well expressed by a man we know who said to his wife, "I like your body because you have curves where I don't, and you don't have hair where I do." The curious gazer discovers beauty in another person and dreams not of conquest but of further discovery of yet deeper beauty. He is like a voyager who, landing on the island of Tahiti, sets out not to conquer the island, nor buy it, nor strip it of its natural resources for his own gain, but rather to explore and delight in its people and climate. It was the curious gaze with which Adam first beheld Eve, a creature like none in his experience who moved him to wonder. Women long to be looked at as the lover in the Song of Songs looks at his beloved: with enraptured pleasure.

> "I am tired of the same old sex roles. I want to do better things."—Marilyn Monroe, announcing the debut of her own production company in 1955[9]

On the other hand, women fear and even feel angry at being looked at as things to be taken and used for someone's pleasure. We also fear being looked at and judged as too fat or too old, and therefore unworthy of respect. The controlling gazer sees not a woman with beauty of body, mind, and spirit—all of which he desires to know—but rather an object. His gaze lays claim both to the object and to the right to judge it. Claiming the right to judge someone is the first step toward domination, and tradition has long accorded men the right to rank women's looks according to their standards. Ranking feels degrading, whether one is ranked a "1" or a "10." Treating a person as a thing violates the command to love one's neighbor as oneself.

Judging women's looks gives men the feeling they're in control, and most often men do it among themselves in order to assert their status among men. Adolescent boys vote on which girl in their class has the best breasts or other feature. Adult men comment on women they observe, or they even ask women to pass judgment on other women. An acquaintance told me (Cinny), "I was talking to a coworker the other day and we were discussing our families. He asked me if I had any children. I told him I have a daughter who is sixteen. The next thing out of his mouth was, 'Is she pretty?' I was so surprised by his remark. Why would that be his first response? I told him, 'Yes, I guess she's pretty. She's also very sweet.' Inside I was so angry that the issue of how she looked would be so important and that he would ask me that question about my daughter—but I'm not surprised. That's the first criterion that comes to many men's minds when evaluating a female."

Anger is a natural response to feeling treated like an object, but psychologist Chris Knippers encourages us to feel sad for North American men. Chris, who works with sex addicts in Southern California, says our culture teaches men to objectify everything. "My own father frequently lectured me on the importance of being objective rather than subjective," he recalls. He remembers being told that a man who wants to have control of his life should think objectively about everything, especially relationships. If men learn to objectify everyone and everything, including other men, "Why should our experience of women be any different?" Chris asks. Women certainly suffer when men treat them like objects, but men suffer, too. Their objectivity cuts them off from true intimacy because a person can be intimate only with another person, not with a dispassionately regarded object. Men are left only with lust, the illusion of intimacy, or with passion directed toward safe objects, such as work or sports.[10]

> "Men look at women. Women watch themselves being looked at."[11]

Treating Some Women as Invisible

When men objectify women, detecting them only with their instinctive beauty radar, certain women become invisible to them. Pastor Stan Thornburg told us that as a younger man he tended to pass the obese or unattractive women at his workplace with hardly a word, while he would give the attractive ones more time and attention. Sara Halprin, a university professor and private therapist in her fifties, writes in *Look at My Ugly Face*, "I'm nearly invisible to many men now, and that experience carries both relief and pain, the relief of freedom from critical standards, the pain of exclusion based on those same standards."[12]

As we saw in Chapter 4, the instinctive radar of the flesh is tuned for fertile women; it's designed to ignore women past their biological prime. That's not evil; it's just nature. Older women are visible to a man and desirable as persons only to the degree that he is developing radar for women in their mental and spiritual prime. To that degree he is growing out of adolescence and into maturity.

> "'I mean,' he says a tad crankily, 'off comes the dress and look at you! It's not really fair.'"—writer Penelope Green, reporting her husband's response to the new butt-boosting and waist-cinching undergarments[13]

Controlling Women's Appearance

Stan Thornburg says most men are aware of the ways in which their wives deviate from the ideal, but they learn to accept it, just as they are aware that they don't have their ideal amount of money but learn to overcome the lust for more. The man who nags his wife about her appearance or leaves her for a younger woman has yielded to idolatry. On the other hand, a man who lovingly confronts his wife for showing no concern about her appearance, or for endangering her health through overeating, is doing his job. The line between nagging and confronting may be blurry; it's up to each man and woman to examine their motives.

Sharlene Hesse-Biber, associate professor of sociology at Boston College, writes in *Am I Thin Enough Yet?* that girls with eating disorders sometimes have fathers who rigidly control their wives' looks. She quotes one girl as saying, "My mother has to go to my dad's functions, and she has to just sit there with a smile on her face and look great at parties. She does everything to please my father . . . my father would get into fights, would not even talk to my mother for like a week, because her toenails weren't painted and she was wearing open-toed shoes."[14] This man's self-respect lives or dies on what the other guys think of his wife.

At the other extreme, some men think they have to control their wives' and daughters' appearance in order to prevent them from being promiscuous. Counselor Tom Whiteman grew up in a conservative Christian denomination in which girls and women wore dresses that covered their ankles and neck, ostensibly in order not to tempt men. However, Dr. Whiteman says, such an atmosphere encouraged kids to get into trouble. Since boys were taught that seeing a leg would make them go crazy, boys generally fulfilled those expectations. They learned to believe themselves incapable of making godly choices, so neither they nor the girls learned to make responsible decisions. In like manner, some jealous husbands think that if they let their wives work or be around men, they'll have affairs. In Whiteman's experience, such prophecies are self-fulfilling and drive wives and teens away.

As women, we would feel odd if our husbands didn't care how much of our bodies other men saw. Why? Because our feminine beauty is the visible symbol of our sexuality that should be kept for one man only, and we know the potent effect the visible symbol has on men. But when that natural husbandly concern becomes controlling, it is idolatry.

Harems, Veils, and Pedestals

These controlling rules are more and more rare in Western culture, where idolatry leans more toward flaunting rather than restricting women's appearance; but in other cultures and eras it has been the norm. Once I (Karen) watched my friend as she put on the Kuwaiti *abiyeh* and *hijab*. To see my friend disappear under all this fabric took my breath away. Kuwaiti women see the world through a black polyester haze. Their male relatives carefully control who may see their faces and bodies, even their eyes. Women belong to their husbands or fathers; no males outside the family may even see their women. This practice carries on the ancient custom of the harem, in which women were locked into cramped, windowless barns in order to insulate them from the gaze and violation of men outside the family. The main goal is to guard access to a woman's reproductive capacity, but since her physical appearance is a strong symbol for men of her femininity, they jealously guard that as well.

The Old Testament is full of Middle Eastern monarchs and their harems: the Egyptian pharaoh and Canaanite sheikh who tried to take Sarah from Abraham; David with his wives and concubines; Solomon with his *seven hundred* wives and *three hundred* concubines;[15] and Xerxes with his unspecified legions. Quantity equaled status and the power to fulfill the male fantasy in the extreme. The kings controlled when their women would be shown off to other men, and when they would be hidden away.

This Eastern custom of harems and veils tends to shock us Western women, but it was not so long ago that American and European women were obliged to cover themselves almost as much. Exposing arms and ankles was improper even as recently as 1910. The nun's habit looks restrictive to us, but it was the garment every woman wore in medieval Europe, wimple and all. This determination to hide women's bodies from men's gaze went hand in hand with the cult of chivalry.

> "Discipline is Liberation"—slogan for Jane Fonda workout tapes[17]

Chivalry has come in and out of fashion since the Middle Ages. Although chivalry seems far more pleasant than the Arab harem (and we are entirely in favor of good manners), the chivalric idolatry of beautiful women controls them just as effectively. Those forty-five-year-old divorced Christian men who want to marry twenty-five-year-old virgins may be looking for brides whom they can put on pedestals to represent the feminine ideal, brides who will incidentally be as mindlessly obedient as Snow White. A woman on a pedestal need not be dealt with personally or admitted to a man's secret soul. A woman worshiped from afar does not require a man to be truly intimate or challenge his misdeeds. And a woman too pure to be touched is too pure to meddle in politics or public life. A woman on a pedestal is a statue, an object, a symbol, not a flesh-and-blood person.

Some sex addicts, often Christians, won't "sully" their wives by having sex with them but instead visit prostitutes. This is called a "Madonna/whore split" because such men have two mental categories for women: either perfect Madonnas or wicked (but desirable) whores. One Christian man blithely said he was dating virginal Christian women because he wanted to marry someone like that, but in the meantime he needed sex, so he frequented massage parlors.[16] Such men are by no means the majority, but those who act like this cause destruction in both themselves and the women they're with.

Using Violent Language About Women's Beauty

Controlling women's dress and access to public life is fairly extreme evidence of idolatry. Pedestals and Madonna/whore splits are pathological. But at the far end of controlling behavior lies violence.

Violence begins in the heart, and one evidence of idolatry in a man's heart is the way he talks about women's beauty. Any man will feel pain when rejected, but an idolatrous man may regard rejection as an attack from women upon his masculinity and may lust for revenge. He may express that lust in many ways, including something as simple as the way in which he talks about women's beauty:

> Sexual language is a tremendous, subconscious indicator of revenge. Men who consider a woman's beautiful appearance to be a threat or a weapon may frequently describe her as "a knockout," "strikingly beautiful," or "dressed to kill." Some men who feel intimidated by a woman's pretty appearance may think that her achievement is a result of sexual behavior. Therefore they believe that if they achieve a level of sexuality with pretty women, they too will gain power and control. If they can't, they consider themselves failures. Then, feeling angry, resentful, humiliated, or shamed, they want to get even for what they perceive has been done to them. Through that revenge, they hope to regain a sense of potency or power.[18]

Verbal violence also includes criticizing or taunting a woman about her appearance in order to tear her down emotionally. Mary Pipher claims that what junior-high girls experience from boys today is much worse than what girls faced in the 1960s and 1970s:

> Girls are taunted about everything from oral sex to pubic hair, from periods to the imagined appearance of their genitals. The harassment that girls experience in the 1990s is

much different in both quality and intensity. The remarks are more graphic and mean-spirited. Although the content is sexual, the intent is aggressive, to be rude and controlling.

Recently the American Association of University Women released a study, "Hostile Hallways," that documents what girls are experiencing. It reports that 70 percent of girls experience harassment and 50 percent experience unwanted sexual touching in their schools. . . . Many girls are afraid to speak up for fear of worse harassment.[19]

Sexual Violence

At its most intense level, a man's drive to control women's beauty may erupt in physical violence. The ultimate form of beauty idolatry in men is forced sex. The Bible offers several vivid examples of this, perhaps because it was and is all too common.

One instance is the story of David and Bathsheba. "In the spring, at the time when kings go off to war," forty-year-old King David was not in the tents with his soldiers, but in his palace relaxing.[20] Middle-aged, aware that his glorious battles were past and another man was leading his troops, David was ripe for an affair that might restore his faith in his manhood. Strolling on his rooftop patio, he looked down and glimpsed someone else's wife bathing in her own back yard.

"The woman was very beautiful, and David sent someone to find out about her."[21] He had never even talked to her, but if he was like many men who have affairs, she represented to him (as was said of the sacred prostitute) "the door to the potential of ongoing life." He worshiped the beauty goddess in his fantasy and demanded that this woman embody her.

Even after learning Bathsheba was married, David sent "messengers" to fetch her. We should not imagine she had any choice about the matter. Oriental monarchs were in the habit of commandeering other men's wives for their harems. Abraham and Isaac lived in fear of losing both their wives and their lives in exactly this way.[22] The writer of 2 Samuel understood this, and throughout his account of the adultery and the subsequent murder of Bathsheba's husband, he never wrote a word of reproach against her. Only David was held responsible; the idolatry, the drive to possess a beautiful woman at all costs, was his.

Tragically, the dynamic repeated itself among David's children. They were a blended family, living in close quarters, when Tamar's body began to fill out in the first curves of young womanhood. Her half brother Amnon watched, week by week. He was the eldest, used to getting anything he desired, but this girl with the swelling breasts and the full lips was his sister and yet not his sister — off limits. His frustration grew into a sickness, his lust into an obsession. He couldn't sleep. Eventually his friend noticed his haggard face, and the two of them hatched a plan that ended in rape.

That day changed everything for beautiful Tamar, daughter of David. She had worn the richly ornamented robe of a king's daughter, but now she tore it in two. She put ashes on her head and went away, "weeping aloud as she went." Until that day she had been a princely prize for some treasured friend of her father, with the hope of marriage and motherhood. But from then on she was "a desolate woman"[23] living childless with another brother.

Of what use was her beauty now that she was defiled, no longer a virgin and hence no longer valuable to a man who might want to own her sexuality? Of what use had her beauty ever been except as something to trade for the security and respect of marriage and motherhood? All beauty had proven to be for Tamar was a curse that marked her as prey for a predatory man. Amnon lusted to possess her beauty, the symbol of her sexuality — so he took it by force.

Experts debate how many young women today are sexually molested before the age of twenty. Some say as many as one in three, while others debate those figures. Whatever the real number, incest is terrifyingly common. Tamar was beautiful, and many young girls are molested because older men think of them as objects and project onto them their fantasy ideals of the virginal young woman. "Date rape also results when a man forces his date to embody the image he lusts for."[24]

On the other hand, many rape victims are ordinary or even elderly. The causes of rape are hotly debated, but it appears that sexual violence is not always about the objective attractiveness of the real woman, but about feelings inside the attacker: perhaps lust for revenge against women whom he believes have rejected or tried to control him, or perhaps a more general craving for power.

This is not an exhaustive treatment of how or why men commit violence against women or try to control them in other ways. We merely intend to sketch the extremes to which some men go when their natural radar for attractive women turns into idolatry.

REACTING TO IDOLATRY

Surveying the damage the worship of beauty causes, well-meaning people have often reacted with disgust. "Women's beauty is a snare," they reason. "It leads only to vice and suffering for both women and men. Women who desire physical beauty are foolish at best and malevolent at worst. Men who respond to women's beauty are lustful beasts. Inner beauty is what really matters."

While this reaction is understandable, it distorts God's desire. Next we will look at two ways in which men and women have rejected beauty, with tragic results.

A CLOSER LOOK

Reflect on how you feel about men after reading all these ways in which they can be idolatrous and controlling. Acknowledging men's potential for evil can hinder us from relating well with real men until we get used to seeing them as whole persons, capable of good and evil. For those of us who have suffered under violence or other controlling behavior, learning this balance can be especially difficult.

If you have found this chapter upsetting, and especially if you have suffered from some of the cruelty described here, take some time to process your feelings. You may want to write, pray, draw, talk to a friend—find a form of expression that works for you. Also, pay attention to any habits you may have for numbing or suppressing painful feelings on this subject. For example, do you feel like eating ice cream or watching television instead of letting yourself feel anxious or angry?

Interview a man you know well. Can he identify with viewing women as objects or with any of the other controlling behaviors? Has this tendency decreased as he has matured in Christ? Or does he think beauty idolatry is fairly rare among the men he has known?

CHAPTER TWELVE

BEAUTY VEILED

Physical beauty in the Bible is like a jewel with many facets. The Song of Songs celebrates it as a source of pleasure both for the beholder and the beheld when the former sees with a curious, loving gaze. Even more than the beauty of land and sky, human beauty points toward the beauty of the Creator, who sculpted men and women in His image. A beautiful woman symbolizes the unblemished Eve of Paradise and the cleansed Bride, the beloved of Christ. On a more prosaic level, beauty was a valuable asset for biblical women who wanted to be married and loved. A woman like Esther could use her power over an instinct-driven man for good purposes.

At the same time, the writers of Scripture never flinched from portraying the dark side of beauty. Beautiful women faced dangers from men, from other women, and from themselves. The stakes were high: love, marriage, children, and social respect were greatly desired; but violence, envy, and arrogance were constant threats. An unscrupulous woman could use her beauty to manipulate men. Further, the prophets understood that a woman born without physical beauty was as vulnerable in a fallen world as a woman born without money or social status. Leah's plainness was a source of sorrow worthy of God's compassion. Precisely because beauty symbolized Paradise and divinity, the foolish too often worshiped the beautiful and scorned the unlovely. If a beautiful woman symbolizes Paradise, then old or plain women have often felt stigmatized, spurned as symbols of barrenness and death. The Bible's symbols communicate richly, but no flesh-and-blood human wants to be reduced to a mere symbol. Women have longed in vain to be seen as divine image-bearers regardless of our age, color, or body shape.

In short, as with all things that God created good, humans can respond to beauty for good or ill. The yearning for beauty can be either a desperate craving for the Paradise that will never come again, or a firm hope for the resurrection that will come soon.

When humans observe something being abused, we often respond by rejecting that thing and all who enjoy it. The closer the abused commodity is to the core of our humanity, the more we respond with fear and rejection. Nothing lies closer to the bone than our sexuality, and masculine or feminine beauty is a visible symbol of the invisible essence of masculinity or femininity. Not surprisingly, many people have fled from it in terror.

We could trace this flight through the history of feminism, Buddhism, or a hundred other movements, but we will concentrate on just three manifestations that may be especially relevant to our readers. We'll begin with the often ignored way in which sexual abuse victims hate their beauty, we'll follow with the virulent anti-beauty sentiment among even the wisest of church leaders, and we'll conclude with the modern tendency to trivialize beauty.

THE VIOLATED

A shocking number of women reach adulthood having run the gauntlet of harassing remarks about their appearance, unwanted fondling, or forced sexual acts. Especially if they were children when the abuse occurred, these women often blame their own beauty for the attack. To young girls, the beauty of soul and body is all one, and the outward symbol of their femininity *is* their femininity. Their beautiful femininity must have allured the molester, they imagine, so the way to protect themselves from any future attack is to erase their beauty. Shame, rage, and fear crystallize into a plan. The violated find myriad ways to violate their God-given loveliness.

Some put on twenty pounds; others lose twenty pounds; both want not to look like women because they want not to be women. Christian recording artist Julie Miller cut her face with glass; it made her feel better. One teenager we know, after fending off the unwelcome advances of a boy in her school, went home and rubbed her face raw with sandpaper.

I (Karen) have already described how one of the ways I used anorexia was to hide from men's gaze. After an extended period of childhood incest, I felt confused and disturbed every time a boy in high school tried to seduce me. Unable to control either my family or boys, I controlled the one thing I could control: my eating. Part of me desperately wanted to be seen; I threw myself into schoolwork and became a Presidential Scholar and an Ivy League star. Another part shrank in terror at the thought of being seen. I wore my spirituality as a veil as thick as any Muslim's shroud.

In the mind of an abuse victim, attractiveness and horror are locked together. It's a visceral response, not a logical one, so while the abuse survivor may understand rationally that her beauty was not to blame, something inside her recoils when a man shows interest in either her inner or outer beauty. It takes hard work for her to overcome this reflexive abhorrence.

Because so many women suffer sexual abuse and because few people understand how abuse affects a woman's attitude toward her femininity and her body, we offer three other examples.

Carol

Molested by one of her mother's boyfriends from the time she was five to the time she was eight, Carol grew up without much warmth from anyone. She compensated for the attention her mother never had time to give her by eating cookies and Twinkies. When she recalled the abuse or felt afraid for some other reason, she comforted herself with food. When the boys in her high school made jokes about her weight, Carol swore she would lose weight but only ate more. After high school she put herself on a rigid diet and managed to lose twenty pounds, but when a man at her first job began to pay attention to her, Carol quickly put the twenty pounds back on. His attention thrilled her on one hand and terrified her on the other. That man eventually lost interest; Carol was sure it was because of her weight. Angry at herself, she stuffed herself with more cookies.

This pattern repeated itself for the next fifteen years. Every time Carol managed to lose enough weight to feel attractive, she would also feel terrified, like a whore trying to allure men. It took a period of listening to what was going on inside her before she realized that she still blamed her feminine attractiveness for causing her mother's boyfriend to molest her, as though it were her fault for being attractive rather than his fault for acting on his lust for sex and power.

Kathleen

Kathleen is a counselor on women's issues and a professor of psychology in a Christian graduate school. Her brother molested her when Kathleen was nine, and again when she was eleven. She grew up blaming herself and vowing, "Never again!"

Competition for boys was fierce in her small Christian high school, so Kathleen dated boys outside her school. In her sophomore year her boyfriend forgot which night was her prom night, so Kathleen waited at home all evening, her hair coiffed and her dress perfect. The following year her new boyfriend stood her up on prom night to punish her for refusing him sex. Kathleen got a bad taste for dressing up for men and concluded, "Forget men because they aren't trustworthy; they will never come through for you. I won't wait. I won't hope."

"Because of the incest I had to trash my beauty and became androgynous in my appearance," she says. In college she gave up dresses and lived in sweat suits, pants, loafers, and oxford cloth button-down shirts. She kept her hair very short and wore no makeup. "I moved through my world like a man," she says. "I didn't even walk like a woman." She says she was trying to look "eternally youthful, in denial and defiance of emerging feminine maturity." If being a mature, sexually available woman meant a man might violate her, Kathleen wanted no part of it.

She was so removed from feelings of being female, she said, that she "used to feel that if I dressed like a woman and wore makeup, someone would pull me over and arrest me for trying to impersonate a woman." She thought, "I can't pull it off, I don't have what it takes. I'm a retard as a woman."

But at thirty-eight she began to explore her inability to live comfortably as a woman. Gradually she realized, "For me, to keep dressing this way was sin." Her sexless style of dress was sinful because it expressed her silent vow to reject the God-given femininity that, in her case, had proven dangerous. "For me, Laura Ashley is repentance," she says of her new flowing skirts. "I bought my first short skirt at forty-two." She also uses makeup and styles her hair as outward expressions of her willingness to embrace femaleness with all its risks.

"When I dress nice, I am displaying something that people can be attracted to, and I have no control over it. If I wear a short skirt and walk through my world and am looked at and enjoyed, some people will do good things with it and some will do bad things. Before, I couldn't handle that vulnerability. I have to trust God that I can display my beauty but can't control what happens."

Kathleen also likes dressing up for her husband. "Now the fact that he enjoys my beauty and wants me feels good, even if I'm too tired tonight." Nonetheless, Kathleen is no slave to her new look. The day we interviewed her, she sat in her office in jeans, loafers, and mostly-rubbed-off makeup—yet she still felt feminine. It's the *feeling* feminine, the ability to relax in our womanhood no matter what we're wearing, that signifies healing for the abuse survivor and any woman.

If it were true that inner beauty was all that mattered, then my, Carol's, and Kathleen's determination to hide our physical beauty might be misread as modesty. But when a desolate woman moves through her world with the face of the unloved, God weeps. While it may be charitable for women to veil their bodies out of compassion for men's weakness, God is saddened when we veil ourselves out of fear. The woman whose inward shame, fear, or rage disfigures her outward countenance deserves our compassion.

As a response to men's idolatry, erasing our beauty is no improvement upon worshiping it with them.

Some abuse victims respond with behavior that is the exact reverse of what I've described: they flaunt their sexuality and become promiscuous. Yet behind their heavy makeup and seductive clothing cringe women who have learned to value their beauty cheaply. To shame them for being bad, wanton women will only confirm what they already believe about themselves; to tell them that their bodies are spiritually irrelevant and they should concentrate on inner beauty will only encourage them to devalue their bodies as their abusers did. Instead, they need us to love them until they believe in the beauty and value of both their souls and their bodies.

> "To lose confidence in one's body is to lose confidence in oneself."
> —Simone De Beauvoir

THE TEMPTED

People who know the damage done by lust often encourage women to believe their beauty is bad, a cause of lust, a source of shame they should veil for their own sake and that of men. This belief has firm roots in Christian tradition, having been voiced by some of our most eminent theologians. Modern Christians often pick it up without recognizing its source. We could quote any number of church fathers, but we will concentrate on Bishop Augustine of Hippo because he laid the foundation of medieval theology, heavily influenced Martin Luther, and is still regarded by many Western Christians as the greatest theologian since the apostle Paul. Most of us owe more of our beliefs to Saint Augustine than we realize; for example, he was the first to articulate the doctrine of original sin. His autobiography, *The Confessions*, has been a bestseller for 1,500 years. Brilliant and devout, he deserves our respect even while we critique his legacy on the subject of women's beauty.

The World in A.D. 400

In the centuries after the apostles' deaths, several factors influenced the way church leaders thought about beauty. First, educated people were taught that the body was bad—a nuisance at best and an absolute evil at worst. The male sex drive in particular was considered a hindrance to rational living. Henry Chadwick, the great historian of the early Church, wrote, "all philosophers with a serious claim to be respected as wise moralists—Plato, Aristotle, the Stoics, the Epicureans—were of one mind in being impressed by . . . the capacity of sexual desire to disrupt and even destroy the most rational of plans and intentions."[1] Pagan philosophers disdained, and Christian pastors were extremely concerned about, the way beauty was worshiped in pagan culture—not just as a sign of status, but in connection with sacred prostitution. Temples like that of the Corinthian Aphrodite flourished as religious brothels. It was extremely hard to wean men off the habit of visiting prostitutes after the men professed faith in Christ. Men lived in a curious paradox: believing their bodies to be evil and their sex drives disrespectable, yet obsessed with bodily pleasures. (Experts in addiction say that hatred of one's body often feeds bodily addictions.)

Further, as Roman society decayed more and more, sexual fidelity became rare among men. To church leaders, who were themselves men, lust seemed one of the biggest threats to men's spiritual health. Unfortunately, many pastors had the male tendency to blame women for tempting men. The greatest Greek-speaking preacher of the fourth century, nicknamed John Chrysostom ("Goldenmouthed"), told women seeking baptism that makeup added nothing to their beauty of face, but would

> destroy the beauty of your soul. . . . Especially are you
> heaping up abundant fire for yourself by exciting the looks
> of young men, and attracting to yourself the eyes of the
> undisciplined; by making complete adulterers of them,
> you are bringing their downfall on your own head.[2]

Undoubtedly, some women truly were tempting men on purpose. Some wanted the ego gratification of seducing men, others worshiped beauty by believing their happiness in life depended upon the husband they could net, and others depended upon their looks for their livelihood. Prostitutes, dancers, courtesans, and concubines represented various social levels of kept women.

Some legally belonged to a man, while others depended upon men's attentions for their income. All of them painted their faces. Decent wealthy women also knew their value was measured by their attractiveness. Journalist Nancy Baker writes,

> It was not unusual for a typical Roman beauty to cover her face with a thick poultice meant to keep her skin from wrinkling and to wear the concoction constantly, except when she left the house. Evidently once she was married, the Roman woman didn't feel that she needed to waste her beauty on her mate alone—outsiders had to be present before she would reveal her face.[3]

In a society driven by competition for social status, noblewomen would do almost anything to win points in public.

Ambrose of Milan

Surveying this situation, Bishop Ambrose of Milan told his flock that the body was a "tattered garment" for the soul[4] and enthusiastically promoted lifelong virginity for men and women as "the one thing that separates us from the beasts."[5] Living as he did, surrounded by promiscuity, it is not surprising that Ambrose was such a fan of celibacy. He was also genuinely grieved for women when he saw them displaying themselves like slaves for sale on the marriage market:

> Look at the ears pierced with wounds, and pity the neck weighed down with burdens. That the metals are different [from the metal in criminal's chains] does not lighten the suffering. . . . It makes no difference whether the body be loaded with gold or with iron. . . . But how wretched a position, that she who is marriageable is in a species of sale put up as it were to auction to be bid for, so that he who offers the highest price purchases her.[6]

Ambrose genuinely thought women would be happier renouncing marriage than pursuing it on the terms available in the fourth century. Unfortunately, it was hard for single women to get jobs or live safely on their own, so convents became the only really viable alternative to the marriage market. But giving up all hope of children and marital relations was a cost few women were willing to pay in order to free themselves from the pressures of self-display.

Augustine's Foibles

Augustine was Ambrose's most famous disciple. A careful student of the Scriptures, Augustine was also influenced by the philosophy of his time and by his personal experiences. At age fifteen he discovered sex and spent two promiscuous years driven by youthful hormones. Then at the age of seventeen, like many of his peers, he took a concubine— a sort of a second-class mistress/housekeeper who lived with him. Marriage laws of the day required that a man marry within his class, and since the young Augustine was planning to rise in the world, he didn't want to shackle himself to a low-class wife. So for fifteen years he lived faithfully with his concubine and had a son. Guilt about his attachment to this woman plagued him, for she was not an intellectual and emotional companion, but merely a concession to his sex drive.

> It's not whether you win or lose; it's how you look playing the game.

At last, by thirty-two he had established himself, and his mother found him an heiress with good connections. He got engaged and sent his concubine away to please his prospective in-laws. But shortly thereafter, Augustine decided to abandon his worldly ambitions and devote himself utterly to God. To him, that meant abandoning relations with women as well, for he had been bowled over by Ambrose's preaching on the glories of celibacy.

In *The Confessions*, Augustine claimed he was grieved to lose his concubine because he loved her dearly, but he never named her in his writings, nor mentioned her again. *The Confessions* are full of his shame for having so much sexual desire that he couldn't manage to remain celibate until marriage. He never expressed guilt for having treated the mother of his son so shamefully because he had only done what was normal in his society. He thought himself virtuous for getting rid of her (she likely never saw her son again), then refraining from marrying the heiress and instead becoming a celibate priest. Any man of his class would have agreed with him.

Years later, when as a priest he faced a congregation full of men with concubines, he condemned the practice strongly. Unfaithful husbands were winked at in that society, and it was considered respectable, even in many Christian circles, for a man to keep a concubine along with his wife. However, rather than simply urging these men to be faithful to their wives, Augustine preached celibacy. His only experience of sexual relations was in using a woman for his own lust, so he had no concept that it might be holy for a man to enjoy a wife's beauty exclusively and with respect. When Augustine looked at a beautiful woman he saw only a reminder of his own shame. It was all but impossible for him to see in her the image of God, a symbol of divine beauty.

In his commentary on John's Gospel he wrote that the image of God is mainly in our souls, although our bodies do reflect it somewhat.[7] He also said our inner beauty reflects God's image more than our outer beauty (though not to the exclusion of our outer beauty). Everything bodily or sensual felt to him like a distraction from God, even food and music. He passionately wanted to see God, and he felt that earthly beauties distracted him from God's beauty. Certainly a great many men around him were utterly distracted from God's beauty by earthly beauty, and being the passionate man he was, he regarded moderation as no option. To God, his Beloved, he wrote the most ardent prose:

> Late have I loved you, beauty so old and so new: late have I loved you. And see, you were within and I was in the external world and sought you there, and in my unlovely state I plunged into those lovely created things you made. . . . The lovely things kept me far from you, though if they did not have their existence in you, they had no existence at all.[8]

"Those lovely things" that had kept Augustine from God were first and foremost women. Generations of men after him have read his *Confessions* and identified his experience as their own. How could a "distraction" be a reflection of God's beauty?

After reading a Greek philosopher named Plotinus, Augustine was persuaded that divine beauty shone like light through all the beautiful things in the world. Beautiful things in the world made the person who looked at them sad because they were so fleeting, so superficial and fading, while one knew in one's soul that beyond them was the Source of all beauty that never faded. Augustine even grew to understand that contemplating the beauties of nature and the heavens could "be turned into a stairway to the immortal and enduring."[9] But while he could imagine mountains and stars touching a man's spirit in pure ways, he still couldn't imagine that the beauty of a woman could be a window into the realm of God, even though she bore the divine image in a way the stars did not at all.

Men in his world who responded spiritually to women's beauty were doing it in temples to Aphrodite, having sex with sacred prostitutes. That one could reject the idolatry, gain control over instinct, and then see a beautiful woman purely was beyond Augustine's imagination—certainly no men he knew were doing it. Hence, he could feel the longing for eternity when he looked at the stars and let their beauty point him toward God, but the face of a woman never sparked that sorrowful longing for a better world; she sparked in him only lust, shame, and anger at himself and her. He did what we often do when some person prompts in us feelings we don't know how to deal with; he came down hard both on himself for having the feelings and on women for "causing" them.

Ambrose had rebuked men for blaming women, "whereas all the while it is man himself who seeks in a woman that which tempts him." Ambrose had understood that "The beauty of woman's body is a great work of God, meant to be a sign of that far greater interior beauty, the special clarity and loveliness of her spirit."[10] But Augustine had had mixed personal experience with women's inner beauty. During most of the time he lived with his concubine, his mother also lived with him. She was so attached to her son that he couldn't escape her even by moving from Africa to Italy; she moved with him. *The Confessions* portray a man who felt guilty for falling short of his mother's expectations and who both loved and felt embarrassed by her. With a clinging mother and a mistress, it's no surprise that Augustine had a low view of women. "What is the difference?" he wrote to a friend, "whether it is in a wife or a mother, it is still Eve (the temptress) that we must beware of in any woman."[11]

Augustine's blazing mind enabled him to sort out many profound theological truths, but it did not help him come to terms with the emotional or carnal part of himself, especially the part of him that responded when he looked at a beautiful woman. He knew only two responses to fleshly instinct: give in to it with that shameful concubine, or clamp down on it. He was utterly unable to see the image of God in women, who all looked like temptresses to him, dragging him away from his focus on God.

> "Sleek, darling, sleek and clean; loooong and classy, indeed, almost classic; lean, yes, certainly, modern and functional, but in a glamorous way."
> —fall 1996 fashion hype[12]

Why should we care what Augustine thought? Because under his influence, Western artists and theologians have consistently linked beauty to sexual temptation. Finding in their worlds and in their hearts the same temptations, they have, like him, responded by telling women that to display our beauty is a sin. We rarely hear sermons that warn us against using our bodies as status symbols, but we do learn to be ashamed of our bodies. By focusing on lust, the Augustinian tradition minimizes the more insidious sin of pride.

THE TRIVIALIZERS

We should not imagine, however, that secular thinkers have done better. As a mature man, the British MP Edmund Burke urged King George III to free the American colonies, but as a young man he wrote the highly influential but patently ridiculous *Philosophical Enquiry into the Origin of our Ideas of the Sublime and the Beautiful*. Burke was so uncomfortable with feminine beauty that he decided *beauty* as a concept applied only to weak, feminine things, while strong, masculine things needed a different term: "sublime." "To call strength by the name of beauty," he wrote, "is surely a strange confusion of ideas."[13] Further, "The beauty of women is considerably owing to their *weakness*, or delicacy, and is even enhanced by their timidity."[14] And finally,

> Observe that part of a beautiful woman where she is per-
> haps the most beautiful, about the neck and breasts; the
> smoothness; the softness; the easy and insensible swell;
> the variety of the surface, which is never for the smallest
> space the same; the *deceitful* maze, through which the
> unsteady eye slides giddily, without knowing where to fix,
> or whither it is carried.[15]

In this last passage, Burke skated just this side of erotic as he described the woman's body, but he was clearly thrown off balance by the sight, not knowing where to look or where his eye (or mind) would be carried. Instead of coming to terms with the power a woman's beauty had to affect him, however, he labored to trivialize it, calling it deceitful and weak. We may laugh, but the writings of Burke and others in the late eighteenth century suc-ceeded in trivializing beauty of all kinds to the point where nobody talks today about modern art or music being beautiful. Many con-temporary artists would be embarrassed to be accused of trying to produce beautiful paintings, sculptures, or songs (their work is "important" or "powerful"), because beauty has been relegated to this weak, "feminine" plane. Beauty is not powerful, Burke insisted (in the teeth of its obvious power over him), so today, beauty is important only for women. We are a long way from the teaching of the Bible, in which beauty is clearly a quality of the magnificent, all-powerful God who stamped some of His splendor into the dust and called it human.

SO WHAT?

What happens when violated women revile their beauty, tempted men recoil from it, and self-styled philosophers trivialize it? They cede a God-created glory to the domain of the Devil.

Should we flee from enjoying mountains and forests because some people worship nature, or turn our gaze from the stars because some practice astrology? We impoverish our lives and narrow the scope of God's kingdom whenever we fall for this scam, but disrespecting human beauty is all the more tragic because it leads us to disrespect women, our physical bodies, and our sexuality. To cheapen beauty is to encourage ugly art and abuse of women's bodies. Feminine beauty now belongs to advertising, media hype, and pornography. Driven underground, the longing for beauty enslaves men and women who have not been taught how to master its power for godly ends.

If as women we are going to move beyond pride and shame to a strong humility regarding our bodies, we must stop listening to the voices that tell us beauty doesn't matter. It does matter that every girl and woman learns to see herself as beautiful and offer her face of love to those around her. How do we get there from here?

A CLOSER LOOK

If you have experienced sexual violence of any kind, you may find it helpful to contemplate the story of Tamar. Read 2 Samuel 13:1-22 aloud slowly, picturing the story in your mind as though it were a movie. Pay attention to what you're feeling, and try to stay present with the story. You may find it difficult to read very far without feeling sick or numb. If you have a strong reaction like that, stop and let yourself feel it. You can come back to the story at another time.

Put yourself in Tamar's place. Did you ever feel like the beautiful daughter of a king? How long ago was that? Can you remember what it was like, or does the idea seem completely alien? Why?

"Tamar put ashes on her head and tore the ornamented robe she was wearing. She put her hand on her head and went away, weeping aloud as she went. . . . And Tamar lived in her brother Absalom's house, a desolate woman." Can you remember feeling like a desolate woman—or do you still? Why? What did you do with your beauty? Did you tear your robe or put ashes on your head? Did you hide your beauty, or did you learn to flaunt it? How has being a Tamar affected the way you have treated your own beauty?

If you have never been violated sexually, you probably know someone who has been. How comfortable are you with hearing a friend recount such experiences and supporting her as she heals?

PART THREE

HOW WE CHANGE

CHAPTER THIRTEEN

HONESTY

A woman who has taken years to perfect a hatred of her body or an obsession with looking good stares out over a canyon between where she is and a distant place where she could feel contented, joyful, and unself-conscious about her appearance. The road to that relaxed joy looks steep and dirty, down to the bottom of why she is the way she is, and up the other side. Each woman's path is unique, but we can map some of the likely roadmarks. At the very least, her path will include becoming aware, grieving, letting herself be loved, and learning to love.

BECOMING AWARE

Becoming aware of how and why we abuse our God-given beauty is both a shock and a relief. I (Cinny) was shocked to discover that, even though I could apply my makeup in five minutes and had worn the same easy-care hairstyle for ten years, I was serving the beauty goddess. I was driving myself to obey her commandment, "Thou shalt not gain weight," and judging my daughters by the same law. I was guilty of pride and envy, and my girls were suffering for it. This was incredible. I didn't even know there was a beauty goddess!

I (Karen) was equally stunned that my lifeless appearance wasn't spiritual and that my self-control around food was called anorexia nervosa. I was dead wrong in my belief that I was above worrying about people's respect. I thought I was a valiant crusader against the beauty goddess, when in fact I was merely angry at men, judgmental of women, and afraid to be seen. It took months for the light to dawn and pierce my pride.

On the other hand, becoming aware has also been a relief. It's a relief to know there are good reasons why we feel angry, ashamed, driven, or fearful in a given situation. It's a relief to have words for what used to be reflex reactions. For instance, I (Karen) recently attended a wedding among relatives I didn't know, and in Hawaii, a social system I'm unfamiliar with. While planning what to wear, I was conscious enough of my feelings and motives to say to myself, "Oh, I see. I'm feeling anxious about what these strangers will think of me. I want to be respected. I want my clothes to help me fit in." Just having words for my feelings, and understanding they were normal, helped to dissipate my anxiety. I could talk to God about my feelings and honestly conclude, "Well, I'll do the best I can within reason. They'll either respect me or they won't. The worst that could happen won't be the end of the world, and the worst is unlikely." That was a relief.

For me (Cinny), it's a huge relief every time I recognize an area in which I've been on the beauty performance treadmill. "You mean I don't *have* to do that in order to be acceptable? I get to choose whether I feel like putting my makeup on or not?" It's also a relief to have words put to the ways I've hurt my daughters and to have received their forgiveness.

> "Now you can have the buns you've always wanted."
> —ad for *Buns of Steel* videotape[1]

Awareness gives us the freedom to choose what we are or are not willing to do to enhance our appearance in any given situation. I (Karen) went to the beach with a man who commented, "You know, you look out of place at the beach in a Speedo when everyone else is wearing bikinis." Thus spake Southern California. My response? "Too bad. I feel comfortable in a Speedo, and I don't like bikinis. If the world doesn't like the way I look, they can avert their eyes." I'm aware that I retain some discomfort about displaying my body in public—I'm not lying to myself as I used to do. But I also believe I get to choose when to push myself beyond my comfort zone, and when I get to say enough is enough for me today. I no longer need to judge or envy the women in bikinis, but I can say with relaxation, "Me, I'm a one-piece girl."

GRIEVING

The shock of awareness naturally leads to grief. We grieve the ways in which we haven't received the love and respect we long for. We're sad when men don't notice us, women look down on us, or business associates think less of us because we don't meet their standards of attractiveness. We're legitimately hurt when people send us negative messages about our bodies. And when aging or illness robs us of beauty we once possessed, we give ourselves permission to mourn.

In her eighth month of pregnancy, my (Cinny's) daughter Charis found the right side of her face paralyzed by Bell's palsy. A virus was attacking her nerves and muscles. It couldn't have come at a worse time. She was struggling with the swelling and weight gain of pregnancy and felt that her face and smile were her only redeeming outward features. The suddenly droopy eye that wouldn't close and the frozen mouth that hindered speaking and eating sent her to the edge. It took all her emotional strength to venture out in public, knowing how her disfigurement would affect people's responses. To be the center of attention at her baby shower and not even be able to smile when she opened a gift! She got laughs when she held up in front of her mouth a picture of a smile, but inside she was crying. Her husband had always said how much he loved her smile; now she feared he would be embarrassed about her looks and sad because he knew she was upset for him. "I feel that all my dignity has been robbed from me," she told me. "I hate the way I look. It has changed my personality and my ability to express myself. I don't want anyone to look at me." That's hard to hear from your daughter.

Her friends tried to comfort her by saying that her looks didn't really matter and they loved her anyway. However, that seemed just to trivialize her pain. One day, someone whom she hadn't seen for a while asked in shock, "What has happened to your face?" Instead of being offended, she thanked the person for noticing. At last someone had recognized that something really bad had occurred and was willing to be honest about it.

Why Grieve?

How we look matters. It is an important part (although only a part) of who we are. It affects how we feel about ourselves and how others feel about us. What others think about how we look matters. It affects our love life, our respect in our communities, and our financial success. In our appearance-obsessed culture especially, looking under par carries real costs.

In order to come to a godly contentment with our bodies, and to help our daughters, sisters, and friends do the same, we must acknowledge how important it is for a human being to believe in her beauty. She doesn't need to look like a *Baywatch* star, not even close; but she does need to believe that she moves through her world under the eyes of a Beholder who sees her beauty and loves her.

Writer Nancy Groom records a friend telling her,

> I don't know any woman of inner beauty who hasn't suffered greatly and done the hard work of the gospel that involves grief. . . . For most of my life I would not grieve, because it was seen as a weakness: Strong women don't grieve. Now I believe *only* strong women can grieve, and it's a weakness *not* to grieve. . . . I don't think Jesus named the Holy Spirit the Comforter just on a whim.[2]

We agree: it takes strength to grieve. But too many women feel ashamed when some loss of their physical beauty stuns them into grief. Marjorie had a mastectomy at forty-five and told Cinny a year later, "I was in shock. I couldn't believe it. . . . I couldn't even say the word *cancer*. . . . I thought I had to be strong. My mother had never shared her feelings with me when she had her mastectomy. I thought I was just supposed to ride through this and that 'the peace that passes all understanding' would be there. However, I didn't float through it like I thought I would, and that made me feel guilty. I didn't expect to be so rattled. . . .

"When I lost my hair, that was worse than when I lost my breast. It was an awful loss because the loss of hair is so obvious. That affected my sense of femininity. My loss of hair affected my relationship to [my husband] Roger. I was very self-conscious of making love to Roger without hair. I used to wear a turban."

To come to terms with a loss like Marjorie's requires a willingness to face both the first overwhelming rush of feelings and later the daily ache that seems to never end. When Marjorie first saw her scar, she said, "I was frightened, but it wasn't as bad as I thought it would be. Still everyday, when I get out of the shower, I see it, make myself look at it, and deal with it."

The loss of a breast should never be trivialized. Nor should that of a woman whose abdomen is scarred by Caesarean section, or any woman whose beauty has been marred. The marring of beauty is a sign that death has invaded our world. It's wrong! It should never have been this way; God wanted better for us.

The writer of Ecclesiastes understood the important role grief plays in helping us deal realistically with our fallen world:

> It is better to go to a house of mourning
> > than to go to a house of feasting,
> for death is the destiny of every man;
> > the living should take this to heart.
> Sorrow is better than laughter,
> > because a sad face is good for the heart.
> The heart of the wise is in the house of mourning,
> > but the heart of fools is in the house of pleasure.[3]

Since this is Hebrew poetry, we should not understand the poet to be disagreeing with the apostle Paul's command to "Rejoice in the Lord always."[4] Rather, we should understand that openly grieving losses is part of genuinely rejoicing in the Lord who Himself suffered, was "overwhelmed with sorrow to the point of death,"[5] and faced the destruction of His body, confident that the Father would raise Him from the dead. Losing a breast or a smile or a good figure means watching part of ourselves die.

At sixty-seven, Sarah doesn't obsess over the loss of her youth, but she does admit she has had to grieve. "I didn't know I was vain until I lost any reason to be. Many of us have lost a friend in the course of life. My mirror used to be my friend, and now I've lost a very close and longtime friend.

> "Jackie, I'd rather have you smoke two packs a day than eat more than 1,000 calories a day."—what comedian Jackie Guerra says a producer told her[6]

"It's an insult to God not to do the best with what we have. I didn't wear makeup until I was fifty—I felt no need for it until then. It's all such a mess, this aging thing, but we have to do the best we can with the wrinkly skin, drooping eyelids, and double chin. We are all conscious that other people have to look at us. I want to say to them, 'I'm sorry I'm not so pleasing to your eyes as I used to be.'"

To hear this woman confess the desire to apologize for her looks moved us to sorrow. We want her to know that she's still attractive to look at, and that the natural process of aging is not a "mess."

How Do We Grieve?

Get physical. The ancient Jews knew how to grieve. They made no apologies for tearing their clothing, dressing in sackcloth, and pouring ashes on their heads. In these ways they used their physical appearance to declare their emotional state. They cried; they wailed; they played sad music. To play a sad love song and have a good cry over lost youth might be a helpful part of a woman's grieving process. To wear black for three months might help a person come to terms with cancer's cruelty to her body.

Sometimes it's important to go public with our grief, while at other times it's wise to mask it. Masking can be life-giving if done with awareness. When her father died, Mary Anne Tabor's skin became dehydrated from stress and crying. She used eye creams to reduce the puffiness and to moisturize and nourish her skin.[7] While she was going through turmoil in her inner life, she used makeup to mask her private struggles while at work. A sales-woman does not have the luxury of exposing her private griefs to her clients. Jesus said, "When you fast, put oil on your head and wash your face" so that only God will know you are fasting.[8] Oil and washing were the rituals of putting on a presentable public face that masked the private spiritual disciplines. When God is taking us through an inner tempest, we can mask when necessary and reveal our struggles only to those who can handle them and be part of our healing process.

Get alone with God. When we're grieving the ways in which people have not treated us as beautiful, it's crucial to bask regularly in the loving presence of the Beholder who sees our beauty more clearly than any human can. The Psalms offer a rich vocabulary with which we can pour out our grief to God:

> My God, my God, why have you forsaken me?
>> Why are you so far from saving me,
>> so far from the words of my groaning?[9]

> They have greatly oppressed me from my youth—
>> let Israel say—
> they have greatly oppressed me from my youth,
>> but they have not gained the victory over me.[10]

They invite us to shout, to cry, and then to still our souls like a child at rest in her mother's arms, the mother who is her face of love.[11]

Get mad. Fear and anger are normal parts of the grieving process. Women who feel themselves constantly under the gaze of judges often walk in fear of failing the test. It's easy to exhort women not to worry if they fail to win husbands or promotions or esteem because they don't look good enough, but God understands the pain when a woman's worst fears come true and, like Leah, she must face her life as the Unchosen.

Some women, when they wake up to the fact that they and their sisters have lived their whole lives in such terror, turn from fear to rage. In *The Beauty Myth*, Naomi Wolf seethes at the men she believes have colluded to keep women under the tyranny of looking okay. We don't agree that the problem is a male conspiracy, but we understand her anger that women are suffering and nobody seems to be doing anything about it. We have felt a lot of anger while researching and writing this book.

It's easy to get mad at men who use women for status, self-esteem, and self-gratification. It's easy to get mad at women who prop up their own egos by shaming other women for not looking good enough. It's very easy to get mad at the people who are making millions on cosmetics, dieting products, and plastic surgery, while young girls are dying of anorexia. *"Who says that a youthful body is the most attractive? Just who made up that rule? . . . Who says that protruding bones look better than cushiony flesh? Who says that angular looks better than round? Just who came up with that crazy idea?"*[12]

> "There's only one thing between you and a perfect body. Your appetite."
> —ad for appetite control formula Inhibitrol[13]

Anger can be useful in shaking us out of denial, and it can energize us to pursue change. The Bible is full of stories in which God gets angry at injustice and idolatry. We can well imagine God being angry at people who tease young girls about their looks and at people who profit from women's fear-driven compulsion to lose weight. But for humans seeking to live with the paradox of beauty, anger can be either productive or unproductive.

Anger occurs when our desire to live in the perfectly just and pleasant Garden of Eden bangs its shins on an outcropping of life in this world. That stab of pain offers us a choice between wise and foolish anger. Wise anger drives us to God with a host of questions: "What's going on? Why are You allowing this to happen? Are You as just and loving as I thought You were?" These are healthful, honest questions about the circumstance and about God's character. The psalmists asked this kind of question frequently:

> Has [God's] unfailing love vanished forever?
>   Has his promise failed for all time?
> Has God forgotten to be merciful?
>   Has he in anger withheld his compassion?[14]

Although these questions seem to express mistrust in God (and, indeed, the psalmists' trust was incomplete), the queries actually honor God by trusting His love enough to pursue Him with hard questions. God blessed Jacob for daring to wrestle with Him.[15] Such honest wrestling leads us to meditate on God's character, and soon we are asking questions that reflect trust in His shrewdness and timing in dealing with injustice: "Should I yield before this wrong, or confront it? Should I confront it now or later? Should I confront it alone or with others? What would a person wise as a snake but innocent as a dove[16] do about this?" We surrender to God, wait for His guidance, and hope in His justice.

On the other hand, the pain of suffering injustice may spark a foolish response. We want justice *now*, our way. We want our oppressors to pay now, and we're not interested in their side of the story. If we don't get what we want, we may lash out at others, or we may turn our anger inward at ourselves. We are victims. No one loves us. Foolish anger makes some of us shrill and many of us mute.

The psalmist exhorts us to be still and wait when we are angry:

> Be still before the LORD and wait patiently for him;
> > do not fret when men succeed in their ways,
> > when they carry out their wicked schemes.
> Refrain from anger and turn from wrath;
> > do not fret—it leads only to evil.[17]

Stillness is not the same as the muteness of a victim. Drs. Dan Allender and Tremper Longman III offer this meditation on what it means to be still and wait:

> When you are angry, wait. Stop, sit, don't move! . . . Detoxification of anger is writhing with the desire to strike out and choosing not to release the anger—either toward another person or toward an inanimate object. Be still. Sit with your rage, let it rack you like a buffeting wind and a harsh rain. Let its fury soak you in the sweat of desire. . . . Waiting does not deny, nor does it pretend. It is not merely taking a timeout. It is entering the very soil that drew the

rage to the surface—the fury against God for requiring us to wait to see His justice and goodness.[18]

Such a silent tempest will probably make us more angry, not less. But at last we are voicing anger at the Person we were angry at all along. God is the One who has made men with this proclivity for slim waists and unlined faces. God is the One who has cursed us with breasts that sag and bellies that bulge. God has left us in this world struggling for jobs, lovers, and respect. Has God forgotten to be merciful? We yell the question, then wait in silence for the answer.

It's essential to own up to how angry most of us are at God for making us live in a fallen world. In his book *Yearning*, minister Craig Barnes says men and women

> are torn by the longing to get life right and the nagging suspicion that they are fatally flawed, and they are torn absolutely apart by the craving to be loved and the terrified fear of being known. . . . So out of compassion, someone [the world of advertising] tells them all of it can be changed because—and this is the seductive part—God [their product] wants to meet their needs.[19]

According to Barnes, yearning "is what one does with a life that falls short of realized wholeness." Humans think they have a right to be whole and complete in themselves, and advertisers play on this belief. Men and women yearn for "a body that won't make us ashamed,"[20] and manufacturers promise they can get that shame-free body through money and hard work. When the perfect body doesn't materialize, people may even blame God for their flawed forms.

But while Genesis 2 suggests that humans were made with glorious bodies not subject to decay and death, not even Adam and Eve had it all. The forbidden Tree symbolized the limitations built into being human. The first man and woman were not gods, and it frustrated them. The reach for the forbidden fruit, or the perfect body, "eternally symbolizes our reach for something more than mere creatures can ever have."[21] That's why the goddess of beauty seduces us: she offers us perfection here and now, while the God of the Bible never does. In order to break her spell over us, we must acknowledge our anger over fallenness and limitation. When we face our anger while clinging to faith in God's ultimate justice, sadness comes as rage melts into tears and we find ourselves able to run to God for comfort.

JOINING TOGETHER

Grieving means slogging through the muck at the bottom of the canyon. It's tough. We should not expect ourselves to do it—or any other significant effort of spiritual growth—alone. Our individualistic culture teaches us from birth to believe that maturing means learning to take care of ourselves, and there's a strain of Christianity which implies that truly godly people get all their spiritual needs met in their quiet times alone with God. Nothing could be further from the picture the Bible paints of following Christ. We need each other, not only to share grief, but also to share joy, hope, and reality checks that reinforce our awareness. A crucial aspect of breaking free from the beauty goddess is learning to love and be loved.

A CLOSER LOOK

The more we honor our bodies as *us*—as intertwined with our spirits, as limbs of Christ, temples of the Spirit, and bearers of God's image—the more we will understand and manage well the power of physical appearance in our lives.

Examine yourself in a mirror. Ideally, undress and look at your whole body, but if you're not ready for that, begin with your face. Look for signs of God's inner work, marks of family genetics, battle scars, and badges of courage. Take time to grieve that figure lost for the good cause of babymaking or maturing; mourn her like a lost loved one. Feel sad that the flower must wither. Don't hurry the process. Cry about it, write about it in your journal, talk about it with a friend. Pray about it to the God of all Comfort.

CHAPTER FOURTEEN

LOVING AND BEING LOVED

One of the bravest things a woman can do is to let herself be loved. Those who have grown up being treated as beautiful may not find it hard to receive this kind of love, but those of us who have endured many negative messages about our bodies often grow thick hides that resist love of all kinds. However, very few of us will acquire the face of love—faces that shine with God's love for others—until we develop a habit of letting God love us both directly and through other people.

RECEIVING GOD'S LOVE DIRECTLY

Many contemporary schools of psychology teach that a person's identity comes from within her. If we look inside ourselves long enough, they say, we will find out who we are and discover our beauty. But the Bible and our experience seem to say that identity is bestowed, not dredged up from within. In the Scriptures God is forever changing someone's name, transforming his identity. God tells us who we are; God declares us beautiful. If we can't hear God, then we naturally turn to the important people around us to tell us who we are. "You're smart." "You're good at sports." "You're stupid." "You're only a woman." "You're ugly." We hear and believe. More often than not, we literally become what we are told we are. We saw in Chapter 2 how Mary Anne Tabor actually became ugly because her mother told her she was ugly, and how Ellen Lambert lost her early beauty when she lost the person who drew it out of her.

God's loving gaze is the one we need the most. It is impossible to overstate the effect of meditating on God's loving gaze until we believe it. What God promised Jerusalem He whispers to each of us:

> The nations will see your righteousness,
>   and all kings your glory;
> you will be called by a new name
>   that the mouth of the LORD will bestow.
> You will be a crown of splendor in the LORD's hand,
>   a royal diadem in the hand of your God.
> No longer will they call you Deserted,
>   or name your land Desolate.
> But you will be called Hephzibah [my delight is in her],
>   and your land Beulah [married]. . . .
> As a young man marries a maiden,
>   so will your sons marry you;
> as a bridegroom rejoices over his bride,
>   so will your God rejoice over you.[1]

No longer will you be called "Ugly" or "Unloved," but you will be named "Beautiful," and "My Delight Is in Her." The eyes of love transform the beloved.

GOD'S LOVE THROUGH PEOPLE

A few great saints have achieved this transformation through solitary meditation alone, but God's standard method is to love us through other people. God intends us to discover our identities and our beauty through healthy, life-giving relationships. This is God's plan for families, friends, and all brothers and sisters in Christ.

Family Bedrock

Anne's family made all the difference for her. Born with what is called a "port wine stain" birthmark covering the left side of her face from her eye to her mouth, Anne told us, "My parents always made me feel beautiful and special. I asked my Mom if she was disappointed when she first saw me as a new baby. She told me when she looked at me for the first time, head full of dark hair with a bow the nurses had tied at the top, she thought I was the most beautiful baby she had ever seen. My parents just loved me and always taught me that beauty really comes from within."

It wasn't as though her mother was in denial about her birthmark. "My Mom always kept me up-to-date with anything new being done cosmetically for birthmarks. However, she always made it clear to me, in a very loving way, that she didn't think there was any reason in the world to ever have anything done to my birthmark. She just wanted me to be informed as to my options, in case at some point in my life I didn't feel the same way."

The acceptance and love of Anne's family and friends made the few circumstances in her life when people did comment on her birthmark memorable, but endurable. "In college I was told by the director of a precision dance team that if and when I did 'make the line' I would have to 'cover that thing on your face.'" Anne was able to take the insult in stride. It only takes one or two clear conduits of love to keep a person like Anne going. At forty-six, she has been able to turn what could have been a harsh liability into a source of character.

If a woman has been wounded around matters of appearance, she might feel ill-equipped to help her children handle their wounds. Nothing could be further from the truth. The more honest we are with our daughters about the struggles we face ourselves, the more free they will feel to face their own struggles honestly. Marjorie, the woman we mentioned in Chapter Thirteen who underwent a mastectomy, remembers how hard it was for her as a child when she saw her mother disfigured by a mastectomy. The ugly scar frightened her when she glimpsed her mother in the bathtub, but because her mother never talked about the surgery, Marjorie was never able to voice her fears. Now, Marjorie is committed to letting her children see and react to her scar so they won't feel frightened by it.

Marjorie is wisely drawing her children into her process of grieving and acceptance. Someday they will need those grieving skills when their world judges them less than perfectly beautiful. We probably can't protect our daughters from outrageous media messages or cruel comments at school; but when their hips begin to spread, we can listen to their fears and tell them about our own. We can be sad and mad with them about how lousy it feels to live in a world that hates big thighs. When they come home from school with bruised hearts, we can cry with them and show them that strong women grieve. Instead of telling them that looks don't matter and they shouldn't be so vain, we can reassure them that we see them as beautiful and others will, too.

The Gift of Friends

For those of us who did not grow up with families like Anne's (and even for those who did), friends can be invaluable companions on the road to change.

A place to unmask: One of the great gifts we can give each other is a place to strip off the mask. Mary Anne Tabor describes a class in which her assignment was "to communicate experientially" with her classmates:

> I played a portion of a tape from my private journal (I used to tape record my journal at night) which revealed some of my fears that stemmed from being hit when I was a child. While the tape played, I stood in front of my classmates and took off my makeup.
>
> I had put on full makeup that day, as if I were going to work. From foundation and rouge to eyeshadow and eyeliner, plus bright lipstick, I looked every bit the cosmetics saleswoman.
>
> I brought a tissue with me and a creme-based makeup remover and took off every bit of makeup from my face while my tape played. When I finished some of my classmates were crying. I had revealed myself without my

mask. . . . I was feeling the fear of being rejected, and feeling very vulnerable when one of the guys in my class said I looked more beautiful at that moment than he had ever noticed before. Then the rest of the class began giving me feedback, saying they saw me as beautiful, sensitive, loving, caring, and possessing other such tender qualities. . . .

For me, at the moment, it was like being bathed in bright sunshine after walking out of a dank, dark cave.[3]

Mary Anne's makeup symbolized her public face: the competent businesswoman. Her bare face represented the secret hurts she didn't normally flaunt in public.

There is no describing the pleasure of being seen at our most vulnerable and disheveled, and being loved. Women tell us how much they like sitting with their girlfriends, unpainted and uncombed, and allowing themselves to be seen and known. The first time a potential mate sees us that way is always a watershed: can he wake up happily to that face every morning? I (Cinny) plead guilty to waking up early for the first six months of my marriage so that I could put my makeup on before Bob saw me. As a Southern girl, I was conditioned never to be seen without my public face. But the truth is, taking off the public face is intimate and risky, and it honors those whom we trust with that revelation. It is far easier to grieve our flaws and losses and come to terms with them when we have people who will do what God does: see us without our masks with the eyes of a loving beholder, and accept us.

> "I never met a dame yet who didn't know if she was beautiful or not without being told."
> —Marlon Brando, *A Streetcar Named Desire*

Words of love: A second thing friends can do is tell each other we're beautiful. Marlon Brando is simply wrong: while there may be a few vain women around who don't need to be told they're beautiful, most of us could stand to hear it a lot more than we do. We know (sort of) that God sees us as beautiful, but God gave us each other so we can speak the words that bring out in each of us the face of the beloved.

Friends made the difference between life and death for me (Karen). They provided a safe place where I could strip off my pious mask to reveal the hurt girl underneath, and they continually encouraged me to grow in beauty. They listened to my grief, hugged me when I cried, and cheered when I took steps forward. I didn't need people to tell me what colors I looked best in so much as I needed people who gave me reasons to wear happy colors instead of sad ones. Often, their words of life spoke of my inner beauty (they might remark upon my courage or passion or loyalty), but such words ignited in me the hope and peace that altered my countenance.

My friends also seemed to know I felt uncertain and self-conscious about being seen and made a point of encouraging me when I took the risk. Once I went to a large meeting full of many strangers and a few of my coworkers. One coworker whispered to me when I arrived, "You look gorgeous!" Somehow, her comment fed humility in me rather than pride. I felt less self-conscious among strangers (self-consciousness is a feature of that pride-shame pendulum), and more able to care about the other people in the meeting. I felt relaxed and grateful. I wasn't used to hearing that I was gorgeous, so I experienced an eight-year-old's pleasure about it.

How different this experience was from the envious spirit so common between women at work. This woman didn't feel in competition with me for approval from the others in the room. She did what the apostle Paul said lies at the core of life in Christ:

> If you have any encouragement from being united with
> Christ, if any comfort from his love, if any fellowship with
> the Spirit, if any tenderness and compassion, then make my
> joy complete by being like-minded, having the same love,
> being one in spirit and purpose. Do nothing out of selfish
> ambition or vain conceit, but in humility consider others
> better than yourselves. Each of you should look not only to
> your own interests, but also to the interests of others.
>
> Your attitude should be the same as that of Christ
> Jesus.[4]

God gave us each other so we could sit together to mourn the loss or lack of physical beauty, and to celebrate the gift of inner beauty. A community of sisters is a place where the angry can declare their anger, the grieving can share their grief, and the joyful can celebrate their joy, all without fear of being judged faithless or vain.

Good men are indeed a scarce and valuable commodity, and not everyone can get a promotion. The decision to treat our colleagues, schoolmates, and the woman next to us in the pew or the ladies room as a sister rather than a rival carries a risk. If we're not looking out for number one, someone else may get the man or the job. Yet the price is worth it: my coworker's kindness added to her beauty as well as my own. Furthermore, what have we really gained if the price we pay for our careers, our husbands, or our status is a driven, anxious, envious, proud-and-easily-shamed heart? What does it profit a woman if she gains the whole world but loses her soul?

Christ had ultimate status and security, but He gave it all up in order to stand alongside us. As sisters of Christ, there is nothing more loving we can do than to "rejoice with those who rejoice" because they have found a faithful man, won a promotion, look great, or are young and beautiful, and to "mourn with those who mourn" because they have lost their hair, had a breast removed, are unnoticed by men, or are unattractive by the world's standards.[5]

A refuge for those who grieve: Marjorie, the woman who underwent a mastectomy, spoke of the compassion she felt from her female doctor, who cared about how she looked after the surgery. Marjorie asked me (Cinny) if I would like to see her mastectomy scar. I felt apprehensive, the natural human response to disfigurement. But Marjorie seemed so eager to show her scar that I felt I should look. Marjorie's doctor had done a wonderful job, leaving a flat chest with one horizontal scar across the area where her breast had once been. In that moment of looking and accepting, I was able to send Marjorie a message she needed: Yes, your loss is real and terrible, not to be healed until heaven; but you are still you, still a beautiful person. For me to say that about Marjorie also meant saying that about myself, so we both gained in that moment of connection.

Grieving and rejoicing with a community also helps us put our own losses in perspective. A woman who has always felt cursed by her size may gain compassion for a petite friend for whom losing her looks in middle age comes as a shock. Women who can afford face lifts would do well to talk with women who struggle to keep their children fed. Women born slim, rich, or white may not know to count their blessings until they hear what it's like to go through life with an appearance the world considers low-status.

A Day of Beauty: Some enterprising friends surprised Nancy, a business attorney in the Seattle area, with a Day of Beauty. As a little girl, Nancy was a tomboy and grew into a highly competitive swimmer of national caliber. As an adolescent, she was too busy climbing mountains and swimming miles to spend time perusing *Seventeen* magazine for makeup tips or shopping at the mall with friends. She was comfortable with herself and focused on school. Boys liked her for sports and friendship.

After graduating from Yale and completing law school, Nancy entered her profession. "In the 1980s, the clothing consisted of dark, tailored suits and bow ties, no silk blouses, dresses, or pearls. I fit into this dress code because I was more interested in progressing in my career than in my wardrobe and didn't want to lose respect from my male clients by focusing on looks. But eventually, as I was gaining confidence in my work and hitting my stride professionally, I didn't have to worry as much about my performance and how I was perceived. I thought I could do more to take care of myself personally."

About this time, Nancy showed up to meet a couple of friends for a birthday breakfast. To her astonishment, she found eight women waiting with a birthday card promising a Day of Beauty. "When I saw this card, it was like a giant warm fuzzy. This was a gift given out of love and fun, and I never felt any judgment, like I needed this improvement. I felt totally loved."

She had her hair cut and colored, eyebrows waxed, upper lip "ripped" (waxed to remove hair), and a manicure and pedicure. "While I was under the hair dryer, my friends were scurrying around Nordstrom's, gathering clothes, scarves, and accessories for me to try on." Her friends had good eyes for color and style and urged Nancy to try on some things she never would have chosen. "I never would have done scarves if I hadn't been shown how to wear them."

Next came a makeover. Nancy had never worn much makeup, even lipstick, unless it was a special event. She had never learned how to apply it, and it just wasn't part of who she was. "I had my makeup done years ago. I remember afterward thinking I looked like a hooker. The gal had loaded the makeup on my face and I couldn't wait to wash it off. But this time it was different. The woman steered me through the process, explaining what she was doing and then encouraging me to participate in putting on the makeup.

"I learned some things about clothes and makeup that were basic and easy, and I felt confident to follow through on them. I got positive affirmations and felt professional and classic in this new look that allowed the strong woman in me to come out.

"These physical changes helped me focus on taking care of myself and affected my personal life. Even though I understand how men think, it made me much more proud to be a woman and to know that being a woman is good. As I embraced my femininity, I felt better about what being a woman brings to the table. I feel more confident enhancing those qualities visually, so I'm able to bring them out personality-wise. I had had more confidence in the professional side of life than in the personal side.

"I see some professionals around town use their sexuality and their looks to get what they want. In the process they lose credibility with men. In my madeover state, I don't wear much makeup. My goal is to be attractive, not sexy. I have never viewed this as a vanity issue. I won't be picked first for the Prom Queen, but I'm very grateful for my other talents and qualities."

Nancy got married seventeen months after the makeover and didn't think it was a coincidence; she had learned to balance her career goals and her femininity, and her appearance reflected that new balance. The outer change expressed the inner one. Now, Nancy says, "It's fun to dress up and have my husband tell me how beautiful I look."

Role models: Fun-loving friends with a healthy perspective on beauty are just as important to the woman who has been overly concerned with looks. Pat, the woman in Chapter 2 who learned as a child to use attractiveness as a tool, says, "When I became a Christian at the age of thirty-three, there was a big turnaround in my feelings about my appearance. I was more relaxed when I went to parties and didn't worry about having the best outfit. Christ really changed my perspective. My daughter thought I looked dowdy."

Christ changed Pat's perspective partly through the example of His followers: "My Christian friends and I were less concerned about our weight. It was a tremendous feeling to be with people and not worry about clothes. I could really get into other people. I found myself less concerned with how people responded to me, and more concerned with how I responded to them."

> "Don't blame me for the way I look— I was drawn this way."
> —Jessica Rabbit, *Who Framed Roger Rabbit?*

Like anyone joining a new community, Pat took her cues for appropriate behavior from the Christians around her. That included what was an appropriate attitude toward appearance. "I remember going to my first Christian retreat," she told us. "I didn't know what to wear. I cut my nails and removed the red polish. When we got there, I saw that the speaker's wife was beautifully dressed and had long, polished nails. I thought, 'Why did I cut my nails?'" What would happen if we all got dressed for church asking ourselves what kind of example we want to set for new Christians?

Significant men: We have emphasized what women can do for women, but of course the men in our lives are just as important. Pat told us that when she first started dating her husband, Jerry, her looks were the first thing that attracted him to her. "Jerry was a star athlete and always went with pretty girls. I was like a prize on his arm." But as Pat has matured spiritually, so has Jerry. Because her looks aren't of great concern to him anymore, she finds it easier to relax about them.

Ellen Lambert found that when she doubted her own continued beauty after losing a breast, it made all the difference to have her mate reassure her. At those vulnerable moments, we may need to see ourselves through a loved one's eyes before we can see ourselves as God sees us.

CHANGING THE WORLD

We live in a world biased against people who are large, aging, blemished, or poorly dressed. Whether caused by instincts wired into the human animal or by cultural conditioning, that bias has existed for a long time and, if anything, is increasing. Call it instinct or call it sin: most people prefer to live, work, and sleep with women who look young, healthy, and fertile.

What can we do about this? We could wring our hands, lamenting that we are victims of society or male oppression. We could campaign for equal rights for the circumferentially gifted or lobby against discrimination based on race, creed, color, gender, size, shape, or symmetry. Some women use the term *lookism* to describe the prejudice they fight. We could form a political action committee to fight this social cancer.

There might turn out to be some wisdom in this, but first let us recognize with Jesus that all politics is local: it starts with the human heart and works outward. If our goal in life is to make men mature enough to see past their hormones, or to stamp out the beauty industry's greed, we may be frustrated by our inability to control what men or corporations do. But if over time we allow ourselves to be loved until we can change how we respond when we look at ourselves in the mirror, we will have made a difference for one person. And as we adjust the messages we send our daughters, our friends, our husbands, and other women in ministry and business, we will have mounted a serious challenge to the beauty goddess. We can begin to change the world just by learning to receive love and pass it on to the next woman.

THE GOOD NEWS

Allowing ourselves to be loved won't make us younger, but it will impart hope, whose glow is agelessly attractive. Receiving and giving love won't necessarily make us thinner (unless it helps take our mind off food), but it will feed our soul hunger and make us the kind of persons whom people will be eager to hug. The best news in all this is that a loving person really is attractive. As Mary Anne Tabor understood at six years old, people really do see as beautiful the face of someone who offers them genuine care:

> I knew what pretty was, or what beautiful was, from my own childish perspective. To me, beauty was a sight that made me feel warm inside . . . made me feel happy for no apparent reason. . . . There was a girl in the first grade I thought was so beautiful. Not because she had blue eyes which reminded me of the sky, but because she just made me feel happy when she looked at me and smiled. I had never felt that happy when anyone else looked at me, so I thought she must be the most beautiful person I knew.[6]

Six-year-old Mary Anne saw her schoolmate as beautiful not because of what we would call physical attributes, but because the girl looked at her with the face of love. The girl's smile was just as outward and physical as the color of her eyes, yet the smile was an outward expression of an inward quality of character. The face of a loving person nearly always strikes the beholder as beautiful, unless the beholder is especially soul-blind.

When *New Woman* asked readers, "What do you want your wardrobe to say about you?" the number one answer was, "Friendly." A smile ranked at the top of the list of physical traits essential to attractiveness.[7]

Pastor Stan Thornburg told us that men often agree with women in their assessment of themselves. He says women who aren't model-gorgeous but like themselves and present themselves as potential persons to be cherished and loved tend to get more respect from men than women who are very attractive but put themselves down. In counseling couples, Stan has found that when a woman complains about some aspect of herself, her husband picks up on it and begins to regard it as a problem. Men don't want to be with a woman who finds herself unattractive. Men, says Stan, want a reason to find a woman attractive if they like her.

So beauty is not just in the eye of the loving beholder; it is also in the face of the one who loves. We are now at a point where we can make sense of the passage in 1 Peter that talks about a gentle and quiet spirit. While to some readers that phrase may conjure up images of mousy and subservient plainness, the truth is far more exhilarating.

A CLOSER LOOK

Who are the people in your life who make you believe in your beauty? If you don't have enough of these people, what can you do about it?

How can you help draw beauty out of someone you know? Does she need a listening ear, a compliment, a Day of Beauty? What action will you take on her behalf?

CHAPTER FIFTEEN

CLEAR MIRRORS

Pride tells us to exploit our beauty to get what we want, or feel ashamed of our ugliness as the proof of our worthlessness. Fear tells us to veil our beauty so we won't draw the envy of other women or the lust of men. But when we choose to become aware of and grieve over our pride, shame, and fear, they lose their grip on us. When we allow ourselves to be loved and invest our energy in loving others, we genuinely grow more beautiful, even as being beautiful becomes less of an obsession. We draw strength from the smiles of loving beholders and begin to smile ourselves, like plants that draw energy from sunlight and photosynthesize it into green leaves. Like the moon, whose beauty is seen only when it reflects light from the invisible sun, we begin to radiate another's light.

The apostle Paul, who by all accounts was under five feet tall and not much to look at,[1] described it like this:

> And all of us, with unveiled faces, seeing the glory of the Lord as though reflected in a mirror, are being transformed into the same image from one degree of glory to another; for this comes from the Lord, the Spirit.[2]

It's as though we look into a mirror, and by the power of the Holy Spirit we cease to see the stressed, aging, bulging body we usually see. Instead, we see the glory of the Lord. And as we continue to focus on that image, we change, more and more resembling it in its glory. The glorious image becomes a truer vision of ourselves than the one we see every day in our clouded mirrors.

Glory is an unfathomable word: God's brilliant, majestic, indescribable beauty. It glowed like a burning cloud when Israel traveled through the wilderness; it shone from Moses' face after he met with God; it manifested in every word and movement of Jesus' sacrificial life, and in His sacrificial death. Glory isn't static, like a model's bland-eyed prettiness. Glory is alive with passionate love.

Glory costs. She who gazes at the face of God until her unveiled face reflects God's glory may not get the husband or the promotion. She may even end up crucified like "the Lord of glory."[3] Not everyone has eyes to see glory. But Paul goes on:

> Therefore we do not lose heart. Though outwardly we are wasting away, yet inwardly we are being renewed day by day. For our light and momentary troubles are achieving for us an eternal glory that far outweighs them all. So we fix our eyes not on what is seen, but on what is unseen. For what is seen is temporary, but what is unseen is eternal.[4]

A GENTLE AND QUIET SPIRIT

When we make the face of God our mirror, rather than constantly comparing ourselves with models and colleagues to see if we measure up, we acquire what the apostle Peter called "a gentle and quiet spirit." But just what did Peter mean when he told women,

> Your beauty should not come from outward adornment, such as braided hair and the wearing of gold jewelry and fine clothes. Instead, it should be that of your inner self, the unfading beauty of a gentle and quiet spirit, which is of great worth in God's sight. For this is the way the holy women of the past who put their hope in God used to make themselves beautiful.[5]

Financial Modesty

Some background will help. The churches who first received Peter's message probably reflected the social divisions that prevailed throughout the Roman world. The vast majority of women were servants, slaves, or manual workers, along with being mothers and wives. They could afford to eat meat only when it was provided free on holidays, and they could afford very little by way of clothing or decoration. They might own two or three plain outfits and a few pieces of cheap jewelry. Their standard of living was roughly equivalent to that of most people in pre-industrial societies today. Outward adornment was definitely not one of their temptations.

One or two percent of the population was far wealthier than the average woman ever dreamed of being. In the church, which was not yet fashionable, there were probably just a few well-to-do women. These wives and daughters of aristocrats and rich businessmen would already have dressed modestly in public in the sense that they covered themselves (no pagan father would have tolerated his daughter being judged as a prostitute by society). However, they were expected to be walking advertisements of their men's wealth and status. Carefully coiffed hair peeked from under demure veils, fabrics were the very best, and jewelry glittered everywhere.

The contrast between rich and poor could not have been more stark. The purpose of all this finery was less to allure men than to compete with the other rich women in flaunting one's father's or husband's wealth. The radiant ones' appearance could only intimidate the low-class women — in fact, out in the world it was supposed to do so. That's how people knew who was important and who was not: by her silks and pearls. But in the church these distinctions undermined the goal of bonding women together as sisters in Christ. Peter had no patience with rich men who wanted to use their wives as status emblems, nor with rich women who wanted to lord it over the poor. He urged women to lay aside their trappings of wealth as a spiritual discipline to train themselves in humility. Their humble appearance would be an outward sign that they considered the other women their full equals.

Paul's instruction was similar:

I also want women to dress modestly, with decency and propriety, not with braided hair or gold or pearls or expensive
clothes, but with good deeds, appropriate for women who
profess to worship God.[6]

Today we may attend churches where everyone is roughly as
affluent as we are. This segregation by income would have annoyed
Peter and Paul, for it encourages the affluent to consider themselves
better than the people on the other side of town. It also encourages
women to dress as advertisements of their husband's status or their
own. Women compete for status in churches today just as they did
1,900 years ago, and a polished appearance that costs more than a
little time and money is often part of the game. While Christians
may decry women who dress immodestly in a sexual sense—in
tight or low-cut outfits—they often admire women who dress
immodestly in the financial sense. We are at much less risk of
tempting men to lust than we are of tempt-
ing other women to envy and shame. If we
want to honor the apostles' instructions,
when we look in the mirror we might be
less concerned with asking, "Do I look too
sexy?" than with asking, "Do I look too
proud?" Humility is an essential element of glory.

> "Beauty is worth just
> what it costs."
> —Professor Robin
> Lakoff

We don't propose to offer a rigid standard of what constitutes
financially immodest dressing. Is $400 the maximum amount that
a godly woman should spend on a complete outfit, or should the
rule be $200, or $800? Is cosmetic surgery financially immodest?
What about jewelry? Rule making like this misses the point that it
is up to every woman to examine herself in the mirror of God's love
and decide what public face she should offer to the world. It is up
to every community of women to help each other sort through this
complex question and cultivate together the habits of humility.

Gentleness

Excessive adornment was the negative that Peter and Paul
wanted to discourage. The positive traits they encouraged were
"good deeds" and "a gentle and quiet spirit." Good deeds stand

in stark contrast to the proud look: less money and time invested in finery and more invested in generosity. The "gentle and quiet spirit" takes more explaining.

There's a funny thing about that Greek word rendered "gentle" or "meek" in English. When commentators define it in the context of 1 Peter 3:4, they say it means something like "not insistent on one's own rights," "not pushy, not selfishly assertive," and "not demanding one's own way."[7] To many women, this sounds like keeping one's mouth shut and being passive. But when the scholars define *praütes* (gentleness, meekness) in the context of the New Testament and the Greek language as a whole, they shade the picture somewhat differently. They use words like,

> benevolent . . . balanced, intelligent, decent outlook in contrast to licentiousness . . . a considerate, thoughtful attitude in legal relationships which was prepared to mitigate the rigours of justice, with its laws and claims, in contrast to the attitude which demands that rights, including one's own, should be upheld at all costs . . . opposed to unbridled anger, harshness, brutality . . . character traits of the noble-minded, wise man who remains meek in the face of insults. . . .[8]

Christ called Himself gentle and humble in this sense.[9] He claimed to be the gentle king foretold by the prophet Zechariah, the king who inaugurated his rule without force or warfare.[10] Paul claimed to be following Christ's example by being meek and gentle in his dealings with stubborn Corinthians.[11] And he repeatedly urged all Christians, women and men, to follow the same example in their dealings both with each other and with outsiders.[12] Peter concurred that gentleness was the best way to draw others to Christ.[13] In short, women are not the only ones who should be more concerned about their responsibilities than their rights. Men, too, should cultivate spirits that bridle their tempers and don't demand their own ways. Peter didn't single out women for a type of behavior that he didn't expect from himself.

Jesus set an example of a gentle and quiet spirit when a soldier hit Him at His illegal trial. Jesus refused to answer the high priest's interrogation because Jewish law required that independent witnesses give testimony of wrongdoing before the accused was required to answer questions. Jesus coolly told the high priest to find some witnesses, and the soldier slapped Him for His impertinence. Jesus then calmly confronted the soldier: "If I said something wrong, testify as to what is wrong. But if I spoke the truth, why did you strike me?"[14] This is how a gentle-spirited person responds to injustice. Jesus' spirit was quiet, but His mouth was not.

Not all bosses and husbands are comfortable around women who speak with this kind of gentle strength. Nor is it easy to acquire Jesus' style of calm assertiveness when threatened. Many of us tend either to become intimidated, lose our voices, and withdraw, or to become angry, lose control over our voices, and attack. Cultivating a gentle spirit requires time and effort in silence alone before God and in sharing grief and joy with others. Slowly but surely, we begin to radiate glory.

Helaine was shopping one day, and a little girl pointed at her and said several times, "Mommy, look at the fat lady." Instead of cringing in shame or lashing out in anger, Helaine went to the child and said, "You know, you're right. I'm probably one of the fattest women you've ever seen. And do you know what? I'm also a mommy and I teach school and I love to swim. What do you like to do in your spare time?" Helaine assured the girl's mother that the child wasn't being rude but simply stating an observation. "Furthermore, by hushing up children . . . you give the impression that there is something unspeakable about fat."[15] Helaine's gentle spirit will go a long way toward helping her deal constructively with her size, whether that involves accepting and embracing it, or seeking ways to change it.

Sandra realized that she and her friends routinely obsessed together about their appearance. "I feel so fat," one friend would say, and another would complain about her thighs. Another would talk about how awful her last haircut was or what a mess her nails were. Putting down their appearance was these women's way of deflecting each other's envy and feeling like comrades: misery loves company, and being uglier-than-thou elicited sympathy rather than jealousy. Bad-mouthing their bodies also enabled them to avoid talking about feelings that lay closer to the bone, such as anxiety over not measuring up at work, or anger at a husband. Sandra decided that in a spirit of gentleness, the next time a friend said, "My stomach is so disgusting," she would say, "I love your body. To me, it's you. And it makes me feel better to know that I'm not the only fabulous woman I know whose waist is bigger than a pencil." Sandra knew that upsetting the status quo like this would draw some flak, but she felt it would be worth it.

Emily's sister got breast implants and kept prodding Emily to do the same. Emily had to cultivate the patience to keep saying things like, "You look terrific, but I like my breasts." To say this honestly without eventually blurting out, "Shut up already! I don't want to be a salt-water bimbo like you!" Emily had to sort out the mixed emotions her sister's words raised in her: defensiveness, shame that maybe her body wasn't okay, envy that her sister now looked better than she did, guilt that she would even contemplate implants for five seconds, fear of the dangerous complications of surgery, concern for her sister's health, judgmentalism about her sister's choice, and the desire to be a godly woman. She sought out friends to help her make sense of it all and received encouragement that her body was indeed okay and her feelings could be embraced by love. Her hard work of awareness, grieving, and receiving love paid off: she found herself on the other side of the canyon with a gentle heart.

QUIETNESS

A quiet spirit is one in which all of those mixed emotions are sorted out, understood, shared with trusted friends, and submitted to a spirit of contentment. The butterflies in our stomachs don't die; we just teach them to fly in formation.

Grief counselors call this stage of grieving "acceptance." When we allow ourselves to be angry and sad over the things that shouldn't be the way they are, we can get to a place of accepting the ones we can't change. There are two kinds of acceptance: one stinks of despair; the other is fragrant with hope. Despair comes when we feel forced to accept that we must do without something we absolutely need for survival, such as love or respect. But contentment and hope bloom when we realize that even without the love and respect we imagine we'd get if we looked the way we'd like, we'll have enough love and respect to thrive on. God loves and respects us, and so do at least a few significant people in our lives.

Acceptance acknowledges that youthful beauty—indeed, all life on this earth—is brief, like the wildflower that delights for a week, then withers.

Charm is deceptive, and beauty is fleeting;
  but a woman who fears the LORD is to be praised.[16]

Notice that the writer of Proverbs 31 does not say, "beauty is wicked" or even "beauty is deceptive." It can be, but it isn't always. What it always is, is fleeting.

Advertisers change models like they change trash bags, throwing out the old ones. Somehow we need to talk about this fact of

> "Only a face lift can make you feel younger."
> —ad for Lift Extrême Nutri-Collagen Concentré[17]

life with our daughters until it sinks in with them and with us. Then we will be able to enjoy the fleeting beauty of youth in the same way we enjoy flowers. We don't get mad or frightened when they fade; we accept that fading is part of the life of flowers. I (Cinny) have come to accept that my youthful beauty is fading as it should be, and I'm encouraged to know that there's plenty of life for me beyond the stage of young womanhood. Accepting what is lets me relax and enjoy what I have.

Quietness includes accepting responsibility for ways in which we've marred our own beauty and letting go of responsibility for things we could never control. For example, a large woman might acknowledge that years of addictive eating and compulsive dieting have left her with extra pounds and the extremely low metabolism of a famine survivor. She may be able to overcome her addictive behaviors, but her body may not shrink much. At the same time, she might accept that she comes from a long line of big women, and there was never anything she could have done about her genes. In Africa she would be a gorgeous prize, but in the West she must learn the delicate art of both grieving and celebrating her body. She might tape a photograph of the Getty Aphrodite or the Venus of Willendorf to her refrigerator to remind herself that in another place and time she would have had to battle vanity.

A woman grieving wrinkles might accept responsibility for the suntans that damaged her skin, but she may also accept the fact that in her family, women wrinkle heavily and early. Bone structure and skin resiliency are largely genetic. She can take comfort in humorist Erma Bombeck's words about her mother:

> She is the most beautiful woman I have ever seen. She should be. She's been working on that face and body for more than sixty years. The process for that kind of beauty can't be rushed.
>
> The wrinkles in the face have been earned . . . one at a time. The stubborn ones around the lips that deepened with every "No." The thin ones on the forehead that mysteriously appeared when the first child was born.[18]

Bombeck wrote this about her own mastectomy:

> We did a lot of thinking about scars that summer . . . emotional and physical. At one time we had looked upon them as disfigurements in an otherwise perfect body. Now they represented detours in a road that spanned the distance between sick and well. They were no longer stigmas, but badges of courage and survival.[19]

Jesus wears scars in His resurrected body as badges of courage—as well as of compassion, His willingness to suffer with and for His people. A C-section scar that marks the day when a woman gave life to a child probably looks a bit like the scar Jesus carries in His side from the day He gave us eternal life.

As with Jesus, our acceptance will be not passive, but gutsy, realistic, and active—a conscious weighing of the pros and cons of each decision, and a willingness to pay the price for our choices. Consider the relatively minor dilemma of a woman with abundant body hair and sensitive skin. Our culture regards body hair as unfeminine and consequently ugly (in many cultures, hair on women's bodies is perfectly acceptable). So when this woman plans a trip to the beach or swimming pool, she faces a decision. In the past she has tried chemical depilatories on her upper thighs; they irritated her skin and failed to remove hair as coarse as hers. Shaving was also painful in that area. Now she is left with two alternatives: a bikini wax, or nothing. Waxing costs $50 and a half-hour of excruciating agony. Not waxing costs social disdain. The "right" choice is not obvious; she has to choose her cost.

Some women would choose the wax automatically; they claim not to mind waxing. Chinese women, likewise, never hesitated to endure bound feet, and Victorian women corseted themselves without blinking. Pain? What pain? Other women really don't care what anybody thinks; their choice is also easy. Let people stare!

However, the real woman who told us this story cared about the money, the pain, and the opinions of those around her. Her choice required grieving that she lived in a culture where such things matter; she even let herself feel angry. Then she began to ask herself questions: How much am I willing to do to make other people comfortable with my appearance? Am I willing to spend $40 on a swimsuit deemed appropriate by my culture? Am I willing to shave my legs and underarms? Am I willing to undergo a bikini wax? Am I willing to have liposuction to smooth out my upper thighs? How much disapproval am I willing to endure, and for what reasons? Am I being worldly here, or culturally sensitive?

There would be pain either way, but because she took the time to grieve this evidence of a far-from-perfect world, she was able to stand on her two feet like a woman and choose her pain. This refusal to deny the harsh realities of the beauty issue enabled her to accept what she could not change without feeling like a victim, make a choice for which she respected herself, and move on. A woman with a quiet spirit doesn't let frustrations like these accumulate in her soul and sap her joy.

We will do her a favor if, as her friends, we are willing to listen to her process of grieving, including the rage or whimpering, without telling her not to be such a crybaby or making her decision for her. We will also be doing ourselves a favor because then she will be more likely to be similarly helpful when we have choices of our own to make. How much should I spend on my wardrobe? Should I color my hair? Should I get only a lumpectomy and hope my breast can be saved? Am I overeating? How much fussing with my looks should I do if I want to get married?

One or two Bible verses will not suffice to answer such questions; we need the whole Bible, plus the Holy Spirit and the community of God's people, to tackle them well.

THE PUBLIC FACE

The woman with a gentle and quiet spirit knows she can't go out among just anybody without her public face (and public thighs). But instead of constructing a public face entirely from what others tell her to be, and then believing that's who she really is, a wise woman consciously selects the elements of her public face and knows it's a mask. She has done the hard work of finding out who God made her to be, and she creates a public face that expresses appropriate parts of that. She may have a different face for different situations: work versus church, for example.

In making decisions about her public face, the gentle and quiet woman sorts through her motives. Am I choosing this in order to manipulate others and get what I want without having to depend on God? Or is this a realistic concession to life in a fallen world? Such discernment isn't easy, and the right answers vary from woman to woman.

For instance, I (Karen) have settled on two lipsticks, two shades of blush, and two eyeshadows—one simple warm look and one cool look, depending upon what I'm wearing. I don't follow the makeup fashions; they don't interest me. For the most part, I paint my face for business, church, dates, and special occasions, and I go barefaced to the gym, to run errands, or to visit friends. This system works for me, and I'm flexible about it. But I respect my friend who loves cosmetics parties and new lipstick shades;

she's entirely capable of examining her own heart and making her own decisions. What I most want people to see when they look at me is not whether I'm pretty or plain, but that I'm alive—living, breathing, and capable of love.

I (Cinny) have one basic look that I use all the time. I'm experimenting with going without makeup occasionally, and I find this practice is spiritually healthy for me, like fasting. I feel I have a long way to go in my journey away from obsession with beauty, but like one of the mothers in *The Joy Luck Club*, I can finally say to my daughters in truth, "I see you. I really see you, and I love what I see." To me, those eyes that can finally see my daughters are more important than the face that others see when they look at me.

Elaine, the newscaster, has learned the appropriate appearance for on-air work, but it's not a high priority for her. It gets tedious, she says, to have to think every day about how your hair and makeup looks. And it's hard for others to take seriously someone who walks around the office all day in heavy stage makeup. Elaine told us, "I don't feel concerned to put on my public face all the time. I put my stage makeup on in a small room standing next to the weatherman as he puts on his. It is truly a reality check." I (Cinny) have known Elaine for a long time and have always been impressed with her lack of concern about presenting an image when she's jogging or shopping for groceries.

"I watch myself aging and am more aware of it than other women because I see myself on camera," Elaine added. "I want to keep my face young, but I like aging. I'm proud of my wrinkles, although I don't like the saggy places. A smile does great things for a wrinkly face. I feel that the lines around one's eyes are the signs of wisdom and courage that come with a woman's aging. I am trying, though, to slow down the aging process, particularly around my eyes. The camera tends to make one look tired. I spend money on an expensive eye cream that really makes a difference.

"I've never compared myself to anyone else. I'm pretty secure about my appearance—I look in the mirror and feel that I look acceptable. Of course, I need feedback and affirmation, but when I don't get it, I can give it to myself."

Three women, three approaches to the public face. All are in process and may be making different decisions this time next year, for our public faces tend to evolve as God leads us through different stages in our lives.

For example, Jan realized that while raising small children, she hadn't done much to look like a girl for a long time. Repentence, for her, meant exchanging what her husband called "concentration camp hair," for a more flattering style and starting to polish her nails. Four years later, however, she was about to go to the Dominican Republic with an aid organization and wondered whether she would have time to keep up her nails. As she prayed, she sensed God telling her that the discipline of nail polish had done its work in her — she was now presenting herself to the world much more like a woman and didn't need to fuss with her appearance so much. Simplicity was the watchword for this new season in her life, so she let the nail polish go, grateful that it had done its job. Jan treated her public face not just as a "look" to be arbitrarily adopted and discarded with every passing fashion, but as a significant way to express what God was doing inside her.

Both of us (Cinny and Karen) like wearing bright colors and playing dress-up occasionally. But we're drawn to Kathleen Norris's description of a nun who has chosen, for healthy rather than fearful or shame-based reasons, to put aside such games so she can concentrate on more important matters. Norris, a best-selling poet and latecomer to Christian faith, writes in *The Cloister Walk:*

I once visited a sister who, next to a shelf that held socks, underwear, and a sweater, had all the clothing she owned hung on several pegs: her spare habit and scapular, both made of denim, a simple kerchief she wore as a veil, a long winter cloak and a lightweight one for spring and fall. It took my breath away. "Thank God for the things I do not own," said Teresa of Avila. I could suddenly grasp that not ever having to think about what to wear was freedom, that a drastic stripping down to essentials in one's dress might also be a drastic enrichment of one's ability to focus on more important things.[20]

CLEAR MIRRORS

The public face of a wise woman lovingly offers her soul to the people around her. She is unafraid to let others enjoy the sight of her, whether her beauty is the young woman's splendor of curves and smooth skin or the mature woman's smile and welcoming eyes. She knows that if someone sees her with lust or fails to see her at all, then the problem lies in his clouded eyes, not in her body. The awareness that she carries God's image and reflects God's glory takes her beyond shame and fear into compassion for the blind. The confidence that God's light is in her face leaves no room for pride. Her humility enables her to let her own and others' beauty matter just enough, neither too much nor too little.

> "'I don't believe we were meant to see ourselves,' said Jane. 'He said something about being mirrors enough to see another.'"
> —C. S. Lewis,
> *That Hideous Strength*

None of us attains this wisdom without help. The habit of beholding the glory of God as in a mirror is not just a solitary discipline—we are each other's mirrors, reflecting back to each other the glorious love of Christ. A lonely woman's mirror is clouded by sorrow, but a loved woman sees a truer reflection in the face of those who love her.

To look deeply into the eyes of those who love us is to contemplate the Lord's glory and be transformed by it. May we have the grace to be clear mirrors for one another, making each woman we meet beautiful in the eyes of a loving beholder.

A CLOSER LOOK

Save some extra time when you're dressing for work or church. When you are completely put together, examine yourself in a full-length mirror and in the mirror of God's love. Ask yourself some questions like these: Do I look too proud? Am I trying to impress people? Why do I want to look my best? Or, Am I trying to be invisible? Why don't I want to be seen?

Gather with a group of women with the purpose of being mirrors for each other. Listen to each woman's thoughts and feelings about her appearance, both what it is and what she would like it to be. Wrestle together over how your looks reflect pride, shame, and humility.

Try an affirmation exercise with your group. Ask for a volunteer to be first in the spotlight. Let each of the other group members tell what they think is beautiful about that person. Then ask for another volunteer, until all members have been in the spotlight. If this exercise seems too intimidating, you could tape a sheet of paper to each woman's back, and write your words of encouragement on those sheets. Alternatively, you could bring each other small gifts that symbolize the beauty you see in one another: *You remind me of a bowl of pure, clear water because. . . .*

NOTES

Chapter One: Does Anyone Else Feel This Way?

1. 1 Peter 3:4.
2. Figures for 1972 and 1985 come from Thomas F. Cash, *What Do You See When You Look in the Mirror?* (New York: Bantam Books, 1995), p. 29. Figures for 1995 come from Barbara Hey, "Fat and Loathing," *Allure*, May 1996, p. 144, quoting Cash.
3. Jan Johnson, "Is Fitness Next to Godliness?" *Discipleship Journal*, issue 90, November/December 1995, p. 81.
4. Naomi Wolf, *The Beauty Myth: How Images of Beauty Are Used Against Women* (New York: William Morrow, 1991), p. 52.
5. Daniel S. Hamermesh and Jeff E. Biddle, "Beauty and the Labor Market," *American Economic Review* 84, no. 5 (December 1994): 1174-1194.
6. A. Eagley, M. Makahajani, R. Ashmore, and L. Longo, "What Is Beautiful Is Good but . . . , A Meta-Analytic Review of the Physical Attractiveness Stereotype," *Psychological Bulletin* 110, pp. 109-129, cited in Mary Anne Tabor, "Being Beautiful: A Study on the Psychology of Beauty Based on Experiences of People Who Work in the Beauty Business" (master's thesis, Sonoma State University, 1990), p. 9.
7. Tabor, p. 10.
8. Clinical psychologist Diana Beliard, quoted in Carol Kleiman, "Too Pretty, Too Heavy—It's All Discrimination," *Chicago Tribune*, 22 July 1991.
9. *"Women's Wear Daily,"* September 6, 1996, p. S18. Data is for the companies' 1996 fiscal year.
10. A 1987 ad featuring a man in a clerical collar eating Land O Lakes Country Morning Blend^R. Eating cholesterol is the "sin" of a new religion. Reprinted in Jean Kilbourne, "Still Killing Us Softly: Advertising and the Obsession with Thinness," *Feminist Perspectives on Eating Disorders*, ed. P. Fallon, M. Katzman, and S. Wooley (New York: Guilford Press, 1993).
11. Maribel Morgan, *The Total Woman* (Old Tappan, N.J.: Revell, 1973), p. 92.
12. Morgan, p. 92.
13. Morgan, pp. 92-93.

14. Morgan, p. 95.
15. Morgan, p. 97.
16. Willard F. Harley, Jr., *His Needs, Her Needs: How to Affair-Proof Your Marriage* (Grand Rapids, Mich.: Revell, 1986, 1994), p. 106.
17. Harley, pp. 107-108.
18. Harley, p. 109.
19. Harley, pp. 109-114.
20. Harley, p. 116.
21. Helena Rubinstein, *My Life for Beauty* quoted in playbill for the Arena Stage production of *The Waiting Room* by Lisa Loomer, December 1995, p. 8.
22. Hopkins, Fischette, and Fadhl stories all cited in Kleiman.
23. "A Stunning Blow-Dry for the Prosecution," *People*, 24 April 1995, p. 104.
24. Laura C. Smith, "Teasing the First Lady," *People*, 3 June 1996, p. 41.
25. 1 Corinthians 13:12, NASB; see also the footnote to the verse.

Chapter Two: The Face of Love

1. Nancy Friday, *The Power of Beauty* (New York: HarperCollins, 1996), p. 20; see also her extensive footnotes on p. 554.
2. Naomi Wolf, *The Beauty Myth: How Images of Beauty Are Used Against Women* (New York: William Morrow, 1991), p. 61.
3. Genesis 29:17-18.
4. Genesis 29:31.
5. Genesis 29:32.
6. Genesis 29:33.
7. Susan Harter, "Causes and Consequences of Low Self-Esteem in Children and Adolescents," in *Self-Esteem: The Puzzle of Low Self-Regard*, ed. R. F. Baumeister (New York: Plenum, 1993), pp. 95-96; quoted in Friday, pp. 223-224.
8. Dr. Nancy Poland, quoted in Friday, pp. 15, 19.
9. Friday, p. 1.
10. Friday, p. 5.
11. Friday, p. 8.
12. Ellen Zetzel Lambert, *The Face of Love* (Boston: Beacon Press, 1995), p. xi.
13. Lambert, pp. 5-6.
14. Lambert, pp. 6-7.
15. Lambert, p. 7.
16. Lambert, p. 11.
17. Ad for Barbie Collectibles™, *Ladies' Home Journal*, June 1996.
18. Mary Anne Tabor, "Being Beautiful: A Study on the Psychology of Beauty Based on Experiences of People Who Work in the Beauty Business" (master's thesis, Sonoma State University, 1990), p. 15.
19. Tabor, pp. 15-16.

Chapter Three: Respect

1. K. Lenerz et al., "Early Adolescents' Organismic Physical Characteristics and Psychosocial Functioning: Findings from the Pennsylvania Early Adolescent Transitions Study (PEATS)," in *Biological-Psychosocial Interaction in Early Adolescence: A Life-Span Perspective*, ed. Richard M. Lerner and T. T. Fochs (Hillsdale, N.J.: Erlbaum, 1987), pp. 225-247; cited in Thomas F. Cash and Thomas Pruzinsky, eds., *Body Images* (New York: Guilford, 1990), pp. 118-119.
2. Patricia Aburdene and John Naisbitt, *Megatrends for Women* (New York: Villard Books, 1992), p. 203.
3. Aburdene and Naisbitt, p. 203.
4. Aburdene and Naisbitt, p. 203.

5. Aburdene and Naisbitt, p. 203.

6. Nancy Friday, *The Power of Beauty* (New York: HarperCollins, 1996), p. 368; citing Irene Hanson Frieze et al., "Attractiveness and Business Success: Is It More Important for Women or Men?" (paper prepared for the 1989 Academy of Management Meetings, Washington, D.C., August 1989); Irene Hanson Frieze et al., "Perceived and Actual Discrimination in the Salaries of Male and Female Managers" (paper presented at the 1986 Academy of Management Meetings, Chicago); Daniel S. Hamermesh and Jeff E. Biddle, "Beauty and the Labor Market," National Bureau of Economic Research, November 1993.

7. Susan Brownmiller, *Femininity* (New York: Ballantine Books, 1984), p. 86. Interestingly, at that time it was the men who decked themselves out for the status competition; their wives and daughters were afterthoughts. This pattern changed in the nineteenth century.

8. Romans 12:10.

9. Ad in *McCall's*, November 1995.

10. Mary Anne Tabor, "Being Beautiful: A Study on the Psychology of Beauty Based on Experiences of People Who Work in the Beauty Business" (master's thesis, Sonoma State University, 1990), pp. 4-5.

11. Clairol ad for hair coloring featuring supermodel Linda Evangelista in four different hair colors, *Ladies' Home Journal*, November 1995.

12. Lois W. Banner, *American Beauty* (New York: Alfred Knopf, 1983), p. 41.

13. Stacey M. Fabricant and Stephen J. Gould, "Women's Makeup Careers: An Interpretive Study of Color Cosmetic Use and 'Face Value,'" *Journal of Psychology and Marketing* 10, no. 6 (New York: John Wiley & Sons, November/December 1993), p. 537.

14. Fabricant and Gould, p. 537.

15. Fabricant and Gould, p. 540.

16. Fabricant and Gould, p. 544.

17. 1 Corinthians 11:3-16.

18. Angela Bonavoglia, "What's *Ms.* Doing at the Fall Fashion Shows?" *Ms.*, September/October 1995, p. 57.

19. Warren Farrell, *Why Men Are the Way They Are* (New York: Berkeley Books, 1988), p. 19.

Chapter Four: Basic Instinct

1. David M. Buss, *The Evolution of Desire: Strategies of Human Mating* (New York: Basic Books, 1994), p. 4.

2. Buss, p. 54.

3. Buss, p. 54.

4. Buss, p. 53.

5. Elizabeth Weil, "What Men Want," *Mademoiselle*, January 1995, p. 110.

6. Buss, p. 55.

7. Buss, p. 54.

8. Weil, p. 110.

9. Spiegel Holiday 1995 catalog, p. 105.

10. Weil, p. 111.

11. Geoffrey Cowley, "The Biology of Beauty," *Newsweek*, 3 June 1996, pp. 64-65.

12. Buss, p. 56.

13. Weil, pp. 111, 145; compare Buss, p. 57.

14. Buss, pp. 56-57.

15. Cowley, p. 65.

16. Susan Brownmiller, *Femininity* (New York: Ballantine Books, 1984), p. 44.

17. Randy Thornhill as quoted in Cowley, p. 66.

18. Cowley, p. 66.
19. Genesis 2:19.
20. Genesis 2:7.
21. Dallas Willard, *The Spirit of the Disciplines* (San Francisco: HarperSanFrancisco, 1988), pp. 86-87.
22. Isaiah 31:3.
23. Galatians 4:23, NASB.
24. Nicolas Berdyaev, *Freedom and Spirit* (London: Bles, 1935), quoted in Willard, p. 87.
25. Judges 14:1-3.
26. Judges 14:16-17.
27. Judges 16:15.
28. Spiegel Holiday 1995 catalog, p. 104.
29. Romans 8:5-6, NEB.
30. Galatians 6:7-8, NEB.
31. Gary M. Gray, *The American Christian Single: Single Saints, Single Sinners, and a Few of Us in Between* (Enid, Okla.: Christian Singles Press, 1996).
32. Personal interview with Stan Thornburg, 12 July 1996.
33. Personal interview with Dr. Tom Whiteman, 11 July 1996.
34. Buss, pp. 80-81.

Chapter Five: Male Status

1. David M. Buss, *The Evolution of Desire: Strategies of Human Mating* (New York: Basic Books, 1994), p. 24.
2. Buss, pp. 59-60.
3. Ad for Diet Sprite that appeals to the career woman who knows respect goes to the thin.
4. "Eye of the Tiger," *People*, 24 June 1996, pp. 90, 92.
5. Jane R. Hirschmann and Carol H. Munter, *When Women Stop Hating Their Bodies* (New York: Ballantine Books, 1995), p. 310.
6. Geoffrey Cowley, "The Biology of Beauty," *Newsweek*, 3 June 1996, p. 65.
7. Guerlain ad, Macy's, June 1996.
8. "The Dark Side: There Is No Safe Way to Tan," *Philadelphia Inquirer*, 28 May 1995.
9. Actually, until the 1960s women continued to covet a tanned look in the summer and a pearly pallor in the winter.
10. Susan Brownmiller, *Femininity* (New York: Ballantine Books, 1984), p. 72.
11. Toni Morrison, *Song of Solomon* (New York: Alfred Knopf, 1977), p. 315.
12. Morrison, p. 316.
13. Brownmiller, p. 71.
14. *Ebony*, October 1996.
15. Esther 1:4.
16. Esther 1:11.
17. Macy's ad, June 1996.
18. Nancy Friday, *The Power of Beauty* (New York: HarperCollins, 1996), p. 174.
19. Willard F. Harley, Jr., *His Needs, Her Needs: How to Affair-Proof Your Marriage* (Grand Rapids, Mich.: Revell, 1986, 1994), p. 109.

Chapter Six: Symbols of Lost Paradise

1. Genesis 2:7.
2. Genesis 1:26.
3. Hans Urs Von Balthasar, *The Glory of the Lord*, vol. 6, *Theology: The Old Covenant*, trans. Brian McNeil, C.R.V., and Erasmo Leiva-Merikakis, ed. John Riches (Edinburgh: T & T Clark, 1991), p. 89. This same idea that "image" refers to a sculpture and a symbol of God's presence on earth occurs in many commentaries, such as

Gerhard Von Rad, *Genesis*, rev. ed. (Philadelphia: Westminster, 1972), p. 58; and Claus Westermann, *Genesis 1–11*, trans. John J. Scullion (Minneapolis: Augsburg, 1984), p. 146.

4. Genesis 1:26.

5. Genesis 2:15.

6. Mary Anne Tabor, "Being Beautiful: A Study on the Psychology of Beauty Based on Experiences of People Who Work in the Beauty Business" (master's thesis, Sonoma State University, 1990), p. 79.

7. Genesis 2:7.

8. Westermann, p. 150, says, "The Old Testament knows nothing at all of the separation of a person's spiritual and corporeal components; it sees the person as a whole."

9. 1 Corinthians 15:35-36,42-45.

10. Luke 24:36-43, John 20:19.

11. 2 Corinthians 5:1-4.

12. 1 Corinthians 6:15.

13. 1 Corinthians 6:19.

14. Ellen Zetzel Lambert, *The Face of Love* (Boston: Beacon Press, 1995), p. 169.

15. Lambert, p. 169.

16. Betty Rollins, *First, You Cry* (New York: New American Library, 1977), p. 146; quoted in Lambert, p. 172.

17. Lambert, p. 172.

18. Irenaeus, *The Demonstration of the Apostolic Preaching*, chapter 11, quoted in Von Balthasar, vol. 2, p. 74; emphasis ours. Compare Irenaeus's book *Against Heresies*, 5.6.1, 5.16.1.

19. Colossians 1:15.

20. John 1:14.

21. Carolyn Warner, *The Last Word: A Treasury of Women's Quotes* (Englewood Cliffs, N.J.: Prentice Hall, 1992), p. 22.

22. Ezekiel 28:17.

23. Interestingly, even some men who don't believe in Christ recognize that their perceptions of real women are shaped by "those larger-than-life shadowy female figures who inhabit our imaginations, inform our emotions, and indirectly give shape to many of our actions"; Sam Keen, *Fire in the Belly* (New York: Bantam Books, 1991), p. 13. Keen goes on to describe this imaginary woman in his mind: "She is the Garden of Eden from which we are exiled and the paradise for which our bodies long," p. 15. Keen, of course, views the exile from Eden as a metaphor rather than an actual past event.

24. *People*, 20 November 1995.

25. C. S. Lewis, *Perelandra* (New York: Macmillan, 1944, 1968), p. 54.

26. Lewis, p. 56.

27. Lewis, p. 63.

28. Lewis, p. 64.

29. Lewis, pp. 54-55.

30. Lewis, pp. 64-65.

31. Ad for Lee Jeans, *New Woman*, May 1996.

32. Robert M. Schindler and Morris B. Holbrook, "Critical Periods in the Development of Men's and Women's Tastes in Personal Appearance," *Journal of Psychology and Marketing* 10, no. 6 (November/December 1993): p. 551.

33. Schindler and Holbrook, p. 561.

34. Warner, p. 20.

35. Song of Songs 6:4.

36. Song of Songs 4:1,3,5.

37. Song of Songs 6:2.

38. Song of Songs 5:1.
39. Von Balthasar, vol. 6, p. 133.
40. Revelation 21:2.

Chapter Seven: The Goddess of Beauty
 1. Warren Farrell, *Why Men Are the Way They Are* (New York: Berkeley Books, 1988),
    p. 19.
 2. Exodus 20:3-4.
 3. Gerald May, *Addiction and Grace* (San Francisco: HarperSanFrancisco, 1988), p. 13.
 4. Romans 1:21-23.
 5. *The Oxford American Dictionary* (New York: Oxford University Press, 1980),
    p. 572.
 6. Quoted by Nina Teischels, *Morning Edition*, National Public Radio, 20 June 1996.
    One-third of Avon's current new business is in Latin America, while India, China,
    and Russia are also growing markets. Selling cosmetics is a respectable way for a
    woman to earn twice what a man can earn through manual labor.
 7. *The Iliad of Homer*, trans. by Richmond Lattimore (Chicago: University of Chicago
    Press, 1951), book 3, lines 156-157.
 8. Aphrodite was sometimes called Cythera because she supposedly came to life near
    that island. This quotation is from "To Aphrodite," in *The Homeric Hymns*, trans.
    Thelma Sargent (New York: W. W. Norton, 1973), no. 6:54, quoted in Ronald
    Schenk, *The Soul of Beauty: A Psychological Investigation of Appearance* (Cranbury,
    N.J.: Associated University Presses, 1992), p. 37.
 9. Nancy Qualls-Corbett, *The Sacred Prostitute: Eternal Aspect of the Feminine* (Toronto:
    Inner City Books, 1988), pp. 57-58.
10. Schenk, pp. 37-38.
11. Romans 1:25.
12. F. F. Bruce, *New Testament History* (New York: Doubleday, 1979), p. 314.
13. Qualls-Corbett, pp. 23-24.
14. "While turning the pages of a pornographic magazine, while in bed with a prosti-
    tute, or when having multiple affairs, the sex addict feels that his or her relationships
    are working and fulfilling. But these relationships are really self-made, seemingly safe
    fantasies structured to be what the addict wants them to be. The addict believes in
    the illusion of control because he or she controls the illusion. 'The centerfold will be
    everything I want her or him to be.' 'The people I'm having affairs with will be coop-
    erative and make me feel great.'" Harry W. Schaumburg, *False Intimacy* (Colorado
    Springs, Colo.: NavPress, 1992), p. 28.
15. Guerlain ad, Macy's, June 1996.
16. Naomi Wolf, *The Beauty Myth: How Images of Beauty Are Used Against Women* (New
    York: William Morrow, 1991), p. 91.
17. "The Famine Within," produced, directed, and written by Katherine Gildad, Kendor
    Productions, Ontario, Canada, aired on WHYY in Philadelphia, 24 October 1994.
18. Bernice Kanner, "What It's Really Like to Be a Top Model," *Mademoiselle*, January
    1995, pp. 103-104.
19. "Mission Impossible," *People*, 3 June 1996, p. 73. Michelle runs the casting agency
    Body Doubles and Parts. She says 85 percent of body doubles have breast implants.
20. M. G. Lord, *Forever Barbie* (New York: William Morrow, 1994), p. 6.
21. Lord, p. 7.
22. Lord, p. 26.
23. Lord, p. 27.
24. Lord, p. 137.
25. Lord, p. 42.
26. Lord, p. 9.

27. Lord, pp. 4, 14, 75.
28. "Mission Impossible," p. 71.
29. Lord, p. 78.
30. Denise Cowie, "Barbie's Her Baby," *Philadelphia Inquirer*, 27 November 1994, pp. H1, H11.
31. Susan J. Douglas, *Where the Girls Are: Growing Up Female in the Mass Media* (New York: Times Books, 1994), pp. 28-29.
32. Douglas, p. 296.
33. Douglas, p. 296.

Chapter Eight: Age, Fat, and Other Sins

1. James Kaplan, "Isabella Unbound," *New Woman*, June 1994, p. 24.
2. Mary Anne Tabor, "Being Beautiful: A Study on the Psychology of Beauty Based on Experiences of People Who Work in the Beauty Business" (master's thesis, Sonoma State University, 1990), pp. 55-56.
3. Tabor, p. 56.
4. Tabor, pp. 57-59.
5. Naomi Wolf, *The Beauty Myth: How Images of Beauty Are Used Against Women* (New York: William Morrow, 1991), p. 55.
6. Danette Carol McEntee, "The Effects of Marital Status on Women's Feelings of Attractiveness, Subjective Age Identity, and Fears of Aging" (master's thesis, Radford University, 1993).
7. P. K. Kim, *Serving the Elderly: Skills for Practice* (New York: Aldine De Gruyter, 1991).
8. J. Greg Getz and Hanne K. Klein, "The Frosting of the American Woman," *Ideals of Feminine Beauty* (Westport, Conn.: Greenwood Press, 1994).
9. Mary Pipher, *Reviving Ophelia: Saving the Selves of Adolescent Girls* (New York: Ballantine Books, 1994), pp. 54-55.
10. "Mission Impossible," *People*, 3 June 1996, p. 71.
11. Pipher, p. 36.
12. Pipher, p. 55.
13. Anne Conover Heller and Maura Rhodes, "Is Your Daughter at Risk for an Eating Disorder?" *McCall's*, November 1994, p. 95.
14. Pipher, p. 170.
15. Pipher, p. 170.
16. Pipher, p. 170.
17. Michelle Stacey, "The Real Waif Look," *Elle*, May 1995, p. 115.
18. Stacey, p. 115.
19. Johann Kinzl, Christian Traweger, Verena Guenther, and Wilfried Biebl, *Family Background and Sexual Abuse Associated with Eating Disorders, American Journal of Psychiatry*, August 1994, vol. 151 [8], pp. 1127-1131; Teresa Hastings and Jeffrey Kern, *Relationships Between Bulimia, Childhood Sexual Abuse, and Family Environment, International Journal of Eating Disorders*, March 1994, vol. 15 [2], pp. 103-111.
20. "Mission Impossible," p. 65. Silverstone's director in *Batman and Robin*, Joel Schumacher, said, "The news coverage was outrageous, disgusting, judgmental, and cruel. What did this child do? Have a couple of pizzas?" Another source told us Silverstone gained 30 pounds; does it matter?
21. Jane R. Hirschmann and Carol H. Munter, *When Women Stop Hating Their Bodies* (New York: Ballantine Books, 1995), p. 13.
22. Jean Kilbourne, "Still Killing Us Softly: Advertising and the Obsession with Thinness," *Feminist Perspectives on Eating Disorders*, ed. P. Fallon, M. Katzman, and S. Wooley (New York: Guilford Press, 1993), p. 7.

23. Galatians 5:23.
24. C. S. Lewis, *The Screwtape Letters* (New York: Bantam, 1982), p. 49.
25. Pipher, p. 184.
26. Galatians 3:2-3.
27. Galatians 6:1-3, NRSV.
28. Lisa Brandt, Hamilton, Ohio, "Mail," *People*, 12 February 1996, p. 8. "How the Stars Fight Fat" ran in *People*, 22 January 1996.
29. Reported on "Is Breast Size the Measure of a Woman?" *20/20*, 26 April 1996.
30. *20/20*, 26 April 1996.
31. *20/20*, 26 April 1996.
32. Comment from a man to a woman named Veronica, who was interviewed on *20/20*, 26 April 1996.
33. Debra Evans has compiled a hair-raising list of surgical complications in *Beauty and the Best*, (Colorado Springs: Focus on the Family, 1993), p. 100.
34. M. G. Lord, *Forever Barbie* (New York: William Morrow, 1994), p. 244.
35. Lord, p. 238.
36. Joyce D. Nash, "Plastic Surgery: When Beauty Hurts: The Truth About Cosmetic Surgery," *Healthline* 13, no. 8 (November 1994): 8.
37. The American Academy of Plastic Surgery, cited in Doug Podolsky and Betsy Streisand, *The Price of Vanity: Cosmetic Surgery's New Risk, U.S. News and World Report*, October 14, 1996, p. 79.
38. Lord, p. 249.
39. Lord, p. 250.
40. Lord, p. 250.
41. "Go Curvy!: The Right Inches/The Right Places," *Mademoiselle*, January 1988, p. 108; quoted in Susan Faludi, *Backlash* (New York: Crown, 1991), p. 217.

Chapter Nine: Pride

1. Philippians 2:3-4.
2. 1 Corinthians 6:20.
3. 2 Kings 9:30.
4. Ezekiel 28:17.
5. Ezekiel 16:7.
6. Ezekiel 16:9-17,25.
7. Ezekiel 16:32-34.
8. Isaiah 3:16-24.
9. Ezekiel 16:49.
10. *Ladies' Home Journal*, June 1996.
11. Marina Rust, "Keeping Up Appearances," *Vogue*, November 1994, p. 260.
12. Nancy Friday, *The Power of Beauty* (New York: HarperCollins, 1996), p. 111.
13. Friday, p. 82.
14. Friday, p. 307.
15. Friday, p. 487.
16. Friday, p. 23.
17. Nancy Baker, *The Beauty Trap* (New York: Franklin Watts, 1984), p. 16; Susan Brownmiller, *Femininity* (New York: Ballantine Books, 1984), p. 35.
18. Michelle Stacey, "The Real Waif Look," *Elle* 10, no. 9 (May 1995): 114-115.
19. Judith Mandelbaum-Schmid, "Coming into Her Own," *Cooking Light*, March 1996, pp. 32-34.
20. Mandelbaum-Schmid, p. 34.
21. Ad as reprinted in Jean Kilbourne, "Still Killing Us Softly: Advertising and the Obsession with Thinness," in *Feminist Perspectives on Eating Disorders*, ed. P. Fallon, M. Katzman, and S. Wooley (New York: Guilford Press, 1993).

22. Mary Pipher, *Reviving Ophelia: Saving the Selves of Adolescent Girls* (New York: Ballantine Books, 1994), pp. 68-69.
23. Esther 4:16.

Chapter Ten: Competition
 1. 1 Corinthians 12:26.
 2. Ellen Zetzel Lambert, *The Face of Love* (Boston: Beacon Press, 1995), p. 20.
 3. Naomi Wolf, *The Beauty Myth: How Images of Beauty Are Used Against Women* (New York: William Morrow, 1991), p. 75.
 4. 1995 National Fluid Milk Processor Promotion Board.
 5. Genesis 29:17-18,30, NASB.
 6. Genesis 30:1-2.
 7. Genesis 30:8.
 8. Wolf, p. 75.
 9. Christie R. Brown, "Look at My Ugly Face: The Cost of Beauty," playbill for the Arena Stage production of *The Waiting Room* by Lisa Loomer.
10. Nancy Baker, *The Beauty Trap*, (New York: Franklin Watts, 1984), p. 16.
11. As quoted in Baker, p. 19.
12. Baker, p. 20.
13. As quoted in Baker, pp. 20-21.
14. Mary Pipher, *Reviving Ophelia: Saving the Selves of Adolescent Girls* (New York: Ballantine Books, 1994), pp. 103, 105.
15. Jane R. Hirschmann and Carol H. Munter, *When Women Stop Hating Their Bodies* (New York: Ballantine Books, 1995), p. 256.
16. Hirschmann and Munter, pp. 11-12.
17. Pipher, p. 105.
18. Susan J. Douglas, *Where the Girls Are: Growing Up Female in the Mass Media* (New York: Times Books, 1994), p. 295.
19. Hirschmann and Munter, p. 16.

Chapter Eleven: When Men Worship Beauty
 1. *Washington Post*, 26 December 1995, quoting the *New York Times*.
 2. Warren Farrell, *Why Men Are the Way They Are* (New York: Berkeley Books, 1988), p. 110.
 3. Leslie J. Friedman, *Sex Role Stereotyping in the Mass Media: An Annotated Bibliography* (New York: Garland, 1977); compare Farrell, p. 111.
 4. Harry W. Schaumburg, *False Intimacy* (Colorado Springs, Colo.: NavPress, 1992), p. 24.
 5. C. S. Lewis, *That Hideous Strength* (New York: Macmillan, 1946, 1968), p. 46.
 6. James 1:14.
 7. Farrell, p. 129, emphasis Farrell's.
 8. Ellen Zetzel Lambert, *The Face of Love* (Boston: Beacon Press, 1995), p. 20.
 9. As quoted in Irene Lacher, "The Starlets Next Door," *Los Angeles Times Calendar*, 9 June 1996, p. 9.
10. Letter from Chris Knippers, 29 July 1996.
11. John Berger, *Ways of Seeing* (London: Penguin Books, 1988), p. 47; quoted in Naomi Wolf, *The Beauty Myth: How Images of Beauty Are Used Against Women* (New York: William Morrow, 1991), p. 58.
12. Sara Halprin, *Look at My Ugly Face: Myths and Musings on Beauty and Other Perilous Obsessions with Women's Appearance* (New York: Viking, 1995), p. 63.
13. Penelope Green, "Image Boosters," *Elle*, December 1995, p. 116.
14. Sharlene Hesse-Biber, *Am I Thin Enough Yet? The Cult of Thinness and the Commercialization of Identity* (New York: Oxford University Press, 1992), page 67.

15. 1 Kings 11:3.
16. Reported by Dr. Tom Whiteman, personal interview.
17. As quoted in Susan J. Douglas, *Where the Girls Are: Growing Up Female in the Mass Media* (New York: Times Books, 1994), p. 259.
18. Schaumburg, p. 27. Compare Timothy Beneke, *Men on Rape*, quoted in Nancy Baker, *The Beauty Trap* (New York: Franklin Watts, 1984), pp. 44-45.
19. Mary Pipher, *Reviving Ophelia: Saving the Selves of Adolescent Girls* (New York: Ballantine Books, 1994), pp. 69-70.
20. 2 Samuel 11:1.
21. 2 Samuel 11:2-3.
22. Genesis 12:10-20, 20:1-18, 26:7-11.
23. 2 Samuel 13:1-20.
24. Dr. Tom Whiteman, personal interview.

Chapter Twelve: Beauty Veiled
 1. See Chadwick's introduction to Saint Augustine's *Confessions*, trans. Henry Chadwick (New York: Oxford University Press, 1991), p. xvii.
 2. John Chrysostom, "The True Adornment of Women," *Baptismal Instructions*, First Instruction, Article 37 (Westminster, Md.: Newman Press), p. 38.
 3. Nancy Baker, *The Beauty Trap* (New York: Franklin Watts, 1984), p. 14.
 4. Ambrose, *Hexameron*, 6.7.42, quoted in Peter Brown, *Augustine of Hippo* (Berkeley and Los Angeles: University of California Press, 1967), p. 84.
 5. Ambrose, quoted in Brown, p. 83.
 6. Ambrose, "To the Virgins," chapter 10, paragraphs 55-56, *Nicene and Post-Nicene Fathers of the Christian Church*, vol. 10, ed. Philip Schaff and Henry Wace (Grand Rapids, Mich.: Eerdmans, 1955), p. 372.
 7. Augustine, *Commentary on the Gospel of John*, 23:10, cited in Patrick Sherry, *Spirit and Beauty* (New York: Oxford University Press), 1992, p. 142.
 8. Augustine, *Confessions*, 10.27.38, translated by Henry Chadwick, p. 201.
 9. Augustine, *On the True Religion*, 54, quoted in Hans Urs Von Balthasar, *The Glory of the Lord*, vol. 2, *Studies in Theological Style: Clerical Styles*, trans. Andrew Louth, Francis McDonagh, and Brian McNeil, C.R.V., ed. John Riches (Edinburgh: T & T Clark, 1984), p. 100. Compare *Confessions*, 10.6.9, p. 183.
10. Thomas Merton, *The Ways of the Christian Mystics* (Boston: Shambhala, 1961, 1993), p. 64. Merton is paraphrasing Ambrose's sermon "On the Education of a Virgin."
11. *The Letters of Augustine* number 243, line 10, quoted in Brown, p. 63.
12. Judy Prouty, "Before and After the Fall," *Los Angeles Times Magazine*, 25 August 1996.
13. Edmund Burke, *A Philosophical Enquiry into the Origin of our Ideas of the Sublime and the Beautiful* (1757) (Notre Dame: University of Notre Dame Press, 1978), p. 106, quoted in Ronald Schenk, *The Soul of Beauty: A Psychological Investigation of Appearance* (Cranbury, N.J.: Associated University Presses, 1992), p. 105.
14. Burke, p. 116, quoted in Schenk, p. 105, italics Schenk's.
15. Burke, p. 115, quoted in Schenk, p. 105, italics Schenk's.

Chapter Thirteen: Honesty
 1. Susan J. Douglas, *Where the Girls Are: Growing Up Female in the Mass Media* (New York: Times Books, 1994), p. 259.
 2. Nancy Groom, *Heart to Heart About Men* (Colorado Springs, Colo.: NavPress, 1995), pp. 97, 103.
 3. Ecclesiastes 7:2-4.
 4. Philippians 4:4.

5. Matthew 26:38.
6. As quoted in "Mission Impossible," *People*, 3 June 1996, p. 73.
7. Mary Anne Tabor, "Being Beautiful: A Study on the Psychology of Beauty Based on Experiences of People Who Work in the Beauty Business" (master's thesis, Sonoma State University, 1990), p. 101.
8. Matthew 6:17.
9. Psalm 22:1.
10. Psalm 129:1-2.
11. Psalm 131:2.
12. Jane R. Hirschmann and Carol H. Munter, *When Women Stop Hating Their Bodies* (New York: Ballantine Books, 1995), pp. 71, 78, italics theirs.
13. *People*, 20 November 1995.
14. Psalm 77:8-9.
15. Genesis 32:22-32.
16. Matthew 10:16.
17. Psalm 37:7-8.
18. Dan B. Allender and Tremper Longman III, *The Cry of the Soul* (Colorado Springs, Colo.: NavPress, 1994), p. 73.
19. Craig Barnes, *Yearning* (Westmont, Ill.: InterVarsity Press, 1992), p. 17-18.
20. Barnes, p. 19.
21. Barnes, pp. 30-31.

Chapter Fourteen: Loving and Being Loved
1. Isaiah 62:2-5.
2. *Allure*, December 1995.
3. Mary Anne Tabor, "Being Beautiful: A Study on the Psychology of Beauty Based on Experiences of People Who Work in the Beauty Business" (master's thesis, Sonoma State University, 1990), pp. 45-46.
4. Philippians 2:1-5.
5. Romans 12:15.
6. Tabor, p. 15.
7. "A Softer, Kinder You," *New Woman*, May 1996, p. 32.

Chapter Fifteen: Clear Mirrors
1. 2 Corinthians 10:10.
2. 2 Corinthians 3:18, NRSV.
3. 1 Corinthians 2:8.
4. 2 Corinthians 4:16-18.
5. 1 Peter 3:3-5.
6. 1 Timothy 2:9-10.
7. Wayne Grudem, *1 Peter* (Grand Rapids, Mich.: Eerdmans, 1988), p. 140.
8. W. Bauder, "Humility, Meekness," *The New International Dictionary of New Testament Theology*, ed. Colin Brown, vol. 2 (Grand Rapids, Mich.: Zondervan, 1976, 1986), pp. 256-259.
9. Matthew 11:29.
10. Matthew 21:5.
11. 2 Corinthians 10:1.
12. Galatians 5:23, 6:1; Philippians 4:5.
13. 1 Peter 3:15.
14. John 18:23.
15. Jane R. Hirschmann and Carol H. Munter, *When Women Stop Hating Their Bodies* (New York: Ballantine Books, 1995), p. 301.
16. Proverbs 31:30.

17. Susan J. Douglas, *Where the Girls Are: Growing Up Female in the Mass Media* (New York: Times Books, 1994), center photo.
18. Erma Bombeck, "Beauty," *If Life Is a Bowl of Cherries, What Am I Doing in the Pits*(New York: McGraw-Hill, 1978), p. 193.
19. Erma Bombeck, *A Marriage Made in Heaven or Too Tired for an Affair* (New York: HarperCollins, 1993), p. 246.
20. Kathleen Norris, *The Cloister Walk* (New York: Riverhead Books, 1996), pp. 327-328.

AUTHOR

KAREN LEE-THORP is a Senior Editor for NavPress, responsible for Pilgrimage small group resources. She was editor for the LIFECHANGE Bible study series and is the author of many study guides. She writes for *EdgeTV*, a video magazine for adolescents, and has been published in *Christianity Today*, *Discipleship Journal*, *The Mars Hill Review*, and *Clarity*. Her books include *The Story of Stories* and *A Compact Guide to the Christian Life*. She holds a B.A. in history from Yale University. Karen lives in Pasadena, California.

CYNTHIA HICKS, "Cinny," is the coauthor of the *Feminine Journey* with her husband, Robert and has coauthored articles on friendship and marriage, which are published in the book *Husbands and Wives*. She attended the University of Florida and did graduate work at Dallas Theological Seminary. Cinny is a popular conference speaker throughout the United States and abroad. She is the proud mother of three and has two grandchildren.

THE FEMININE JOURNEY SHOULDN'T BE A RAT RACE

Social mores, the feminist movement, the church, and the media have given women a myriad of messages about who they should be. But when women try to fulfill all these expectations, they often feel more frantic than fulfilled. So what's the answer?

A woman needs an identity that goes beyond self-fulfillment, relationships, or any of the possibilities in between, say Cynthia and Robert Hicks. Her true identity is found in who she is as an individual designed by her Creator—and that may look different at various stages of her life.

The Feminine Journey explores the biblical terms and examples that shed light on the stages of a woman's life, providing a compelling look at the real essence of womanhood No matter where you've been or where you are now in your journey as a woman, *The Feminine Journey* will give you a sense of direction—and make it a trip worth taking.

The Feminine Journey
(Cynthia and Robert Hicks)
$15/Hardback
0-89109-770-8

The Feminine Journey Discussion Guide
$6/Paperback
0-89109-830-5

Available at your local bookstore, or by calling (800) 366-7788.

NAVPRESS⬤
BRINGING TRUTH TO LIFE